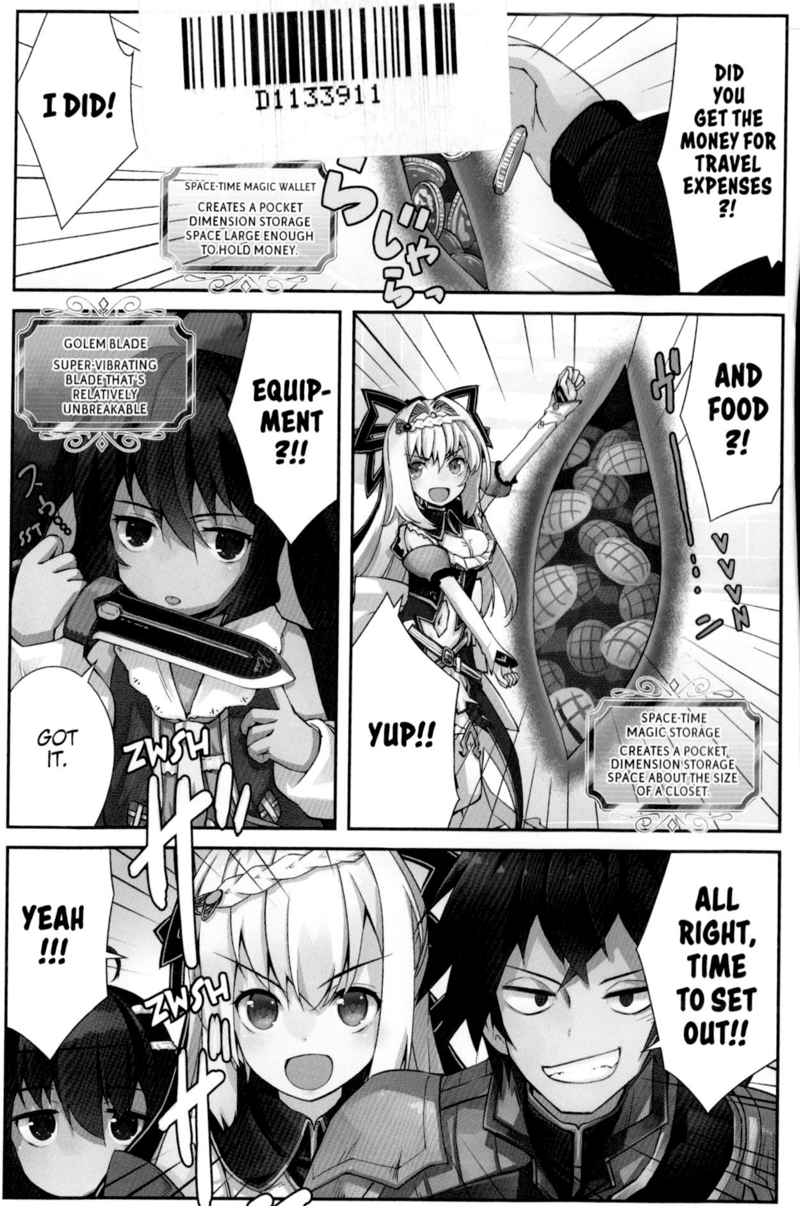
DID YOU GET THE MONEY FOR TRAVEL EXPENSES?!
I DID!
SPACE-TIME MAGIC WALLET
CREATES A POCKET DIMENSION STORAGE SPACE LARGE ENOUGH TO HOLD MONEY.
じゃらっ
AND FOOD?!
YUP!!
SPACE-TIME MAGIC STORAGE
CREATES A POCKET DIMENSION STORAGE SPACE ABOUT THE SIZE OF A CLOSET.
VVVVN
EQUIPMENT?!!
GOLEM BLADE
SUPER-VIBRATING BLADE THAT'S RELATIVELY UNBREAKABLE
SST
GOT IT.
ZWSH
ALL RIGHT, TIME TO SET OUT!!
YEAH!!!
ZWSH

Chapter 12 Management Policy

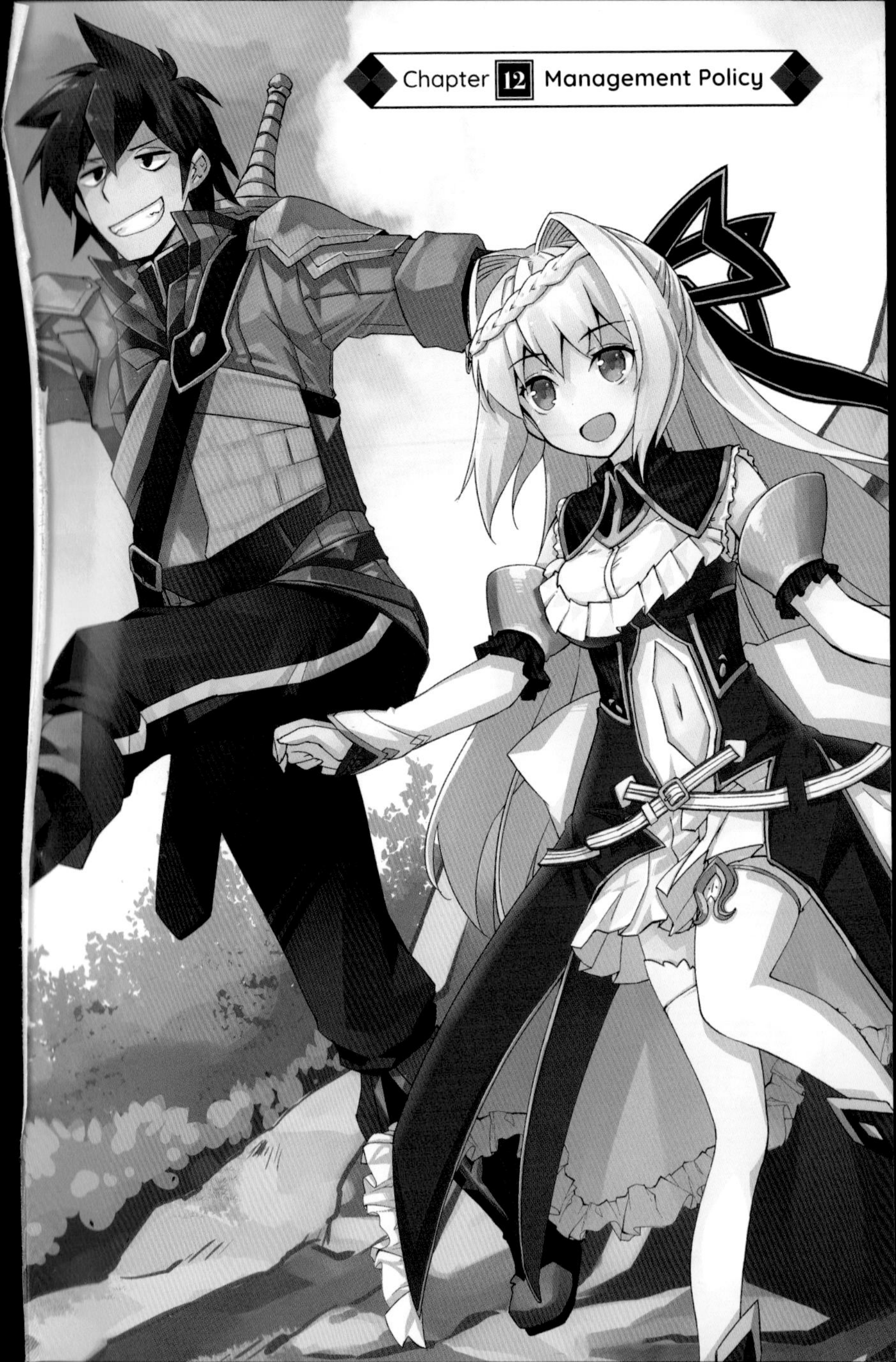

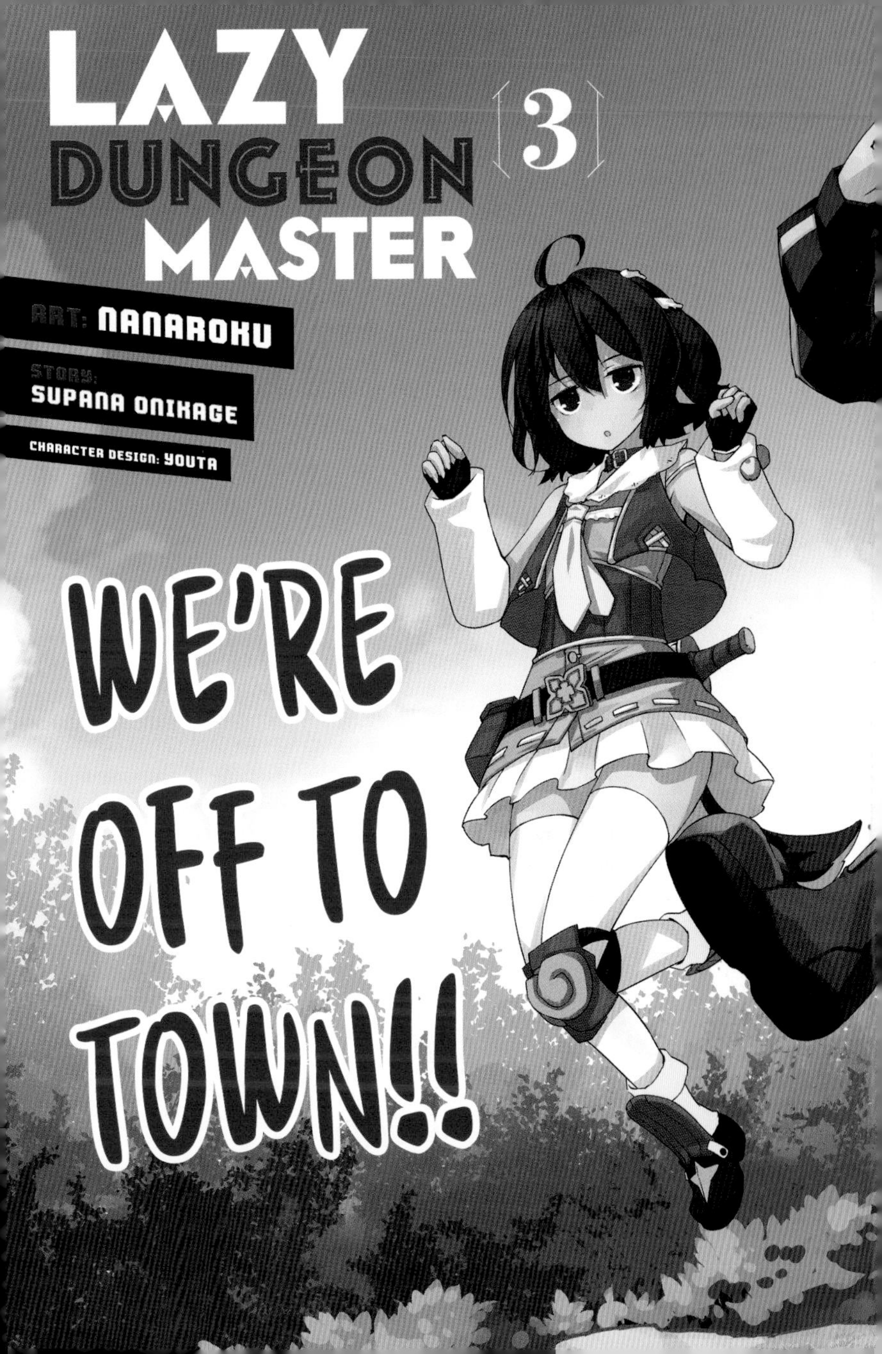
LAZY DUNGEON MASTER
3
ART: NANAROKU
STORY: SUPANA ONIKAGE
CHARACTER DESIGN: YOUTA
WE'RE OFF TO TOWN!!

LAZY DUNGEON MASTER

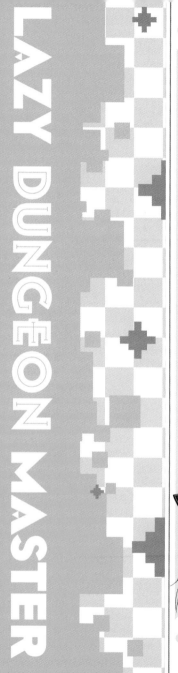

CONTENTS

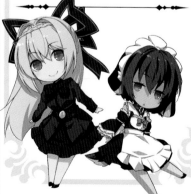

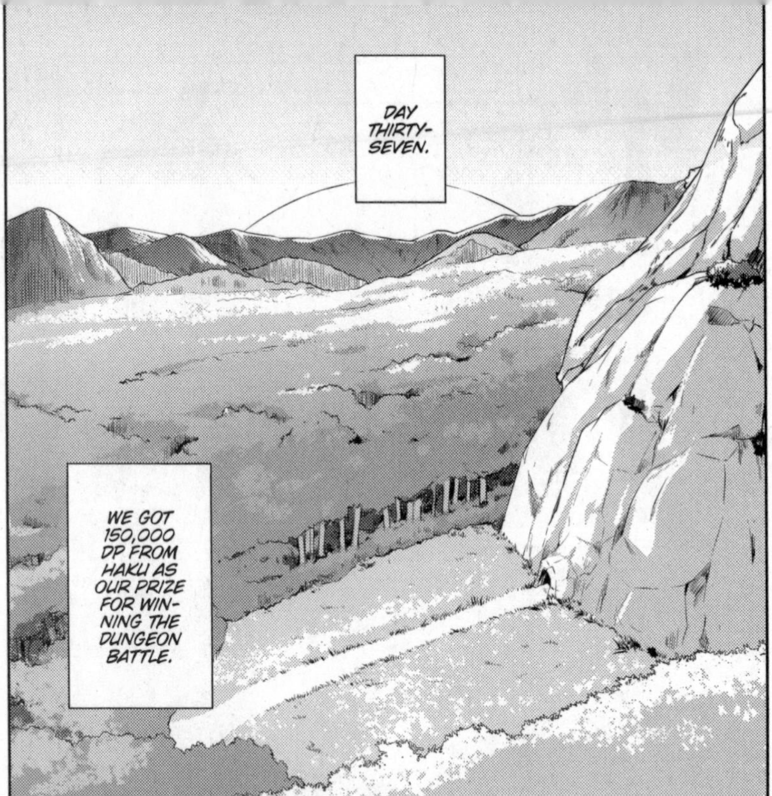
DAY THIRTY-SEVEN.
WE GOT 150,000 DP FROM HAKU AS OUR PRIZE FOR WIN-NING THE DUNGEON BATTLE.

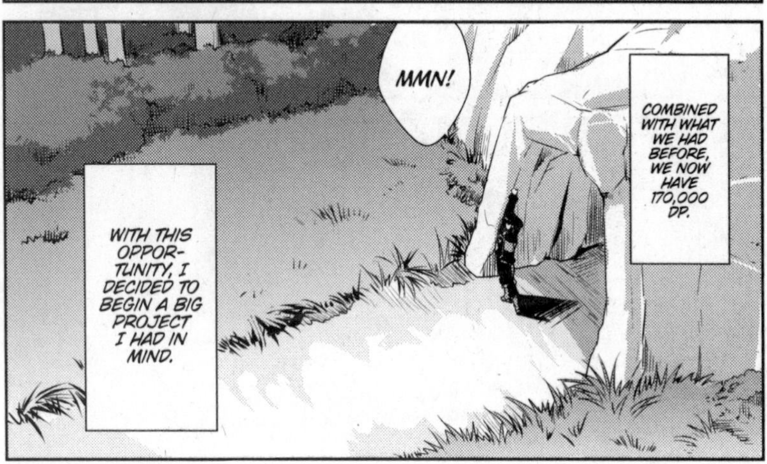
COMBINED WITH WHAT WE HAD BEFORE, WE NOW HAVE 170,000 DP.
MMN!
WITH THIS OPPOR-TUNITY, I DECIDED TO BEGIN A BIG PROJECT I HAD IN MIND.

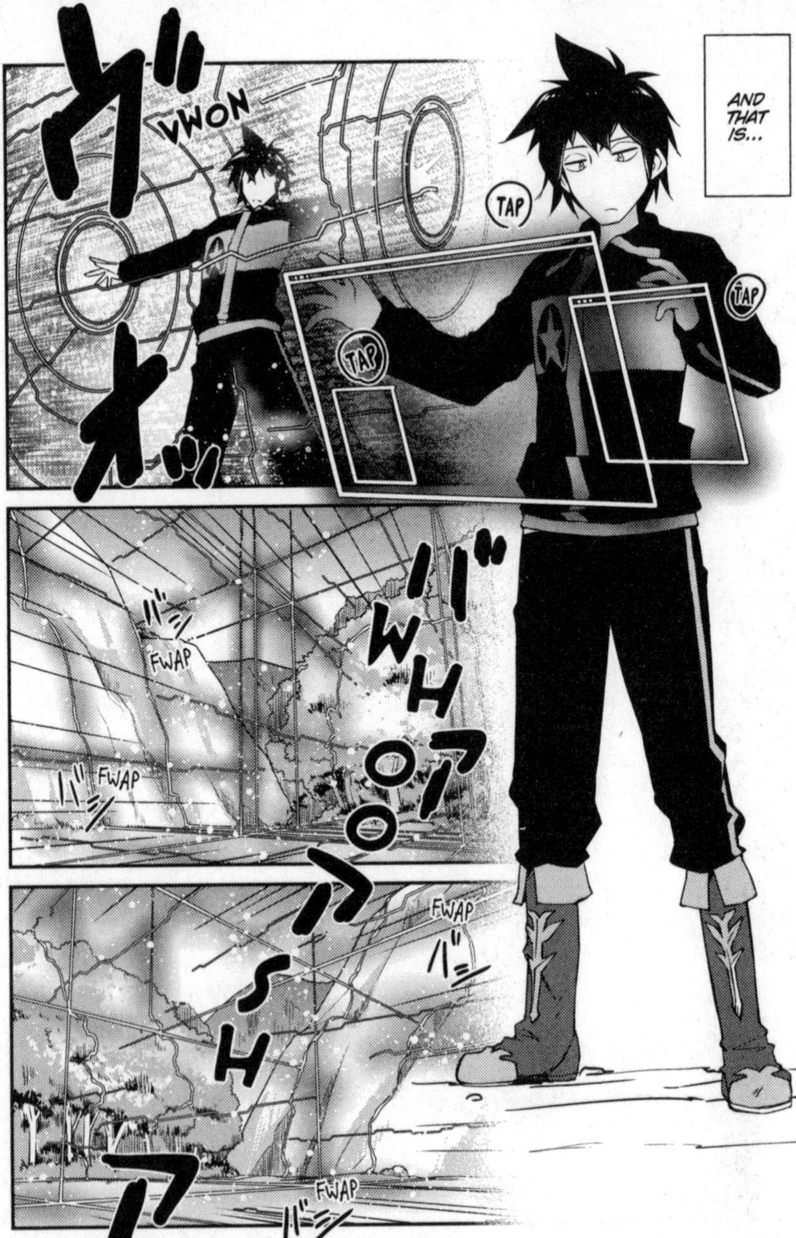
AND THAT IS...
TAP
TAP
TAP
VWON
WHOOSH
FWAP
FWAP
FWAP
FWAP

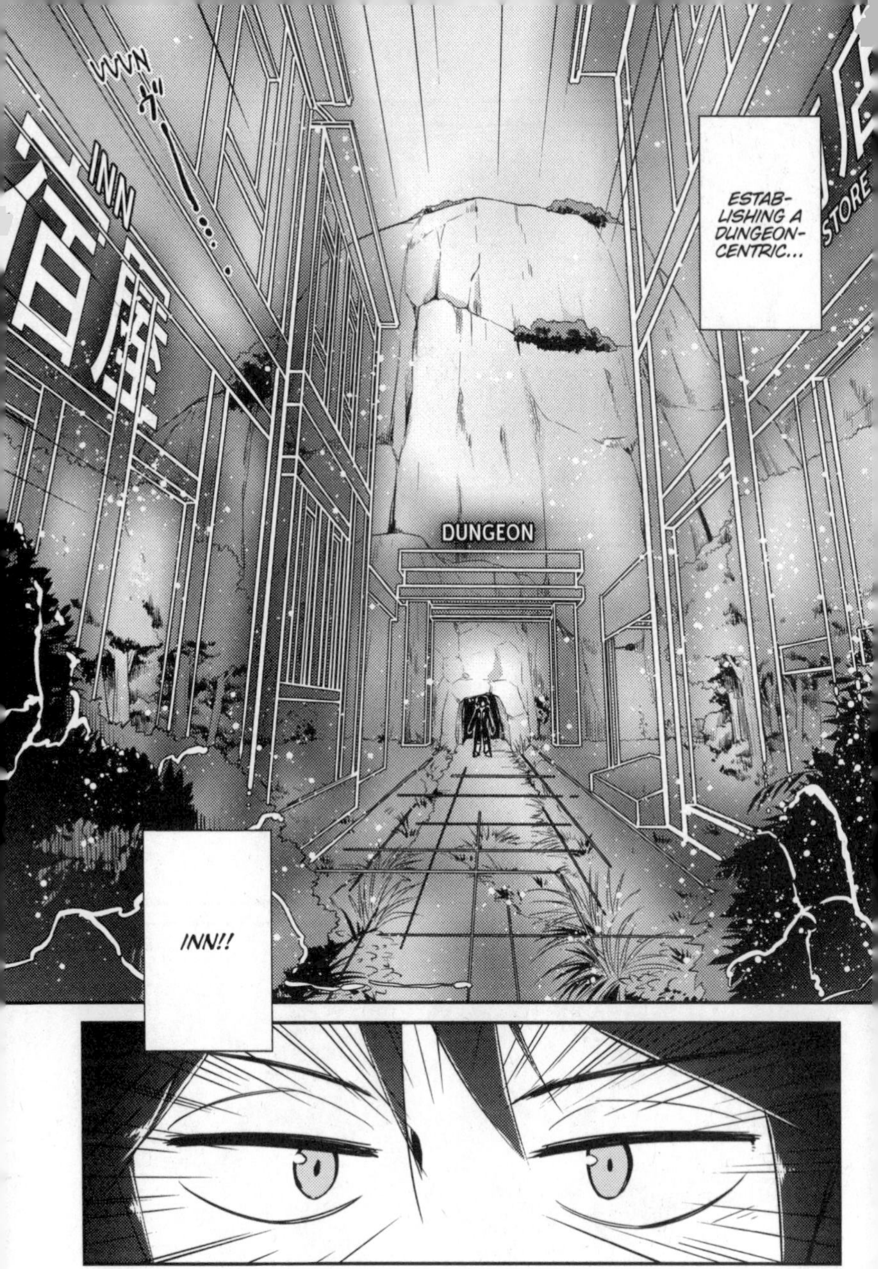
STORE
ESTAB-LISHING A DUNGEON-CENTRIC...
VVVN
INN
DUNGEON
INN!!

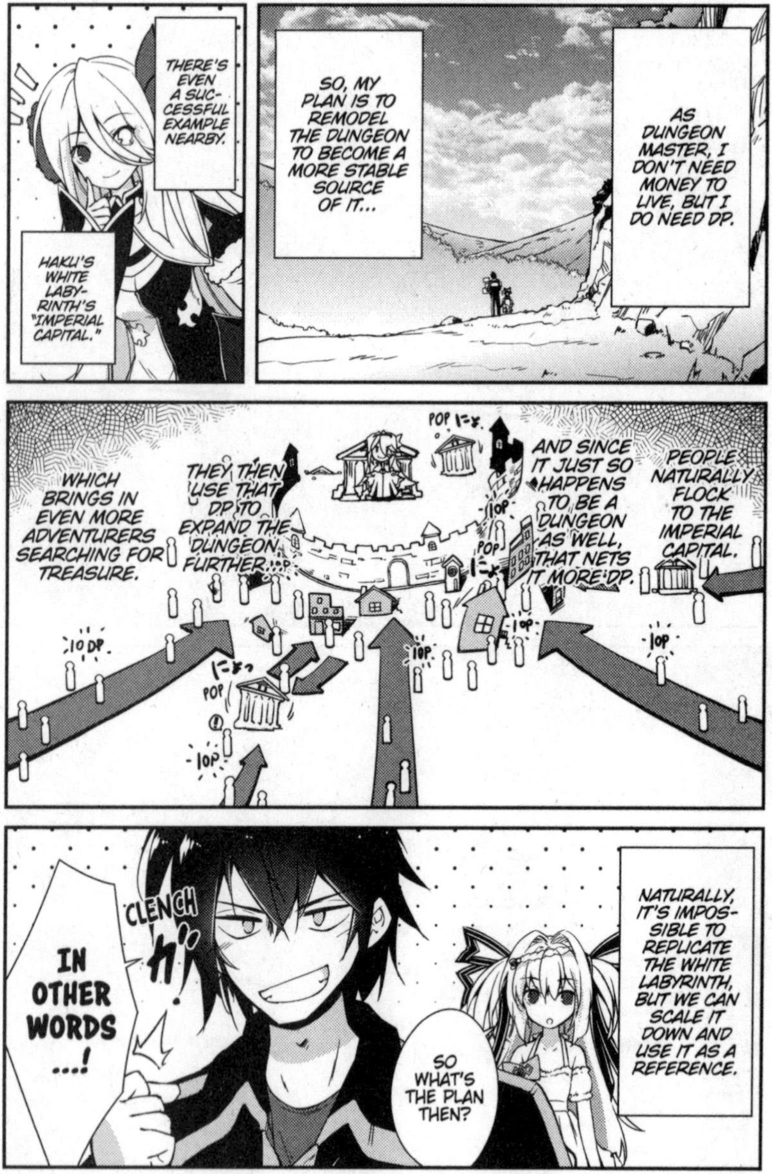
AS DUNGEON MASTER, I DON'T NEED MONEY TO LIVE, BUT I DO NEED DP.
SO, MY PLAN IS TO REMODEL THE DUNGEON TO BECOME A MORE STABLE SOURCE OF IT...
THERE'S EVEN A SUCCESSFUL EXAMPLE NEARBY.
HAKU'S WHITE LABYRINTH'S "IMPERIAL CAPITAL."
PEOPLE NATURALLY FLOCK TO THE IMPERIAL CAPITAL.
AND SINCE IT JUST SO HAPPENS TO BE A DUNGEON AS WELL, THAT NETS IT MORE DP.
THEY THEN USE THAT DP TO EXPAND THE DUNGEON FURTHER...
WHICH BRINGS IN EVEN MORE ADVENTURERS SEARCHING FOR TREASURE.
POP
1DP
10 DP
NATURALLY, IT'S IMPOSSIBLE TO REPLICATE THE WHITE LABYRINTH, BUT WE CAN SCALE IT DOWN AND USE IT AS A REFERENCE.
SO WHAT'S THE PLAN THEN?
CLENCH
IN OTHER WORDS...!

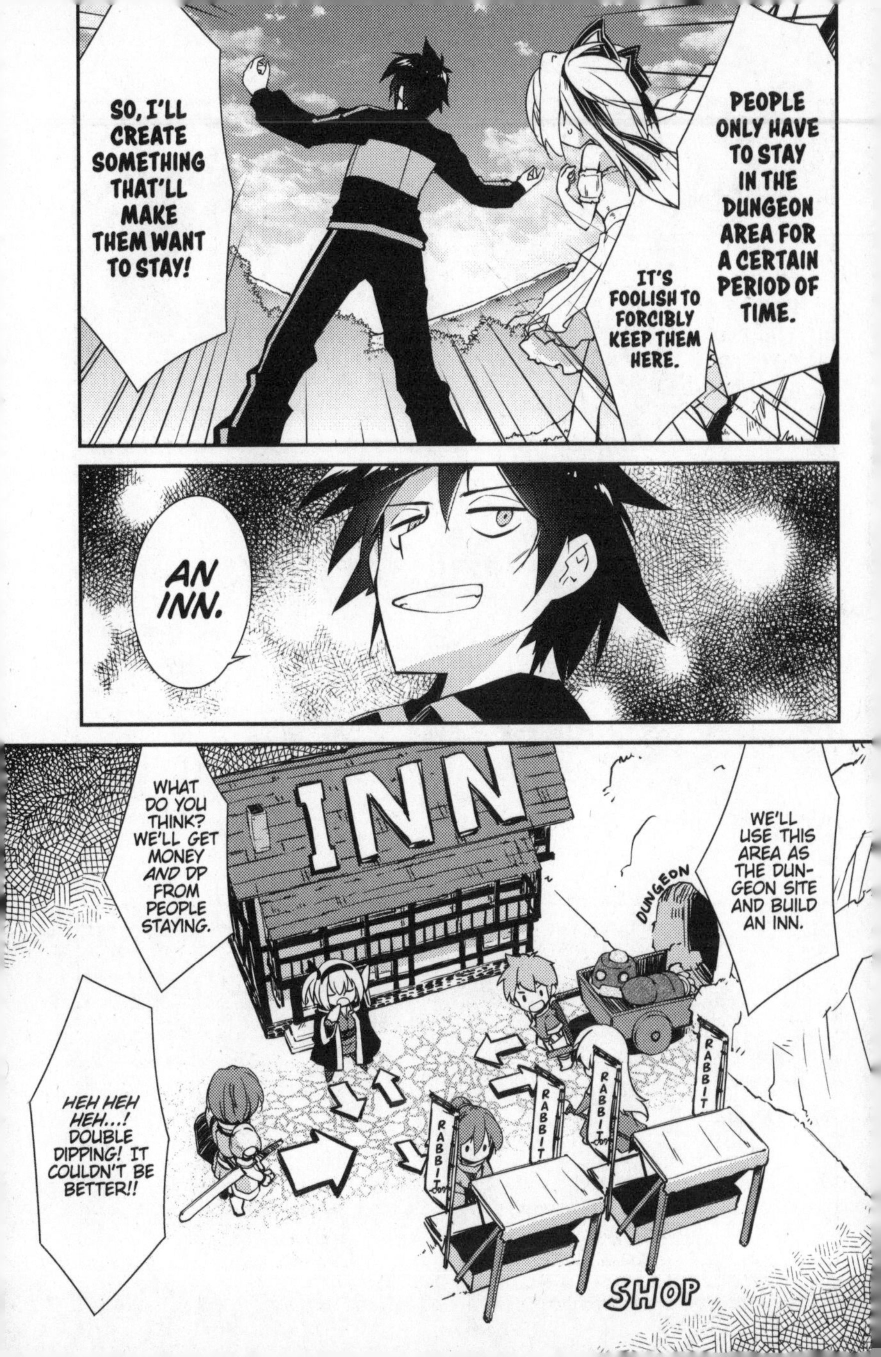
PEOPLE ONLY HAVE TO STAY IN THE DUNGEON AREA FOR A CERTAIN PERIOD OF TIME.
IT'S FOOLISH TO FORCIBLY KEEP THEM HERE.
SO, I'LL CREATE SOMETHING THAT'LL MAKE THEM WANT TO STAY!
AN INN.
WE'LL USE THIS AREA AS THE DUN-GEON SITE AND BUILD AN INN.
DUNGEON
INN
WHAT DO YOU THINK? WE'LL GET MONEY AND DP FROM PEOPLE STAYING.
RABBIT
RABBIT
RABBIT
RABBIT
HEH HEH HEH...! DOUBLE DIPPING! IT COULDN'T BE BETTER!!
SHOP

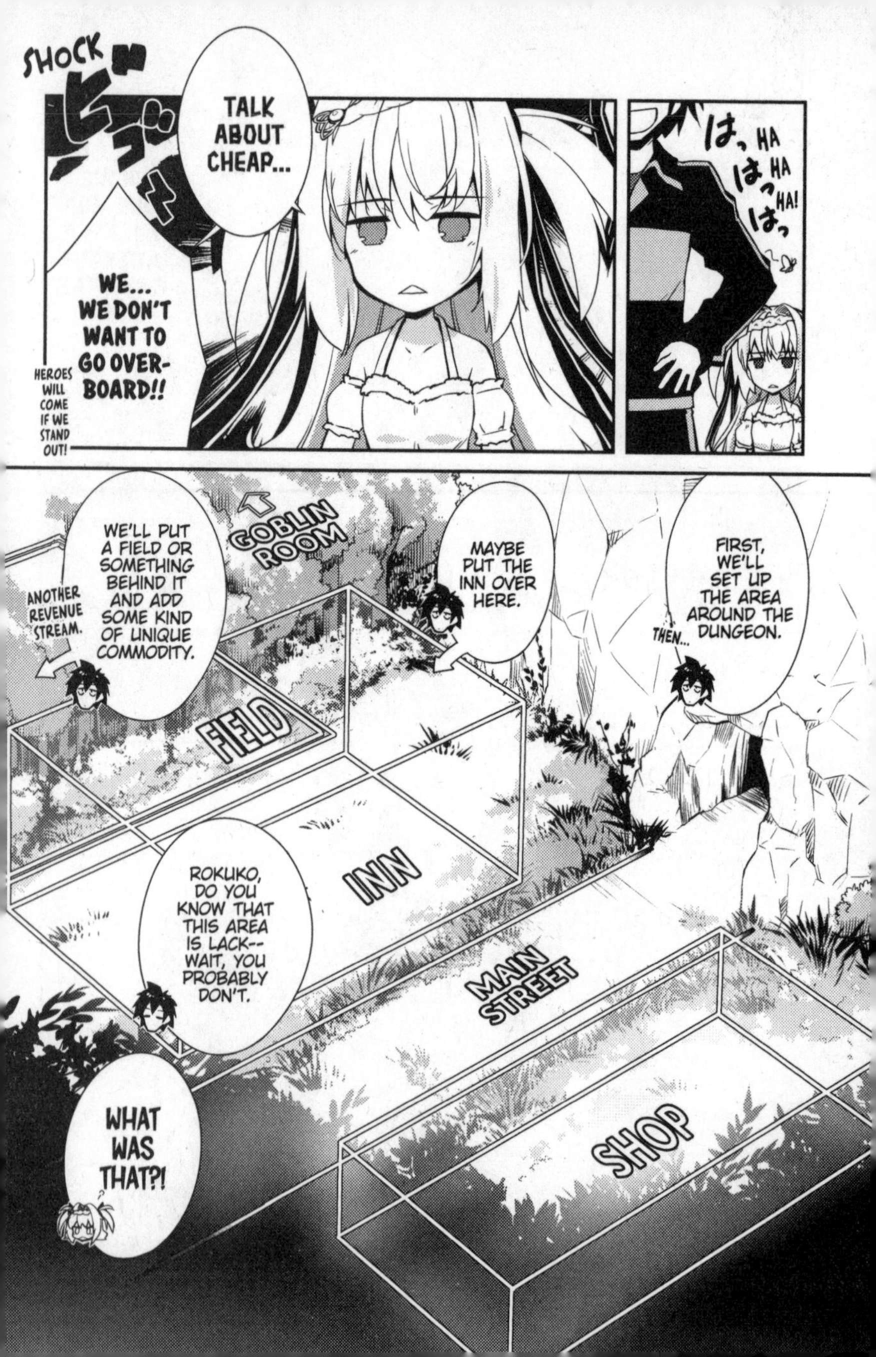
HA HA HA!
TALK ABOUT CHEAP...
SHOCK
WE... WE DON'T WANT TO GO OVER-BOARD!!
HEROES WILL COME IF WE STAND OUT!
FIRST, WE'LL SET UP THE AREA AROUND THE DUNGEON.
THEN...
MAYBE PUT THE INN OVER HERE.
GOBLIN ROOM
WE'LL PUT A FIELD OR SOMETHING BEHIND IT AND ADD SOME KIND OF UNIQUE COMMODITY.
ANOTHER REVENUE STREAM.
FIELD
INN
MAIN STREET
ROKUKO, DO YOU KNOW THAT THIS AREA IS LACK-- WAIT, YOU PROBABLY DON'T.
SHOP
WHAT WAS THAT?!

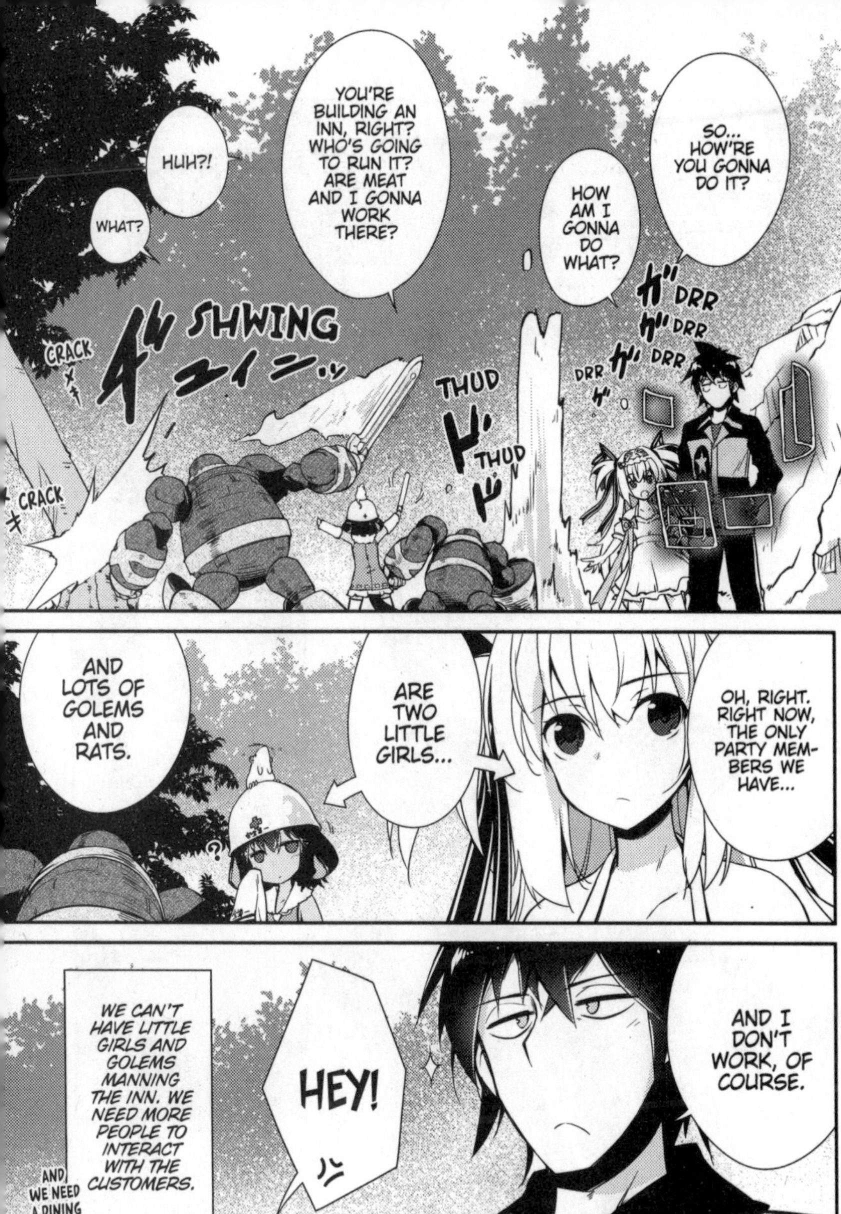
SO... HOW'RE YOU GONNA DO IT?
HOW AM I GONNA DO WHAT?
YOU'RE BUILDING AN INN, RIGHT? WHO'S GOING TO RUN IT? ARE MEAT AND I GONNA WORK THERE?
HUH?!
WHAT?
DRR
DRR
DRR
DRR
THUD
THUD
SHWING
CRACK
CRACK
OH, RIGHT. RIGHT NOW, THE ONLY PARTY MEM-BERS WE HAVE...
ARE TWO LITTLE GIRLS...
AND LOTS OF GOLEMS AND RATS.
AND I DON'T WORK, OF COURSE.
HEY!
WE CAN'T HAVE LITTLE GIRLS AND GOLEMS MANNING THE INN. WE NEED MORE PEOPLE TO INTERACT WITH THE CUSTOMERS.
AND WE NEED A DINING AREA TOO...

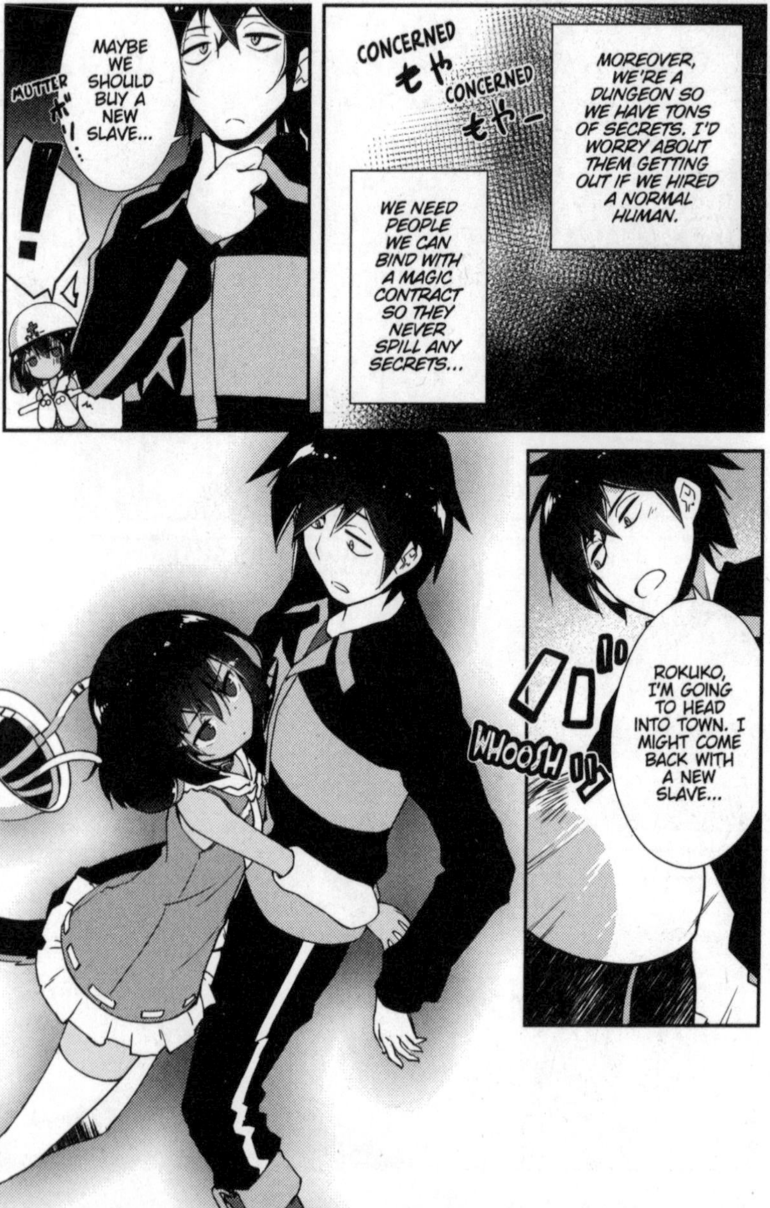
CONCERNED
もや
CONCERNED
もやー
MOREOVER, WE'RE A DUNGEON SO WE HAVE TONS OF SECRETS. I'D WORRY ABOUT THEM GETTING OUT IF WE HIRED A NORMAL HUMAN.
WE NEED PEOPLE WE CAN BIND WITH A MAGIC CONTRACT SO THEY NEVER SPILL ANY SECRETS...
MUTTER
MAYBE WE SHOULD BUY A NEW SLAVE...
!
ROKUKO, I'M GOING TO HEAD INTO TOWN. I MIGHT COME BACK WITH A NEW SLAVE...
WHOOSH

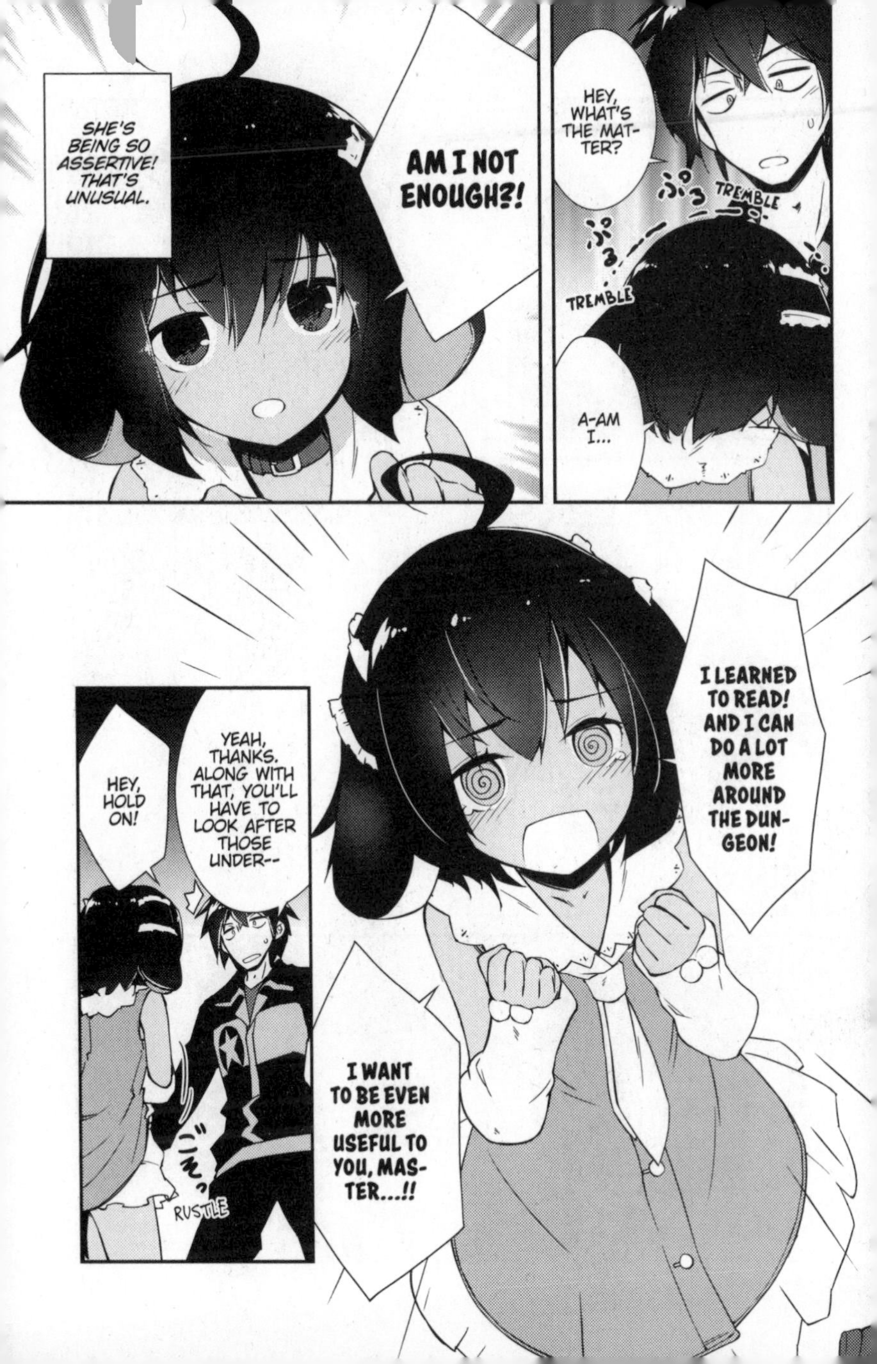
HEY, WHAT'S THE MAT-TER?
TREMBLE
TREMBLE
A-AM I...
AM I NOT ENOUGH?!
SHE'S BEING SO ASSERTIVE! THAT'S UNUSUAL.
I LEARNED TO READ! AND I CAN DO A LOT MORE AROUND THE DUN-GEON!
I WANT TO BE EVEN MORE USEFUL TO YOU, MAS-TER...!!
YEAH, THANKS. ALONG WITH THAT, YOU'LL HAVE TO LOOK AFTER THOSE UNDER--
HEY, HOLD ON!
RUSTLE

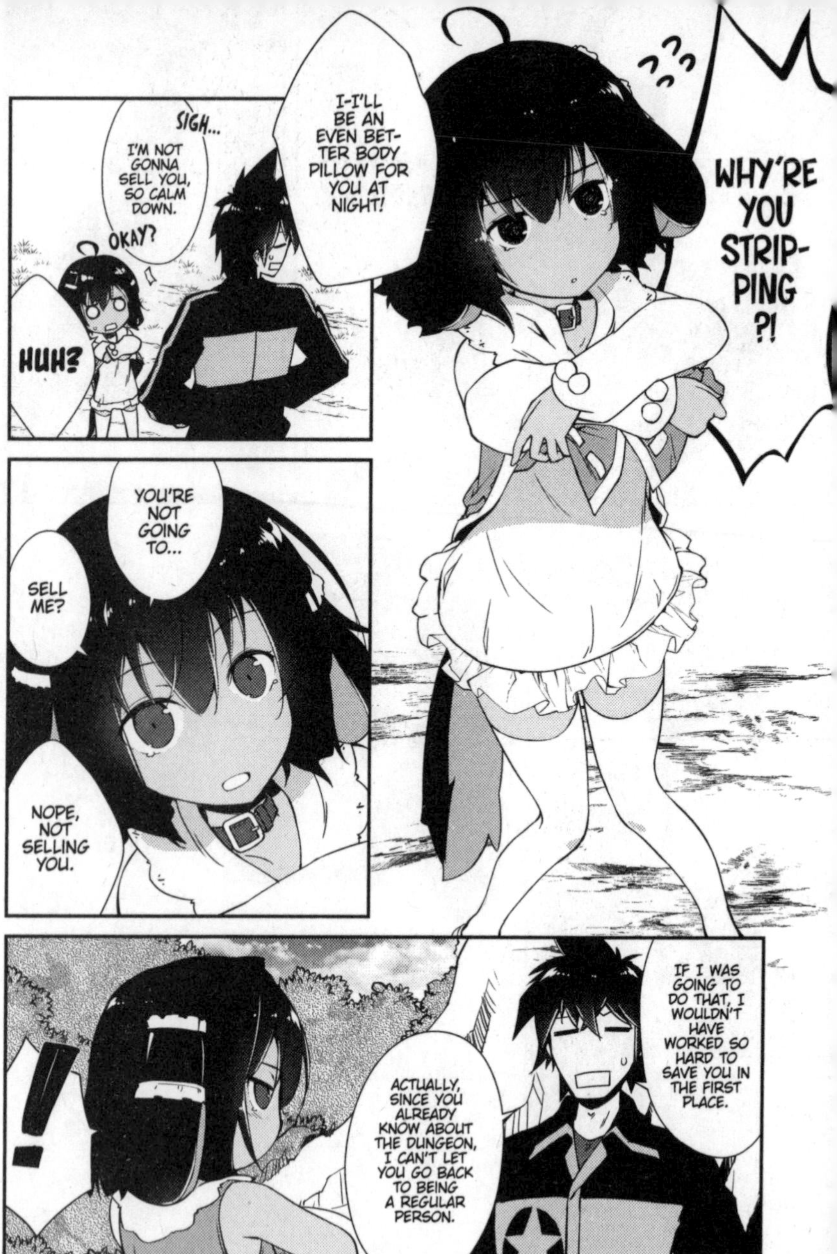
I-I'LL BE AN EVEN BET-TER BODY PILLOW FOR YOU AT NIGHT!
WHY'RE YOU STRIP-PING?!
SIGH...
I'M NOT GONNA SELL YOU, SO CALM DOWN.
OKAY?
HUH?
YOU'RE NOT GOING TO...
SELL ME?
NOPE, NOT SELLING YOU.
IF I WAS GOING TO DO THAT, I WOULDN'T HAVE WORKED SO HARD TO SAVE YOU IN THE FIRST PLACE.
ACTUALLY, SINCE YOU ALREADY KNOW ABOUT THE DUNGEON, I CAN'T LET YOU GO BACK TO BEING A REGULAR PERSON.
!

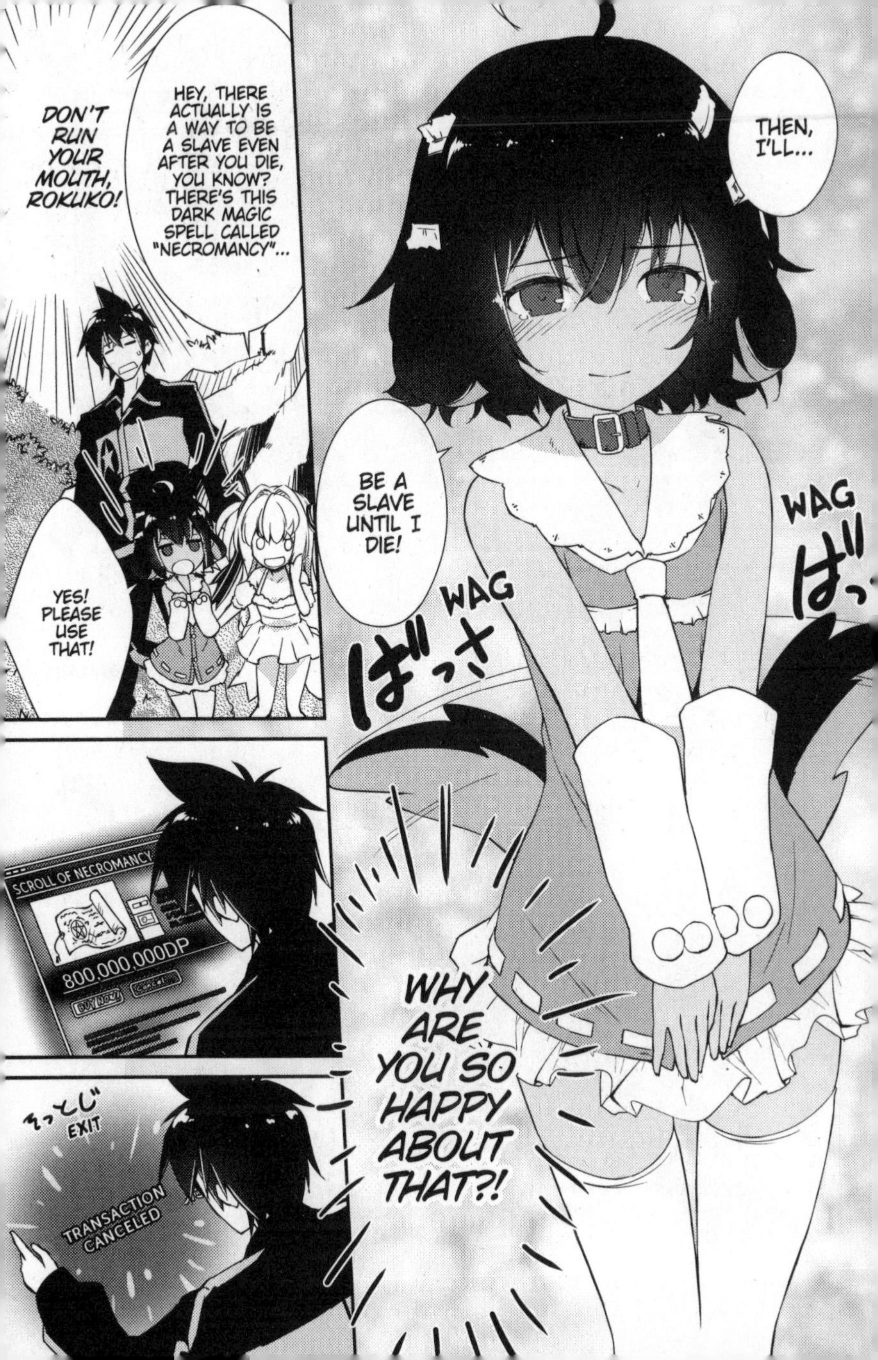
THEN, I'LL...
BE A SLAVE UNTIL I DIE!
WAG
ばっさ
WAG
ばっ
WHY ARE YOU SO HAPPY ABOUT THAT?!
HEY, THERE ACTUALLY IS A WAY TO BE A SLAVE EVEN AFTER YOU DIE, YOU KNOW? THERE'S THIS DARK MAGIC SPELL CALLED "NECROMANCY"...
DON'T RUN YOUR MOUTH, ROKUKO!
YES! PLEASE USE THAT!
SCROLL OF NECROMANCY
800,000,000DP
BUY NOW!
そっとじ
EXIT
TRANSACTION CANCELED

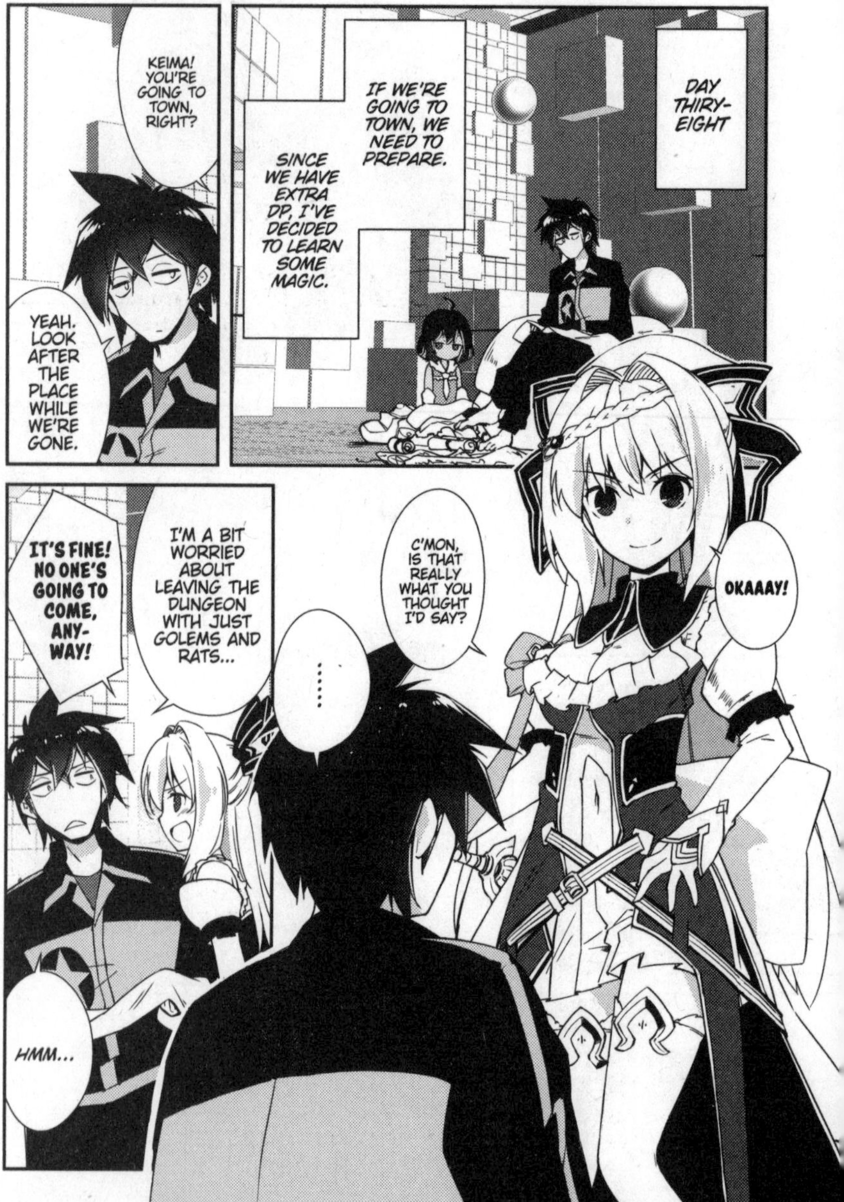
DAY THIRY-EIGHT
IF WE'RE GOING TO TOWN, WE NEED TO PREPARE.
SINCE WE HAVE EXTRA DP, I'VE DECIDED TO LEARN SOME MAGIC.
KEIMA! YOU'RE GOING TO TOWN, RIGHT?
YEAH. LOOK AFTER THE PLACE WHILE WE'RE GONE.
OKAAAY!
C'MON, IS THAT REALLY WHAT YOU THOUGHT I'D SAY?
......
I'M A BIT WORRIED ABOUT LEAVING THE DUNGEON WITH JUST GOLEMS AND RATS...
IT'S FINE! NO ONE'S GOING TO COME, ANY-WAY!
HMM...

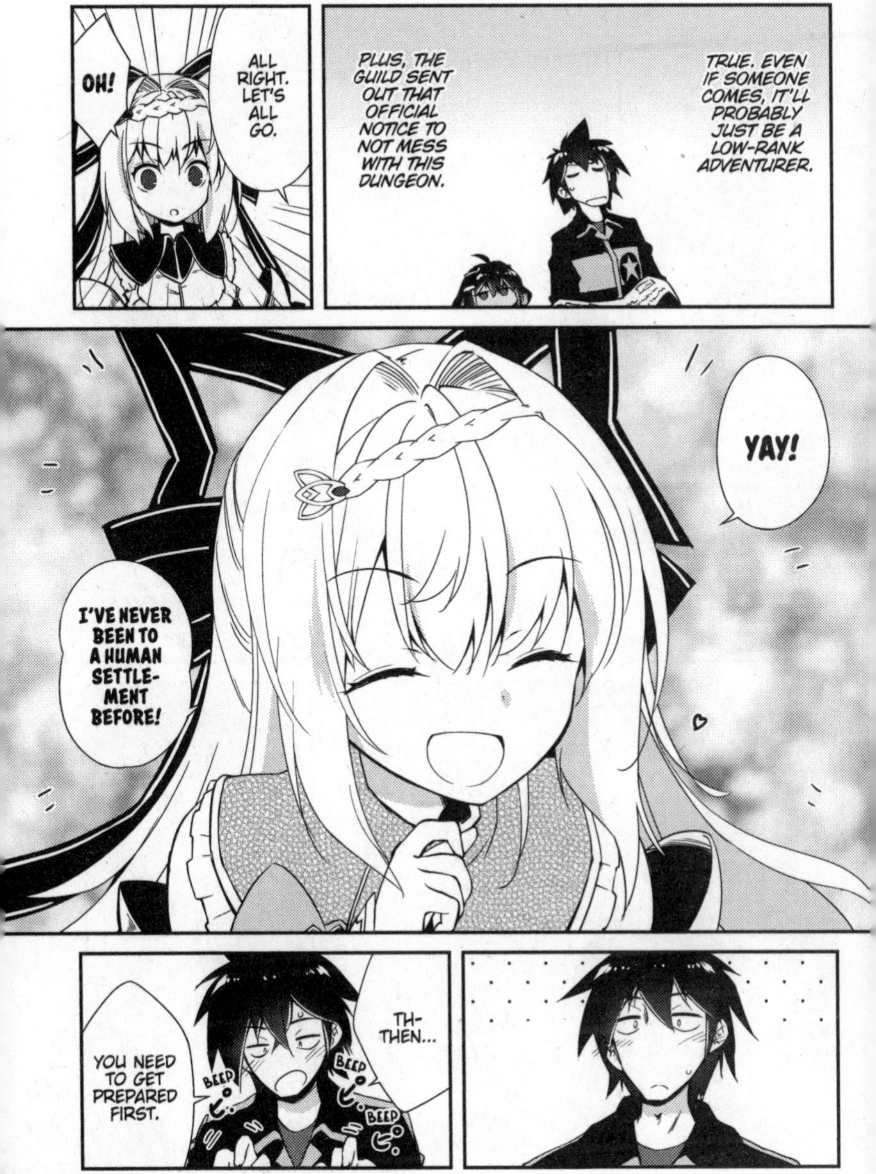
TRUE. EVEN IF SOMEONE COMES, IT'LL PROBABLY JUST BE A LOW-RANK ADVENTURER.
PLUS, THE GUILD SENT OUT THAT OFFICIAL NOTICE TO NOT MESS WITH THIS DUNGEON.
ALL RIGHT. LET'S ALL GO.
OH!
YAY!
I'VE NEVER BEEN TO A HUMAN SETTLEMENT BEFORE!
TH- THEN...
BEEP
BEEP
YOU NEED TO GET PREPARED FIRST.
BEEP

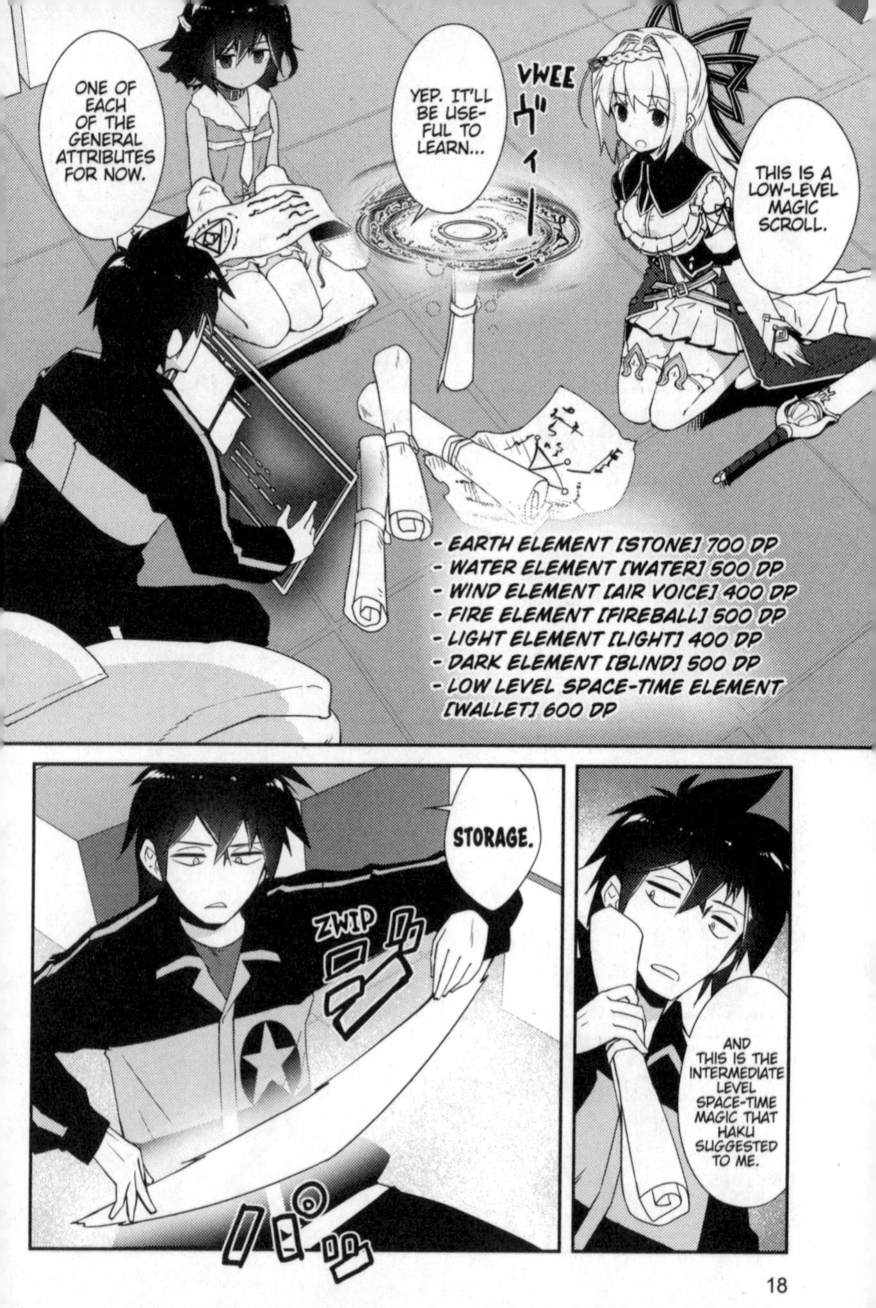

THIS IS A LOW-LEVEL MAGIC SCROLL.
VWEE
ヴィーー
YEP. IT'LL BE USE-FUL TO LEARN...
ONE OF EACH OF THE GENERAL ATTRIBUTES FOR NOW.
- EARTH ELEMENT [STONE] 700 DP
- WATER ELEMENT [WATER] 500 DP
- WIND ELEMENT [AIR VOICE] 400 DP
- FIRE ELEMENT [FIREBALL] 500 DP
- LIGHT ELEMENT [LIGHT] 400 DP
- DARK ELEMENT [BLIND] 500 DP
- LOW LEVEL SPACE-TIME ELEMENT [WALLET] 600 DP
AND THIS IS THE INTERMEDIATE LEVEL SPACE-TIME MAGIC THAT HAKU SUGGESTED TO ME.
STORAGE.
ZWIP

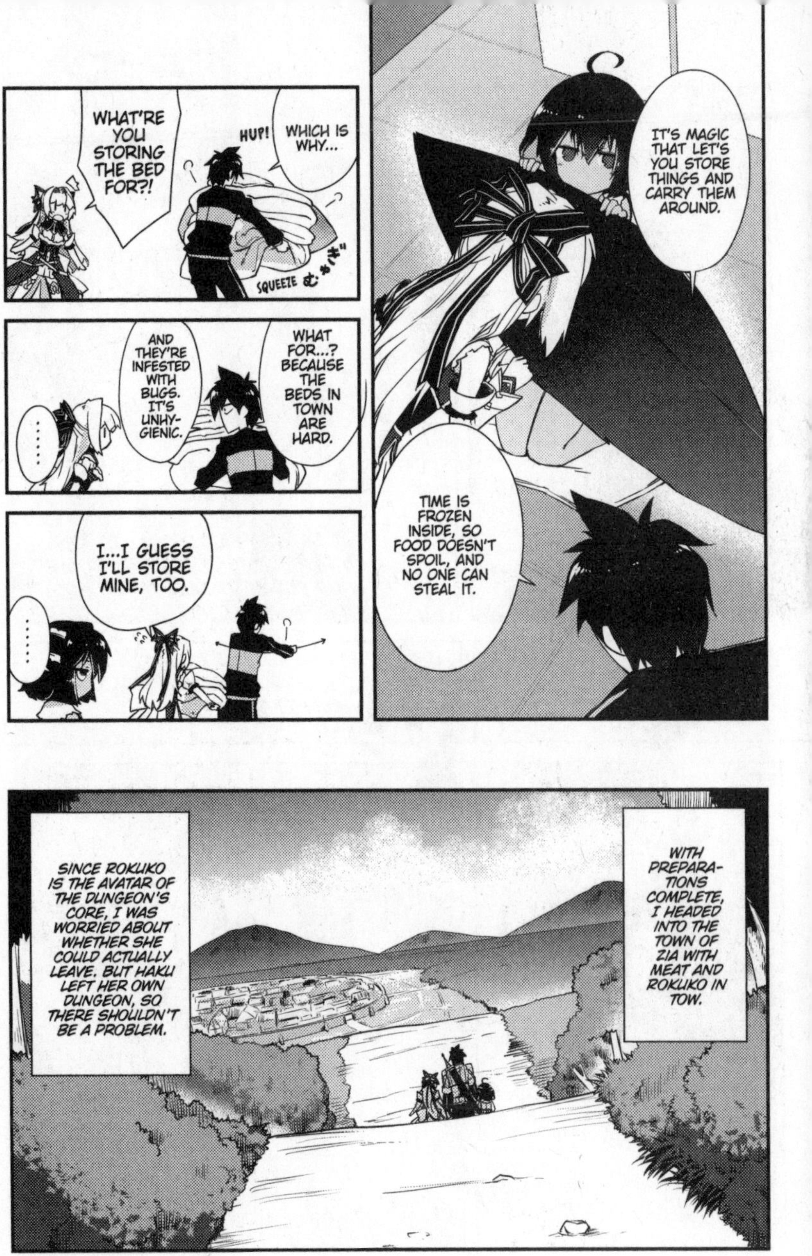
IT'S MAGIC THAT LET'S YOU STORE THINGS AND CARRY THEM AROUND.
TIME IS FROZEN INSIDE, SO FOOD DOESN'T SPOIL, AND NO ONE CAN STEAL IT.
WHICH IS WHY...
HUP!
WHAT'RE YOU STORING THE BED FOR?!
SQUEEZE
WHAT FOR...? BECAUSE THE BEDS IN TOWN ARE HARD.
AND THEY'RE INFESTED WITH BUGS. IT'S UNHYGIENIC.
......
I...I GUESS I'LL STORE MINE, TOO.
......
WITH PREPARATIONS COMPLETE, I HEADED INTO THE TOWN OF ZIA WITH MEAT AND ROKUKO IN TOW.
SINCE ROKUKO IS THE AVATAR OF THE DUNGEON'S CORE, I WAS WORRIED ABOUT WHETHER SHE COULD ACTUALLY LEAVE. BUT HAKU LEFT HER OWN DUNGEON, SO THERE SHOULDN'T BE A PROBLEM.

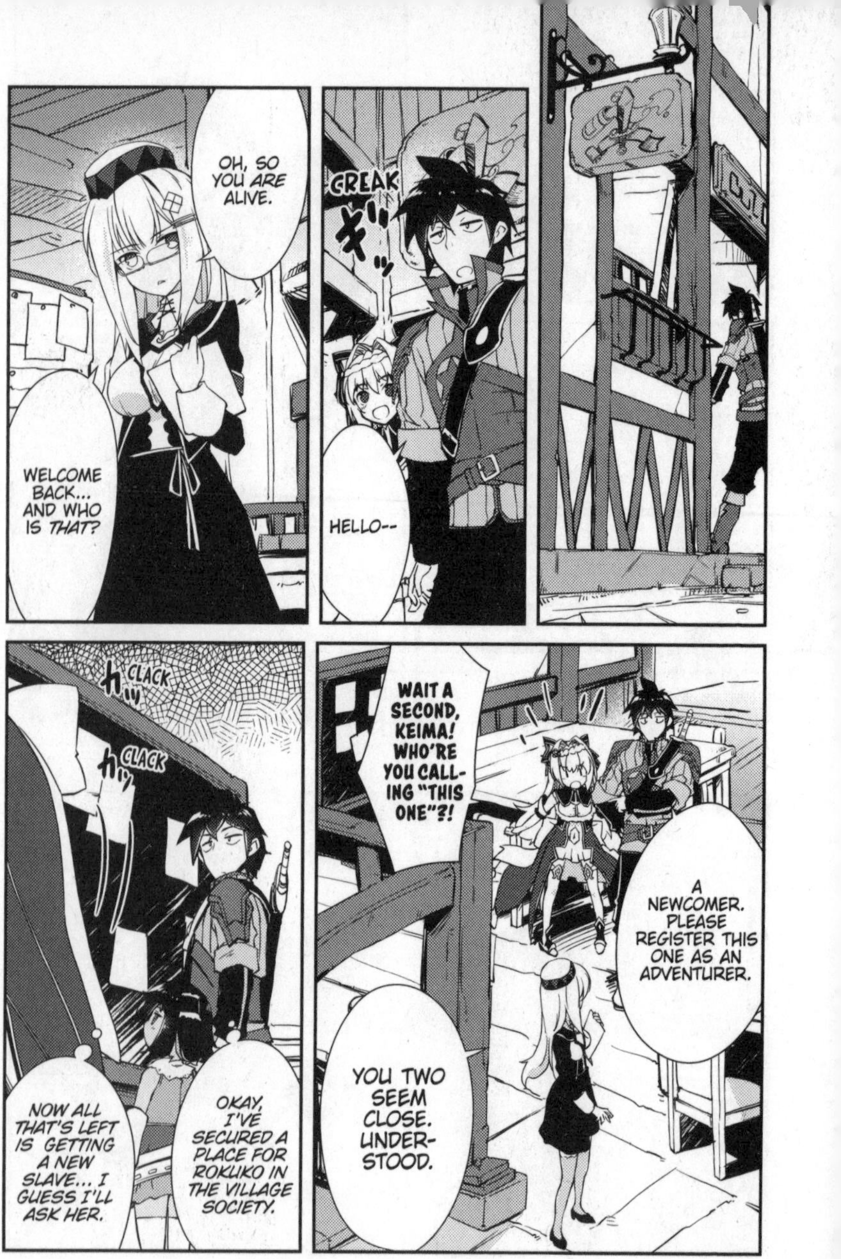
CREAK
ギッ
HELLO--
OH, SO YOU ARE ALIVE.
WELCOME BACK... AND WHO IS THAT?
A NEWCOMER. PLEASE REGISTER THIS ONE AS AN ADVENTURER.
WAIT A SECOND, KEIMA! WHO'RE YOU CALLING "THIS ONE"?!
YOU TWO SEEM CLOSE. UNDER-STOOD.
CLACK
カッ
CLACK
カッ
OKAY, I'VE SECURED A PLACE FOR ROKUKO IN THE VILLAGE SOCIETY.
NOW ALL THAT'S LEFT IS GETTING A NEW SLAVE... I GUESS I'LL ASK HER.

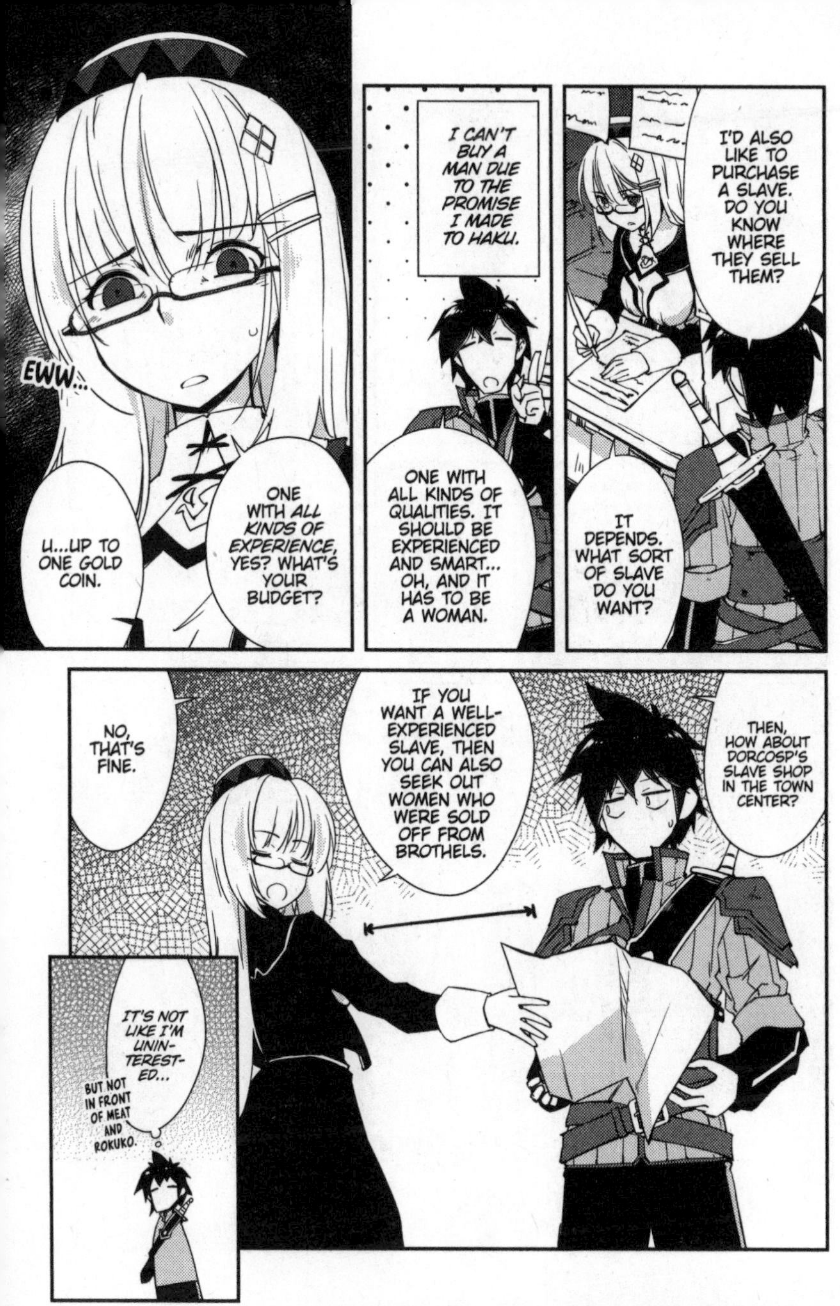
I'D ALSO LIKE TO PURCHASE A SLAVE. DO YOU KNOW WHERE THEY SELL THEM?
IT DEPENDS. WHAT SORT OF SLAVE DO YOU WANT?
I CAN'T BUY A MAN DUE TO THE PROMISE I MADE TO HAKU.
ONE WITH ALL KINDS OF QUALITIES. IT SHOULD BE EXPERIENCED AND SMART... OH, AND IT HAS TO BE A WOMAN.
EWW...
ONE WITH *ALL KINDS OF EXPERIENCE,* YES? WHAT'S YOUR BUDGET?
U...UP TO ONE GOLD COIN.
THEN, HOW ABOUT DORCOSP'S SLAVE SHOP IN THE TOWN CENTER?
IF YOU WANT A WELL-EXPERIENCED SLAVE, THEN YOU CAN ALSO SEEK OUT WOMEN WHO WERE SOLD OFF FROM BROTHELS.
NO, THAT'S FINE.
IT'S NOT LIKE I'M UNIN-TEREST-ED...
BUT NOT IN FRONT OF MEAT AND ROKUKO.

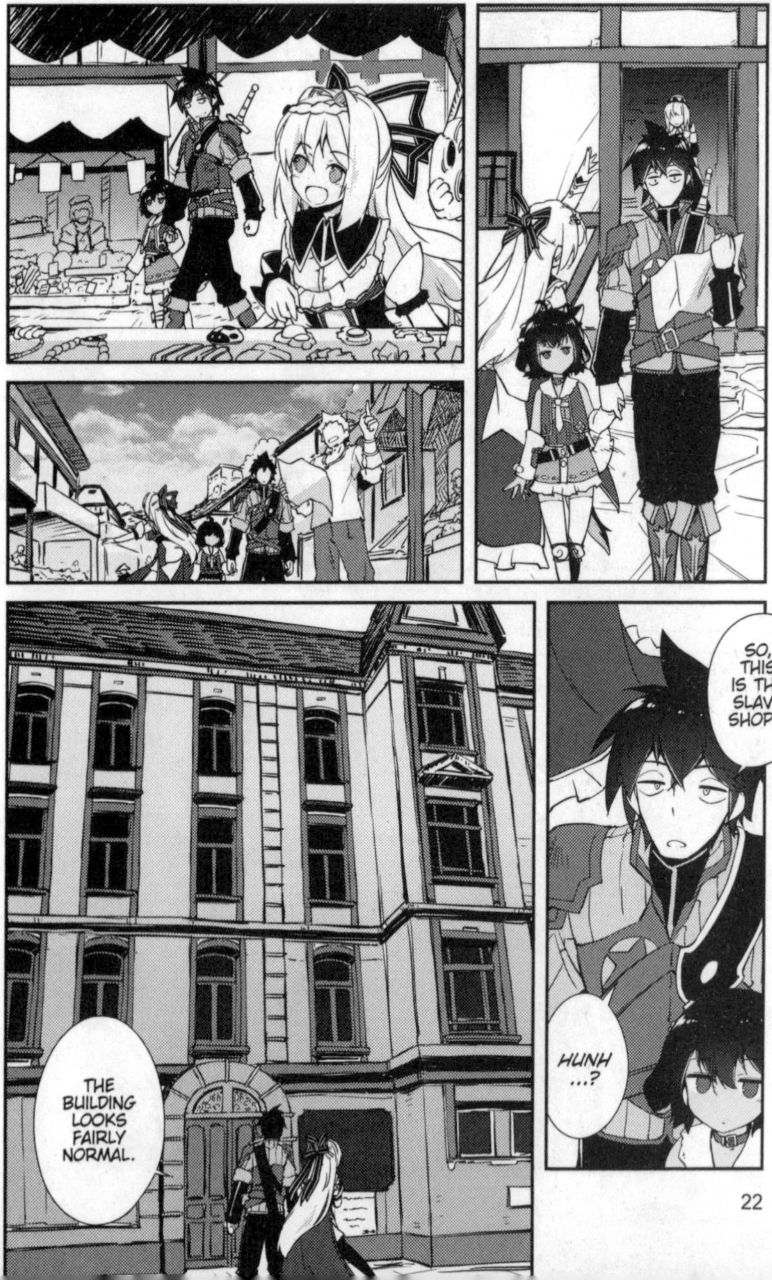
SO, THIS IS THE SLAVE SHOP...
HUNH ...?
THE BUILDING LOOKS FAIRLY NORMAL.

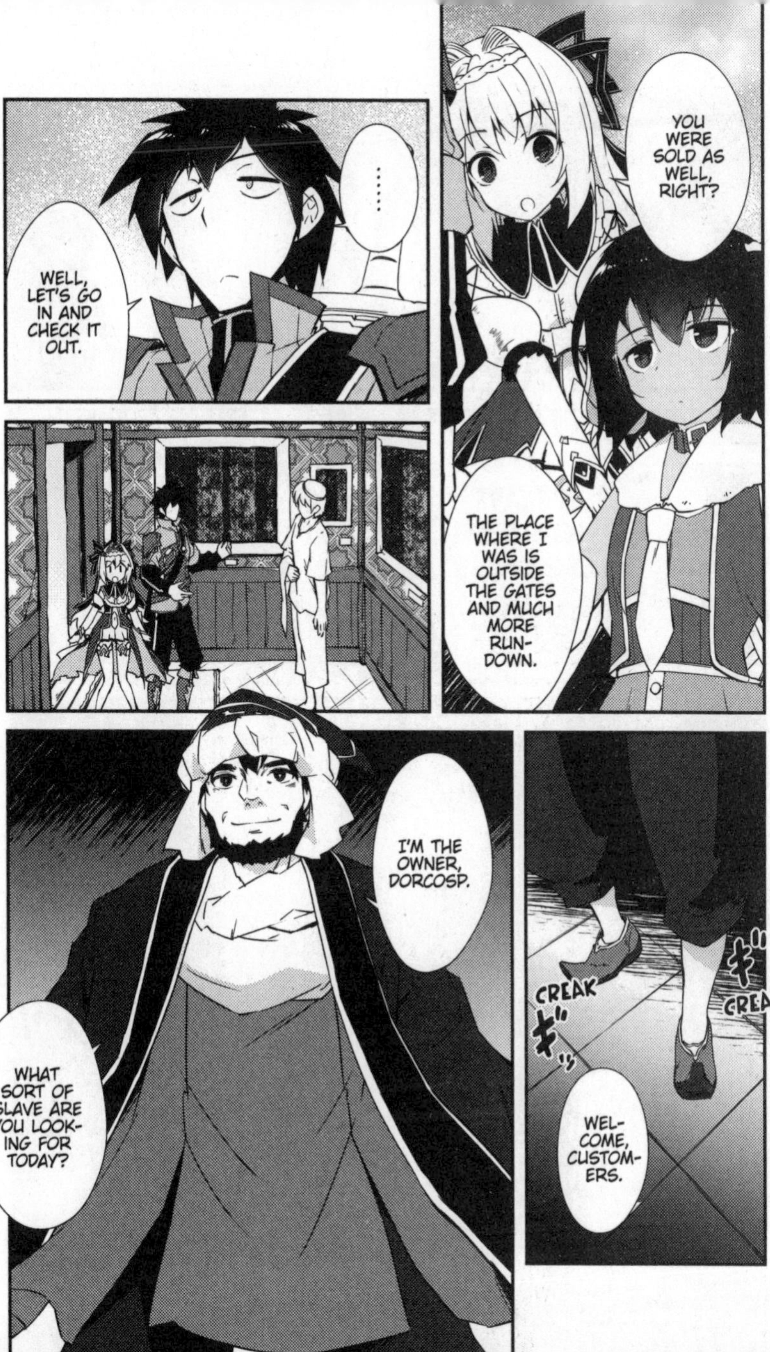
YOU WERE SOLD AS WELL, RIGHT?
THE PLACE WHERE I WAS IS OUTSIDE THE GATES AND MUCH MORE RUN-DOWN.
......
WELL, LET'S GO IN AND CHECK IT OUT.
ギッ
CREAK
CREAK
ギッ
WEL-COME, CUSTOM-ERS.
I'M THE OWNER, DORCOSP.
WHAT SORT OF SLAVE ARE YOU LOOK-ING FOR TODAY?

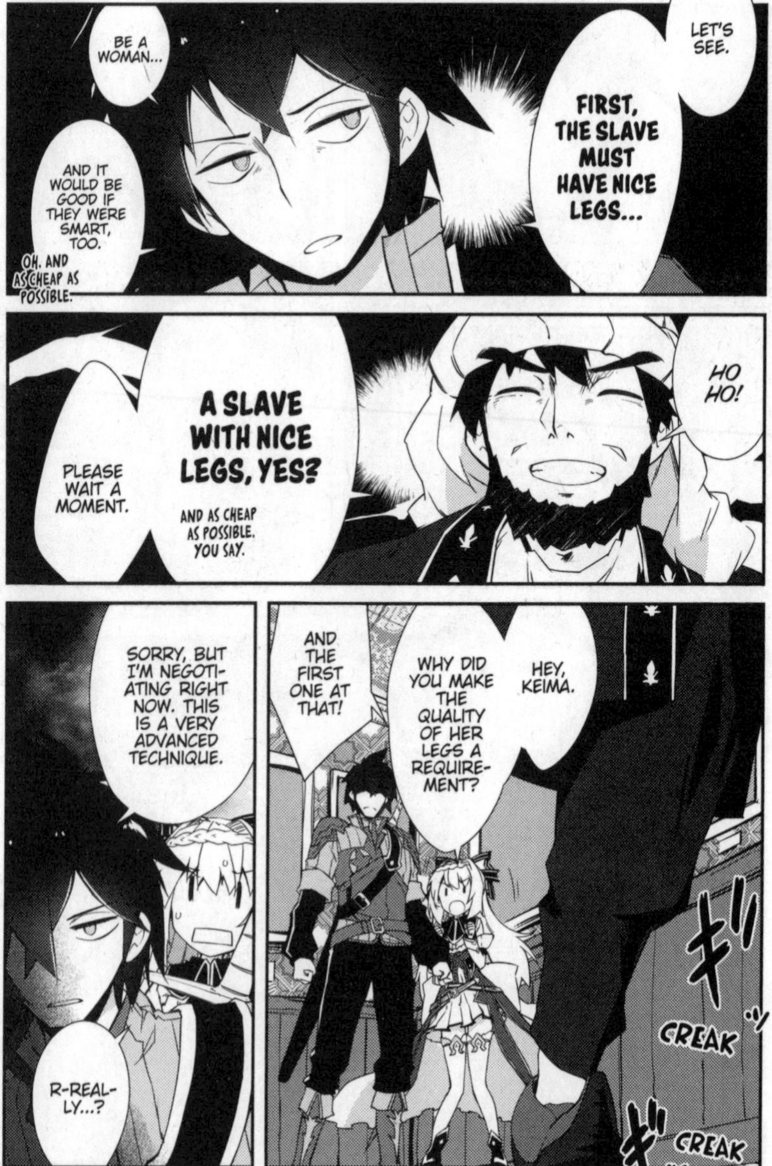
LET'S SEE.
FIRST, THE SLAVE MUST HAVE NICE LEGS...
BE A WOMAN...
AND IT WOULD BE GOOD IF THEY WERE SMART, TOO.
OH. AND AS CHEAP AS POSSIBLE.
HO HO!
A SLAVE WITH NICE LEGS, YES?
AND AS CHEAP AS POSSIBLE. YOU SAY.
PLEASE WAIT A MOMENT.
HEY, KEIMA.
WHY DID YOU MAKE THE QUALITY OF HER LEGS A REQUIREMENT?
AND THE FIRST ONE AT THAT!
ギリッ
CREAK
ギッ
CREAK
SORRY, BUT I'M NEGOTIATING RIGHT NOW. THIS IS A VERY ADVANCED TECHNIQUE.
R-REALLY...?

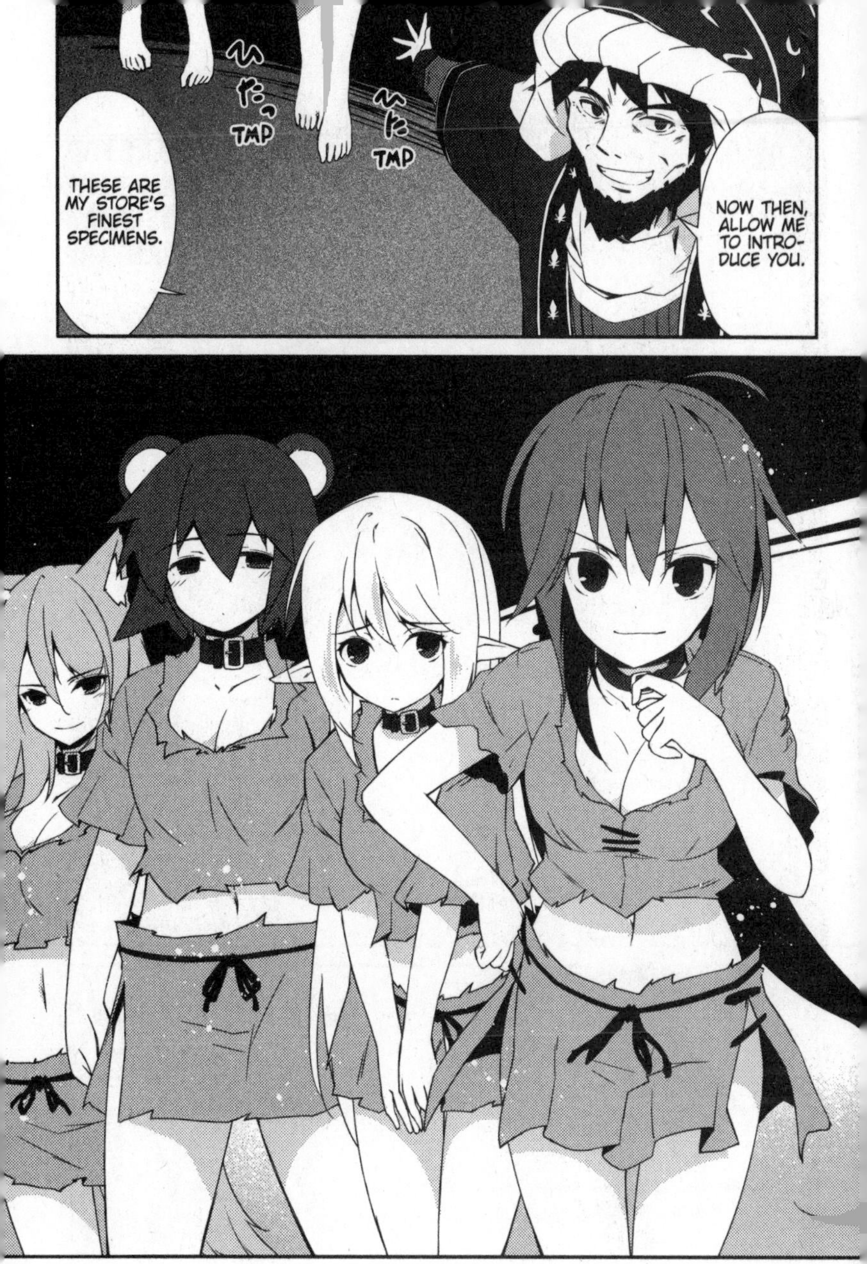
NOW THEN, ALLOW ME TO INTRO-DUCE YOU.
TMP
TMP
THESE ARE MY STORE'S FINEST SPECIMENS.

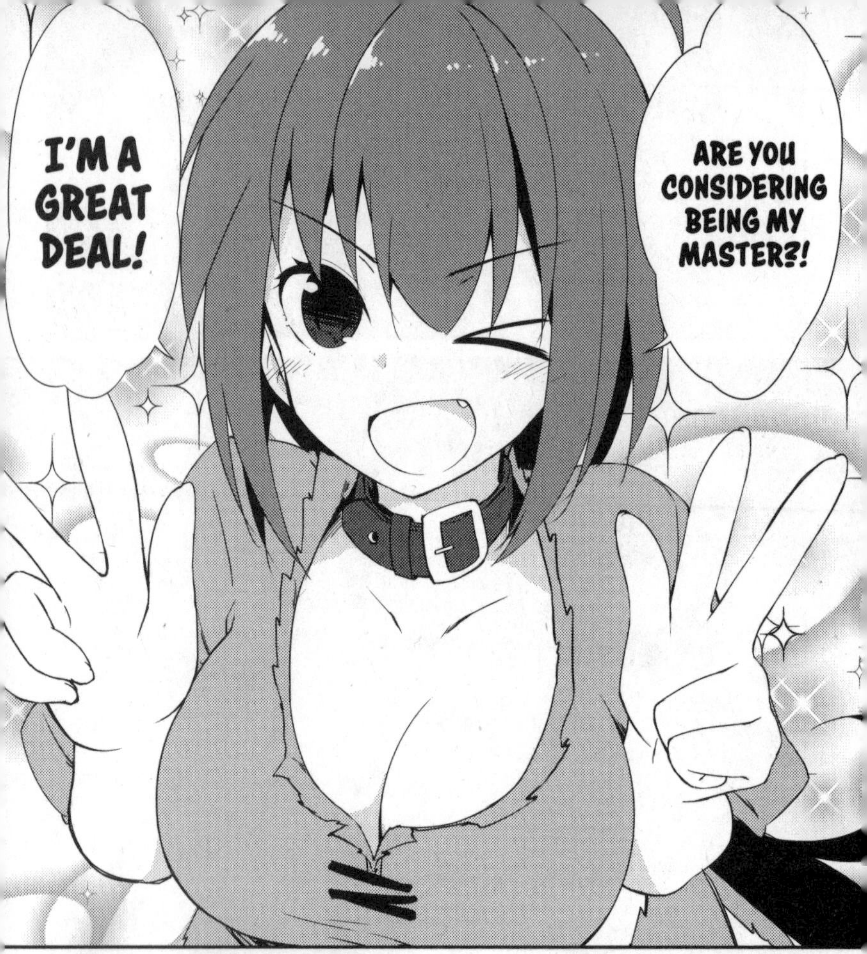
ARE YOU CONSIDERING BEING MY MASTER?!
I'M A GREAT DEAL!

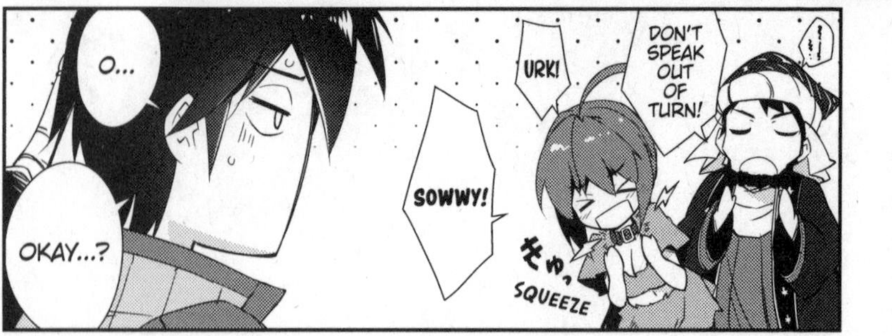
DON'T SPEAK OUT OF TURN!
URK!
SOWWY!
ぎゅっ
SQUEEZE
O...
OKAY...?

LAZY
DUNGEON
MASTER

LAZY
DUNGEON
MASTER

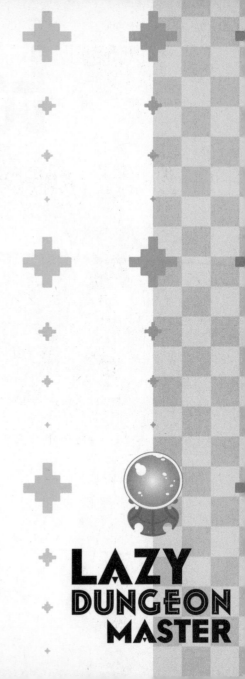

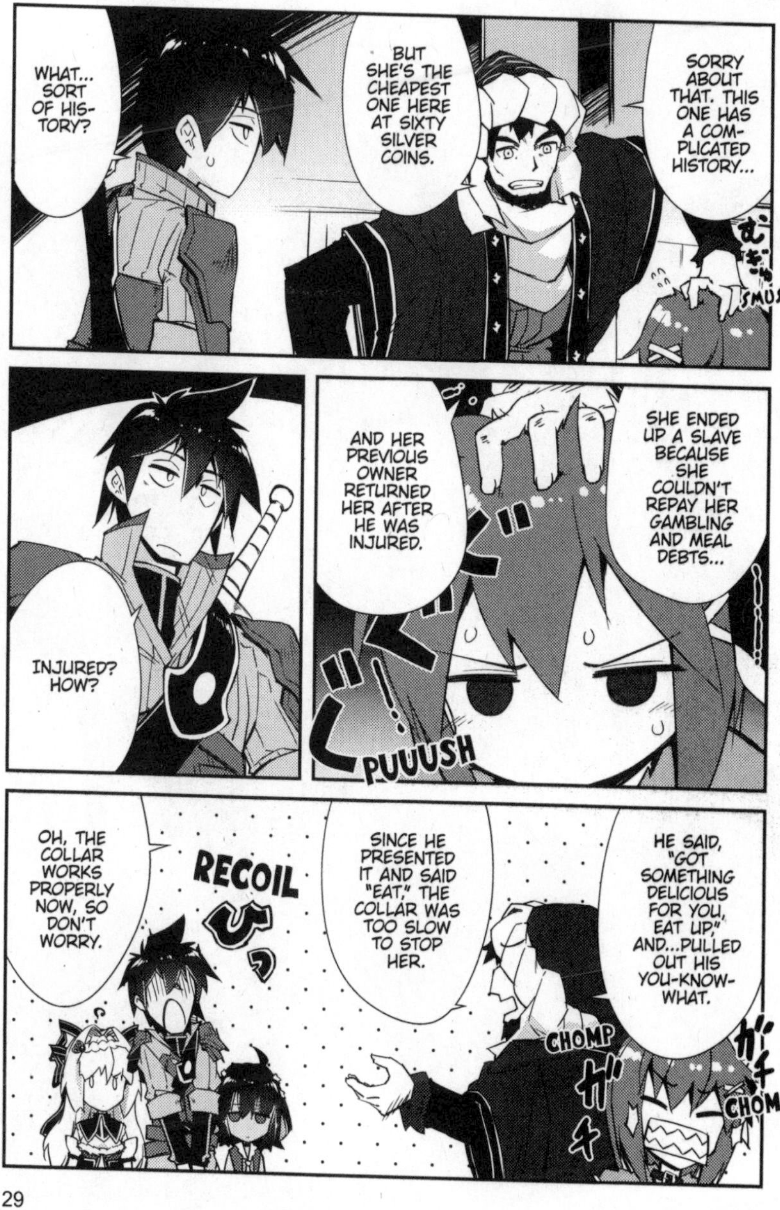
SORRY ABOUT THAT. THIS ONE HAS A COMPLICATED HISTORY...
BUT SHE'S THE CHEAPEST ONE HERE AT SIXTY SILVER COINS.
WHAT... SORT OF HISTORY?
SMUSH
SHE ENDED UP A SLAVE BECAUSE SHE COULDN'T REPAY HER GAMBLING AND MEAL DEBTS...
AND HER PREVIOUS OWNER RETURNED HER AFTER HE WAS INJURED.
PUUUSH
INJURED? HOW?
HE SAID, "GOT SOMETHING DELICIOUS FOR YOU, EAT UP," AND...PULLED OUT HIS YOU-KNOW-WHAT.
SINCE HE PRESENTED IT AND SAID "EAT," THE COLLAR WAS TOO SLOW TO STOP HER.
OH, THE COLLAR WORKS PROPERLY NOW, SO DON'T WORRY.
RECOIL
CHOMP
CHOMP

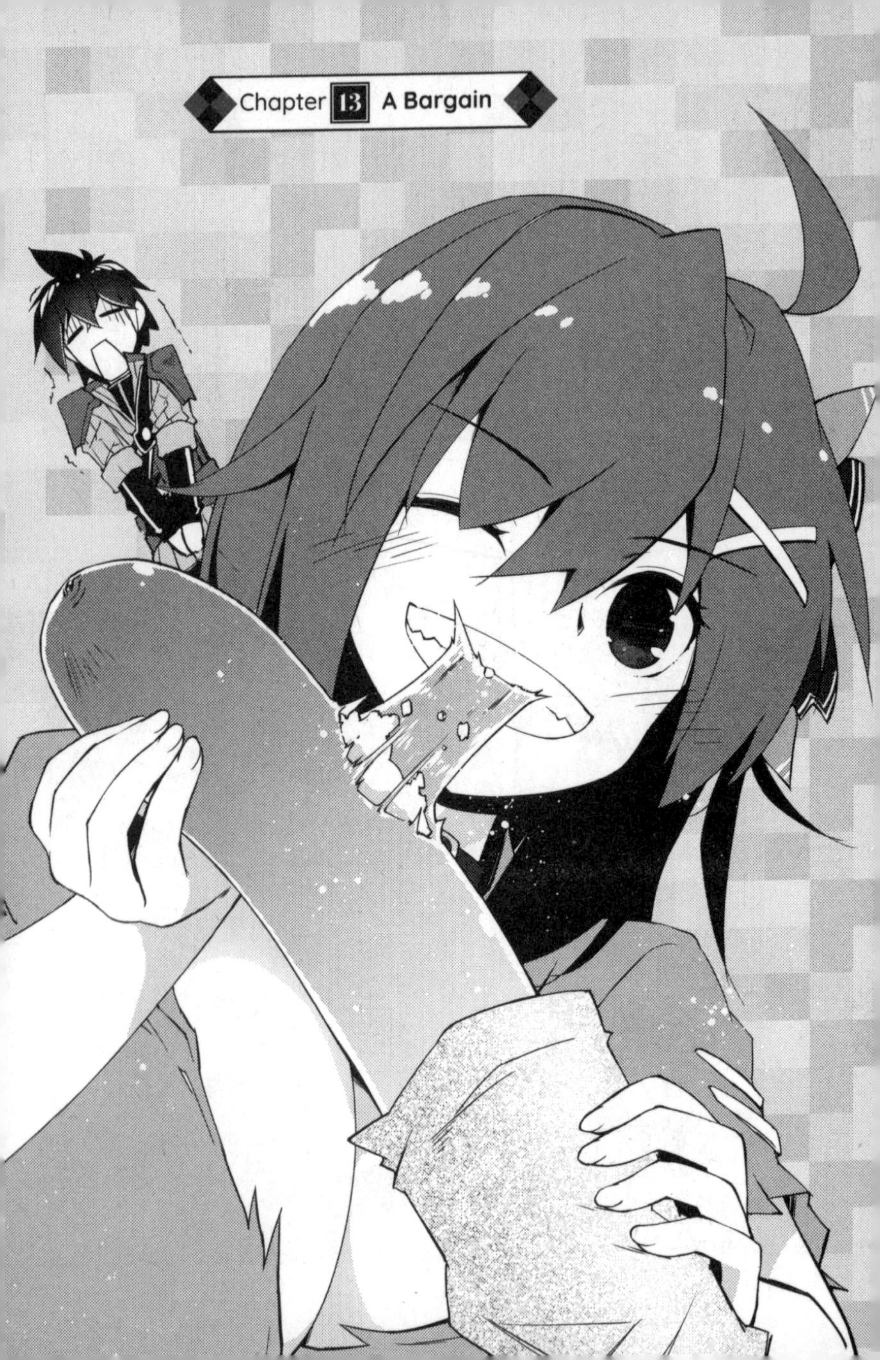
Chapter 13 A Bargain

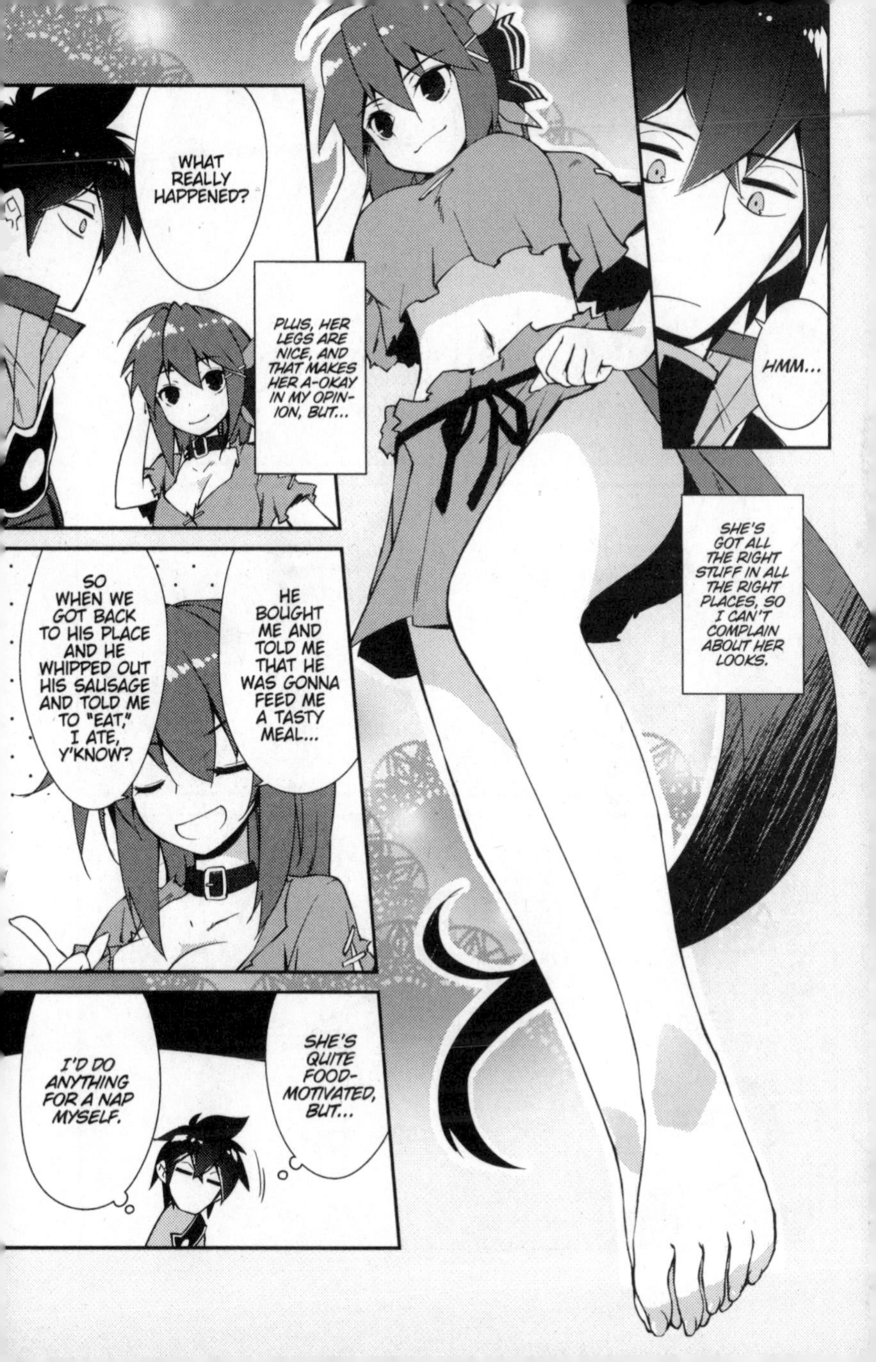
HMM...
SHE'S GOT ALL THE RIGHT STUFF IN ALL THE RIGHT PLACES, SO I CAN'T COMPLAIN ABOUT HER LOOKS.
PLUS, HER LEGS ARE NICE, AND THAT MAKES HER A-OKAY IN MY OPINION, BUT...
WHAT REALLY HAPPENED?
HE BOUGHT ME AND TOLD ME THAT HE WAS GONNA FEED ME A TASTY MEAL...
SO WHEN WE GOT BACK TO HIS PLACE AND HE WHIPPED OUT HIS SAUSAGE AND TOLD ME TO "EAT," I ATE, Y'KNOW?
SHE'S QUITE FOOD-MOTIVATED, BUT...
I'D DO ANYTHING FOR A NAP MYSELF.

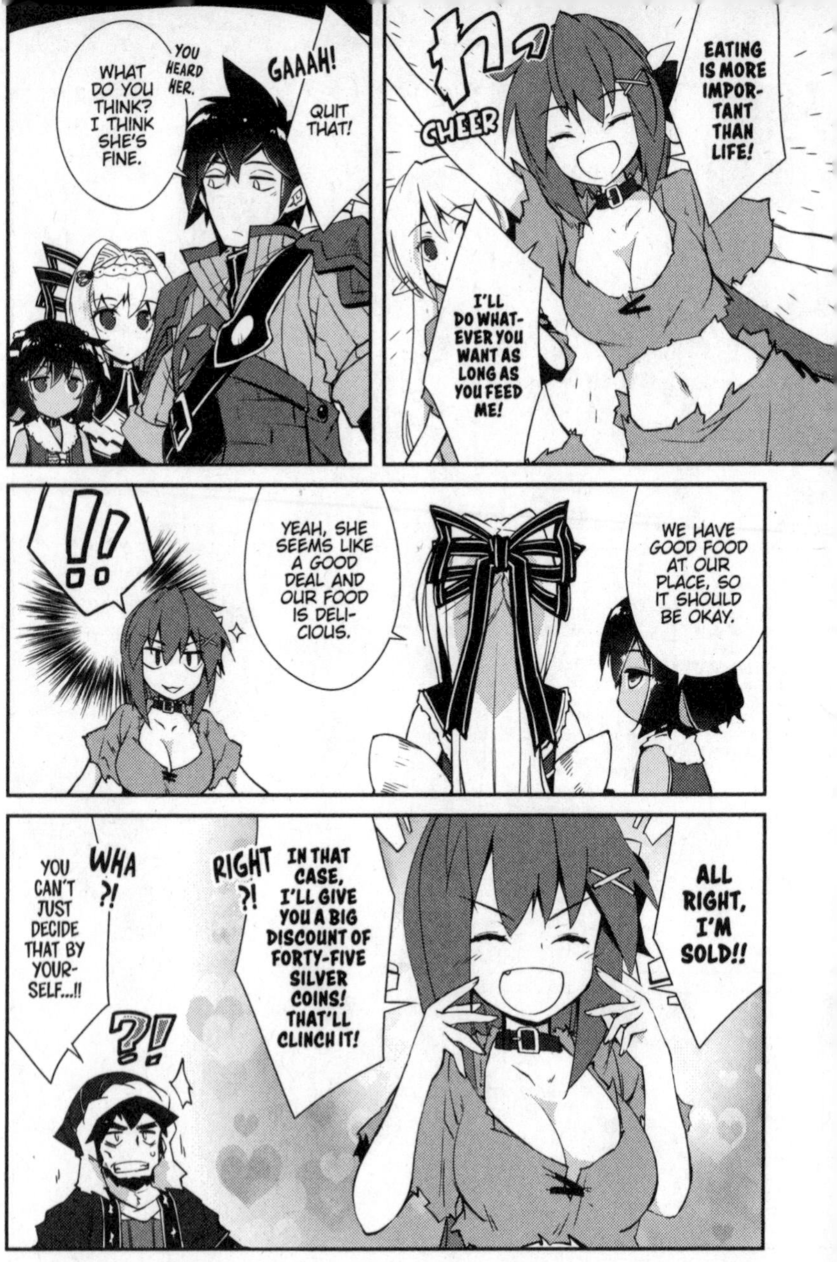
EATING IS MORE IMPOR-TANT THAN LIFE!
わ
CHEER
I'LL DO WHAT-EVER YOU WANT AS LONG AS YOU FEED ME!
GAAAH!
QUIT THAT!
YOU HEARD HER.
WHAT DO YOU THINK? I THINK SHE'S FINE.
WE HAVE GOOD FOOD AT OUR PLACE, SO IT SHOULD BE OKAY.
YEAH, SHE SEEMS LIKE A GOOD DEAL AND OUR FOOD IS DELI-CIOUS.
!!
ALL RIGHT, I'M SOLD!!
IN THAT CASE, I'LL GIVE YOU A BIG DISCOUNT OF FORTY-FIVE SILVER COINS! THAT'LL CLINCH IT!
RIGHT ?!
WHA ?!
YOU CAN'T JUST DECIDE THAT BY YOUR-SELF...!!
?!

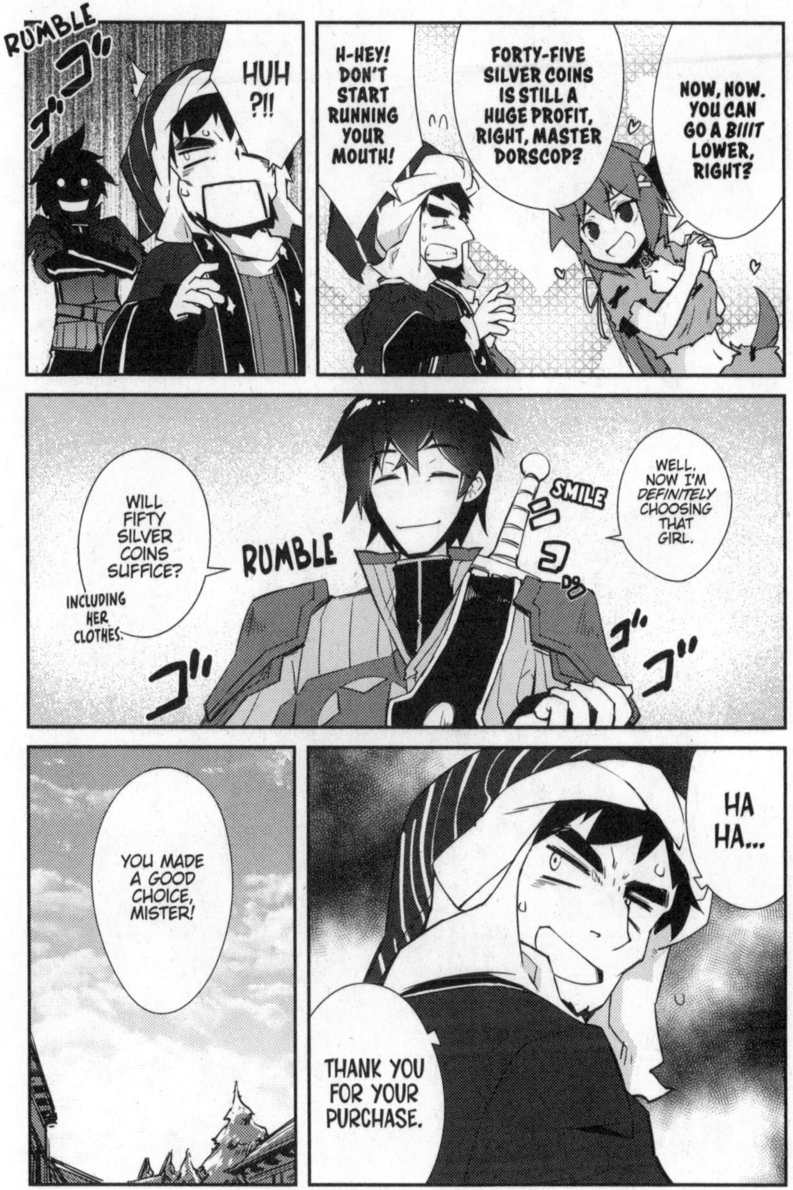
NOW, NOW. YOU CAN GO A *BIIIT* LOWER, RIGHT?
FORTY-FIVE SILVER COINS IS STILL A HUGE PROFIT, RIGHT, MASTER DORSCOP?
H-HEY! DON'T START RUNNING YOUR MOUTH!
HUH ?!!
RUMBLE
WELL. NOW I'M *DEFINITELY* CHOOSING THAT GIRL.
SMILE
WILL FIFTY SILVER COINS SUFFICE?
INCLUDING HER CLOTHES.
RUMBLE
HA HA...
THANK YOU FOR YOUR PURCHASE.
YOU MADE A GOOD CHOICE, MISTER!

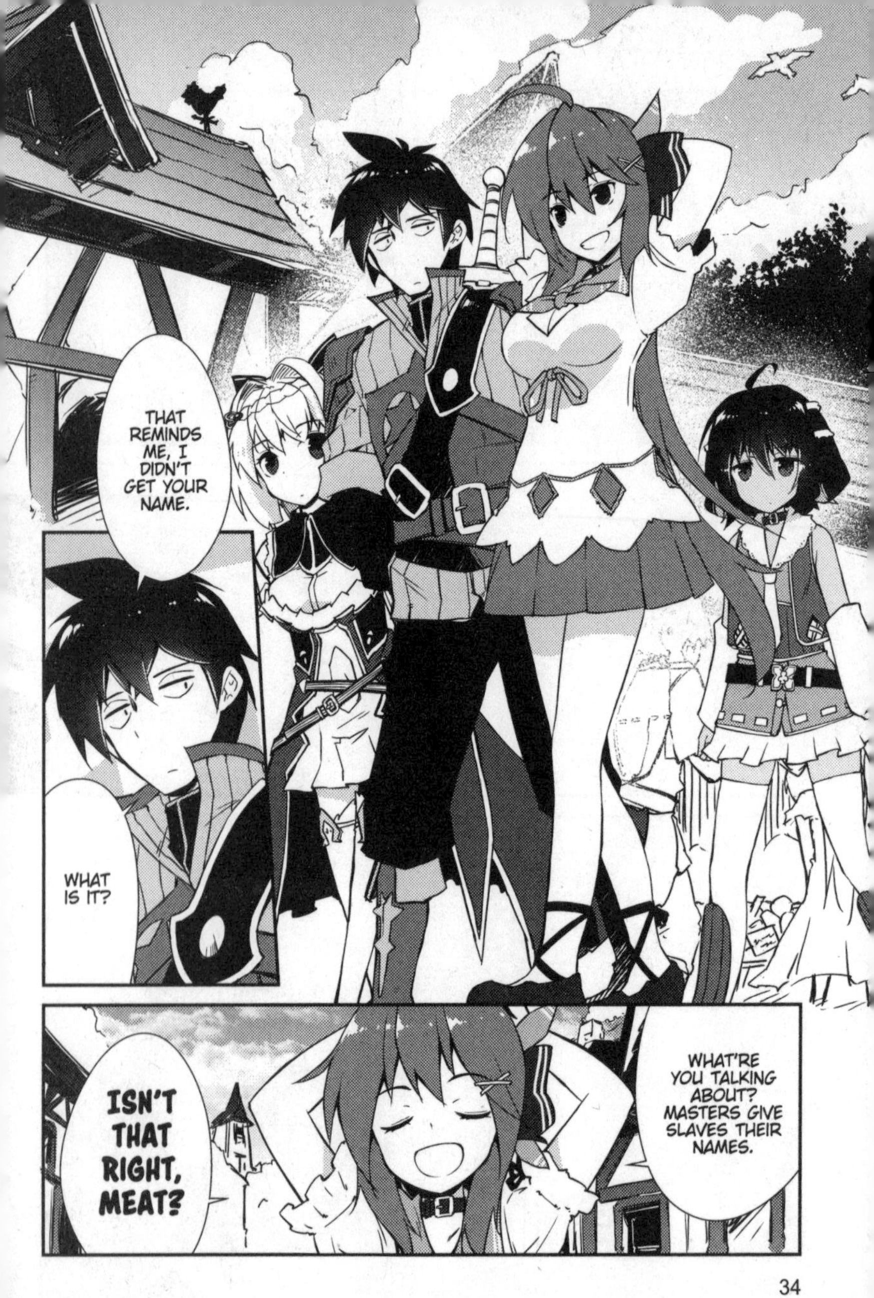
THAT REMINDS ME, I DIDN'T GET YOUR NAME.
WHAT IS IT?
WHAT'RE YOU TALKING ABOUT? MASTERS GIVE SLAVES THEIR NAMES.
ISN'T THAT RIGHT, MEAT?

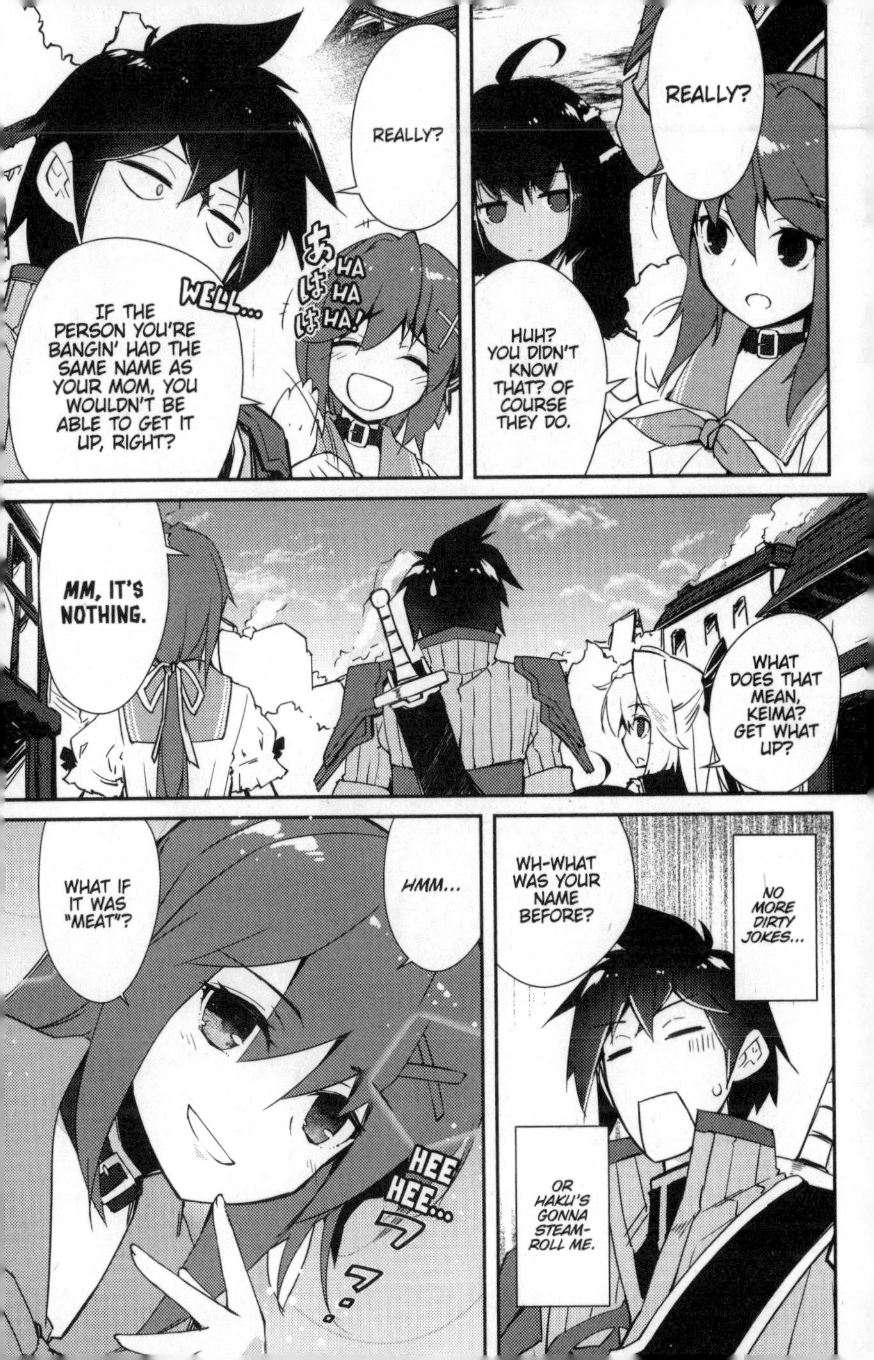
REALLY?
HUH? YOU DIDN'T KNOW THAT? OF COURSE THEY DO.
REALLY?
あはは HA HA HA!
WELL...
IF THE PERSON YOU'RE BANGIN' HAD THE SAME NAME AS YOUR MOM, YOU WOULDN'T BE ABLE TO GET IT UP, RIGHT?
WHAT DOES THAT MEAN, KEIMA? GET WHAT UP?
MM, IT'S NOTHING.
NO MORE DIRTY JOKES...
WH-WHAT WAS YOUR NAME BEFORE?
OR HAKU'S GONNA STEAM-ROLL ME.
HMM...
WHAT IF IT WAS "MEAT"?
HEE HEE...

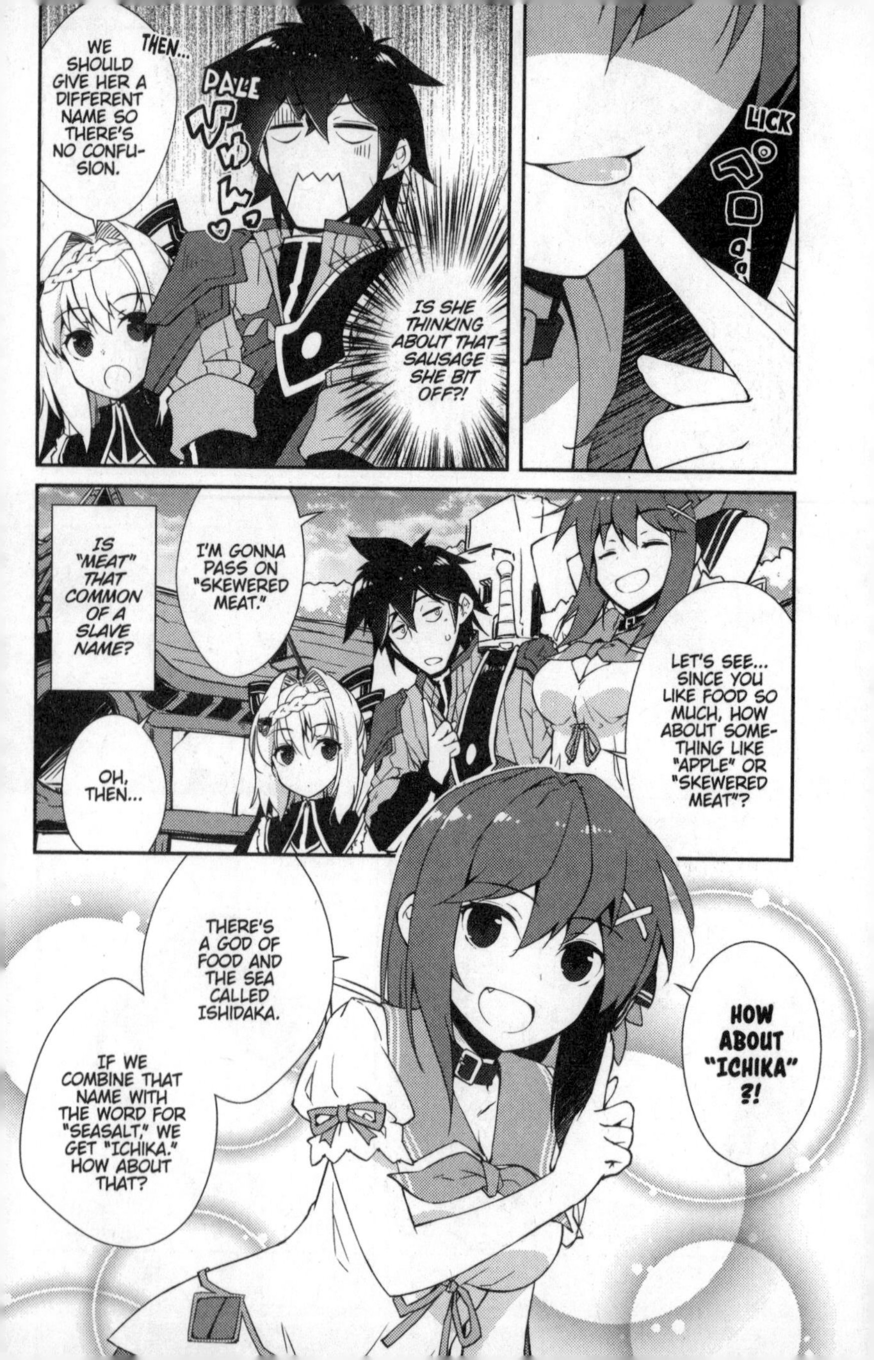
LICK
THEN...
WE SHOULD GIVE HER A DIFFERENT NAME SO THERE'S NO CONFUSION.
PALE
IS SHE THINKING ABOUT THAT SAUSAGE SHE BIT OFF?!
LET'S SEE... SINCE YOU LIKE FOOD SO MUCH, HOW ABOUT SOMETHING LIKE "APPLE" OR "SKEWERED MEAT"?
I'M GONNA PASS ON "SKEWERED MEAT."
IS "MEAT" THAT COMMON OF A SLAVE NAME?
OH, THEN...
HOW ABOUT "ICHIKA" ?!
THERE'S A GOD OF FOOD AND THE SEA CALLED ISHIDAKA.
IF WE COMBINE THAT NAME WITH THE WORD FOR "SEASALT," WE GET "ICHIKA." HOW ABOUT THAT?

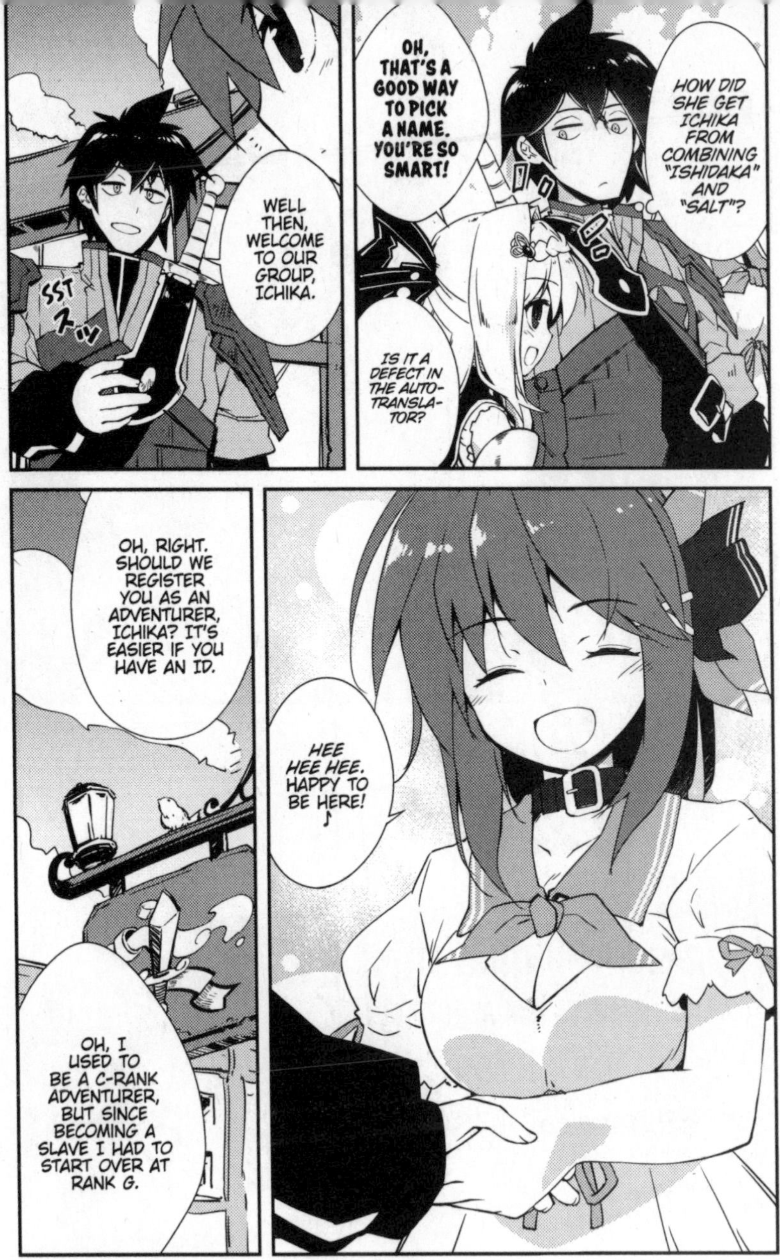
HOW DID SHE GET ICHIKA FROM COMBINING "ISHIDAKA" AND "SALT"?
OH, THAT'S A GOOD WAY TO PICK A NAME. YOU'RE SO SMART!
IS IT A DEFECT IN THE AUTO-TRANSLATOR?
WELL THEN, WELCOME TO OUR GROUP, ICHIKA.
SST
スッ
HEE HEE HEE. HAPPY TO BE HERE! ♪
OH, RIGHT. SHOULD WE REGISTER YOU AS AN ADVENTURER, ICHIKA? IT'S EASIER IF YOU HAVE AN ID.
OH, I USED TO BE A C-RANK ADVENTURER, BUT SINCE BECOMING A SLAVE I HAD TO START OVER AT RANK G.

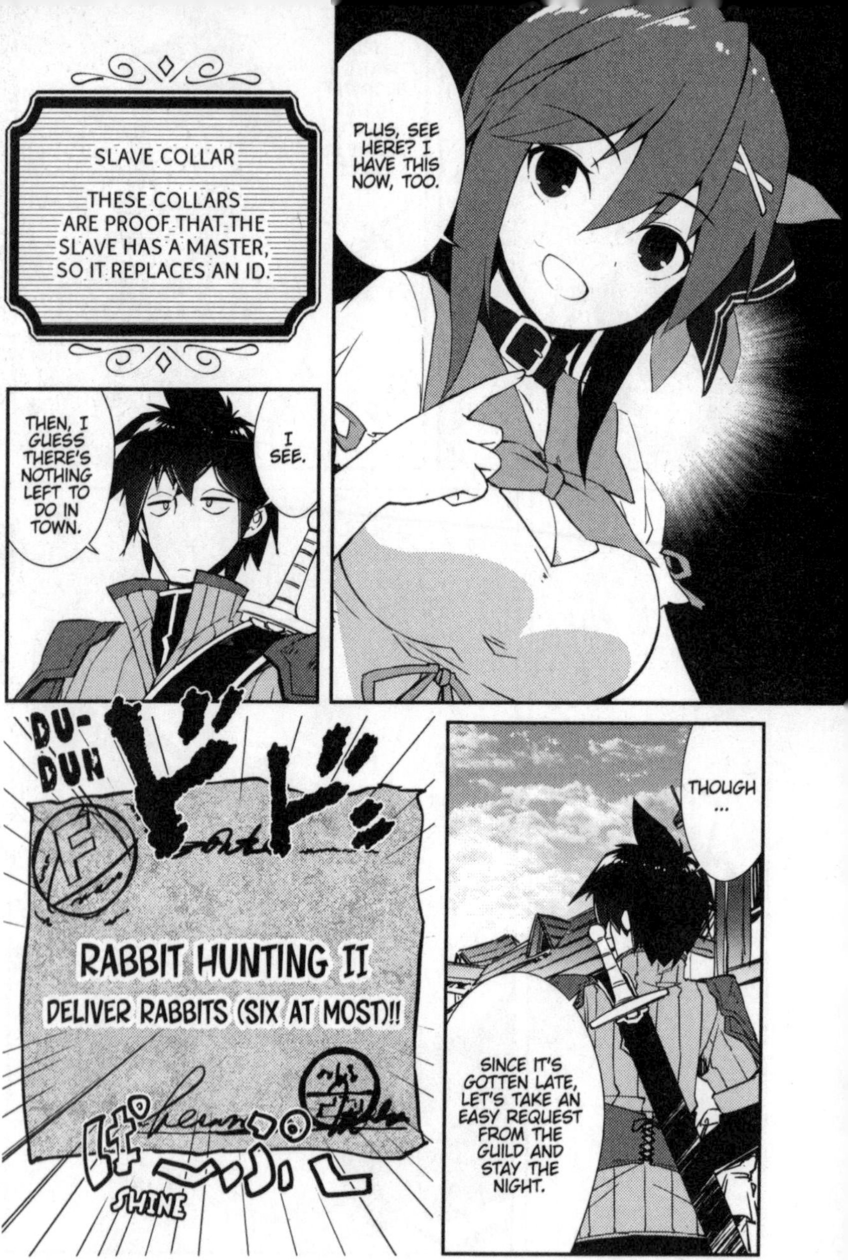
PLUS, SEE HERE? I HAVE THIS NOW, TOO.
SLAVE COLLAR
THESE COLLARS ARE PROOF THAT THE SLAVE HAS A MASTER, SO IT REPLACES AN ID.
I SEE.
THEN, I GUESS THERE'S NOTHING LEFT TO DO IN TOWN.
THOUGH ...
SINCE IT'S GOTTEN LATE, LET'S TAKE AN EASY REQUEST FROM THE GUILD AND STAY THE NIGHT.
DU-DUN
F
RABBIT HUNTING II
DELIVER RABBITS (SIX AT MOST)!!
SHINE

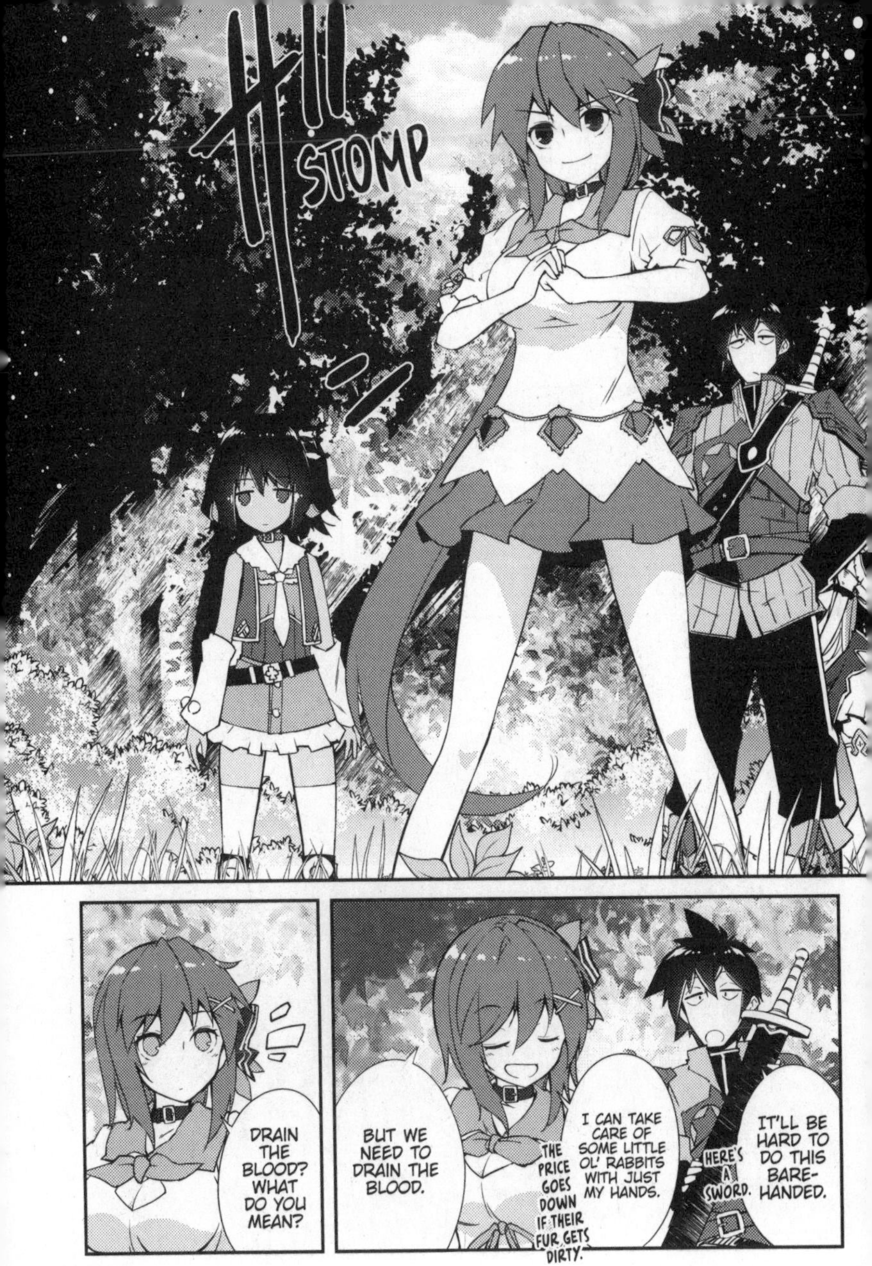
STOMP
IT'LL BE HARD TO DO THIS BARE-HANDED.
HERE'S A SWORD.
I CAN TAKE CARE OF SOME LITTLE OL' RABBITS WITH JUST MY HANDS.
THE PRICE GOES DOWN IF THEIR FUR GETS DIRTY.
BUT WE NEED TO DRAIN THE BLOOD.
DRAIN THE BLOOD? WHAT DO YOU MEAN?

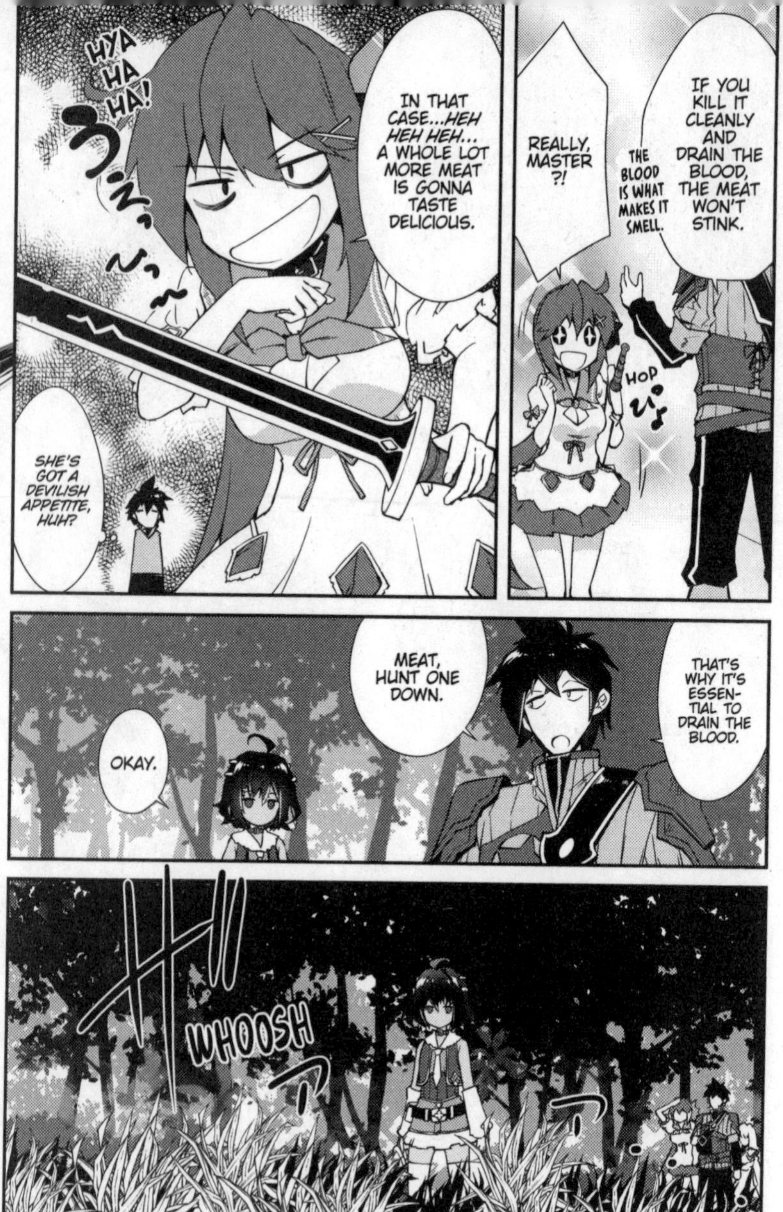
IF YOU KILL IT CLEANLY AND DRAIN THE BLOOD, THE MEAT WON'T STINK.
THE BLOOD IS WHAT MAKES IT SMELL.
REALLY, MASTER?!
HOP
IN THAT CASE...HEH HEH HEH... A WHOLE LOT MORE MEAT IS GONNA TASTE DELICIOUS.
HYA HA HA!
SHE'S GOT A DEVILISH APPETITE, HUH?
THAT'S WHY IT'S ESSEN-TIAL TO DRAIN THE BLOOD.
MEAT, HUNT ONE DOWN.
OKAY.
WHOOSH

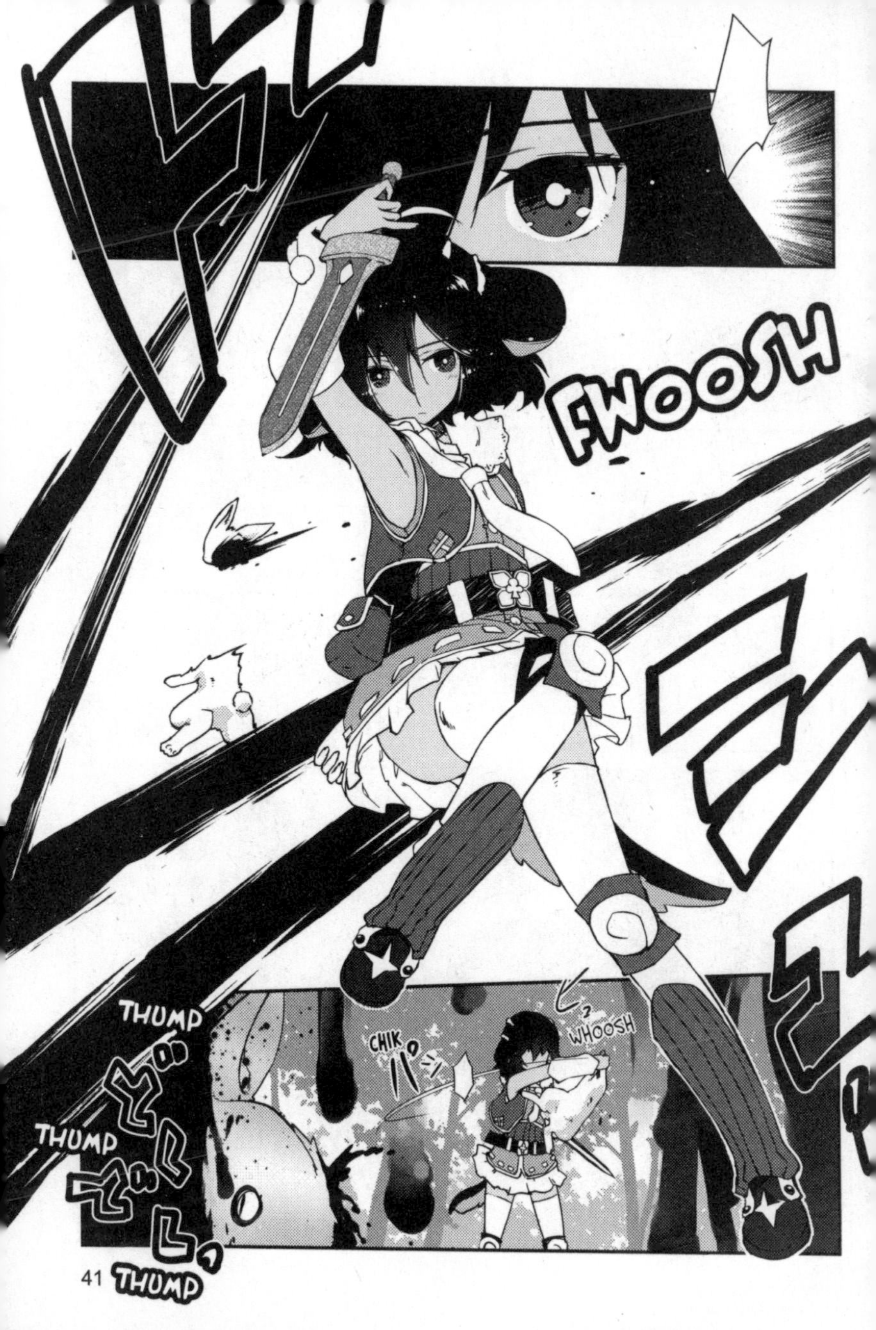
FWOOSH
WHOOSH
CHIK
THUMP
THUMP
THUMP

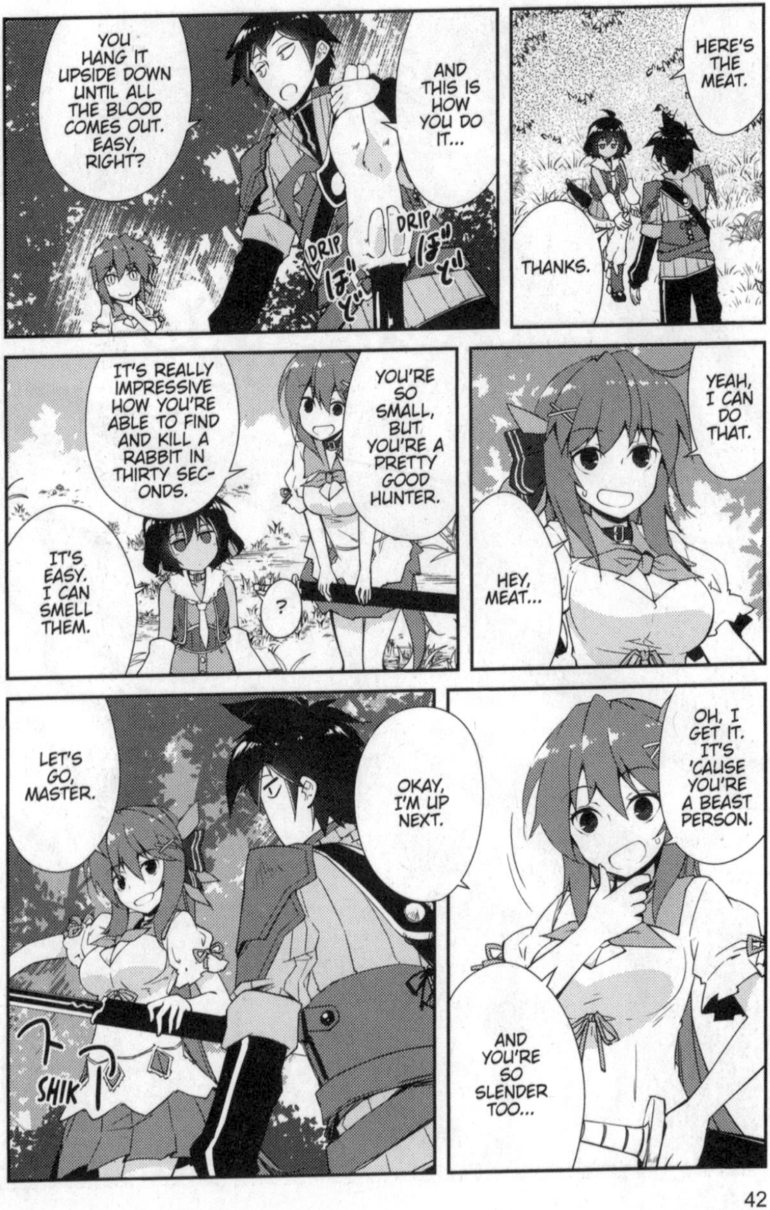
HERE'S THE MEAT.
THANKS.
AND THIS IS HOW YOU DO IT...
YOU HANG IT UPSIDE DOWN UNTIL ALL THE BLOOD COMES OUT. EASY, RIGHT?
DRIP
DRIP
YEAH, I CAN DO THAT.
HEY, MEAT...
YOU'RE SO SMALL, BUT YOU'RE A PRETTY GOOD HUNTER.
IT'S REALLY IMPRESSIVE HOW YOU'RE ABLE TO FIND AND KILL A RABBIT IN THIRTY SEC-ONDS.
?
IT'S EASY. I CAN SMELL THEM.
OH, I GET IT. IT'S 'CAUSE YOU'RE A BEAST PERSON.
AND YOU'RE SO SLENDER TOO...
OKAY, I'M UP NEXT.
LET'S GO, MASTER.
SHIK

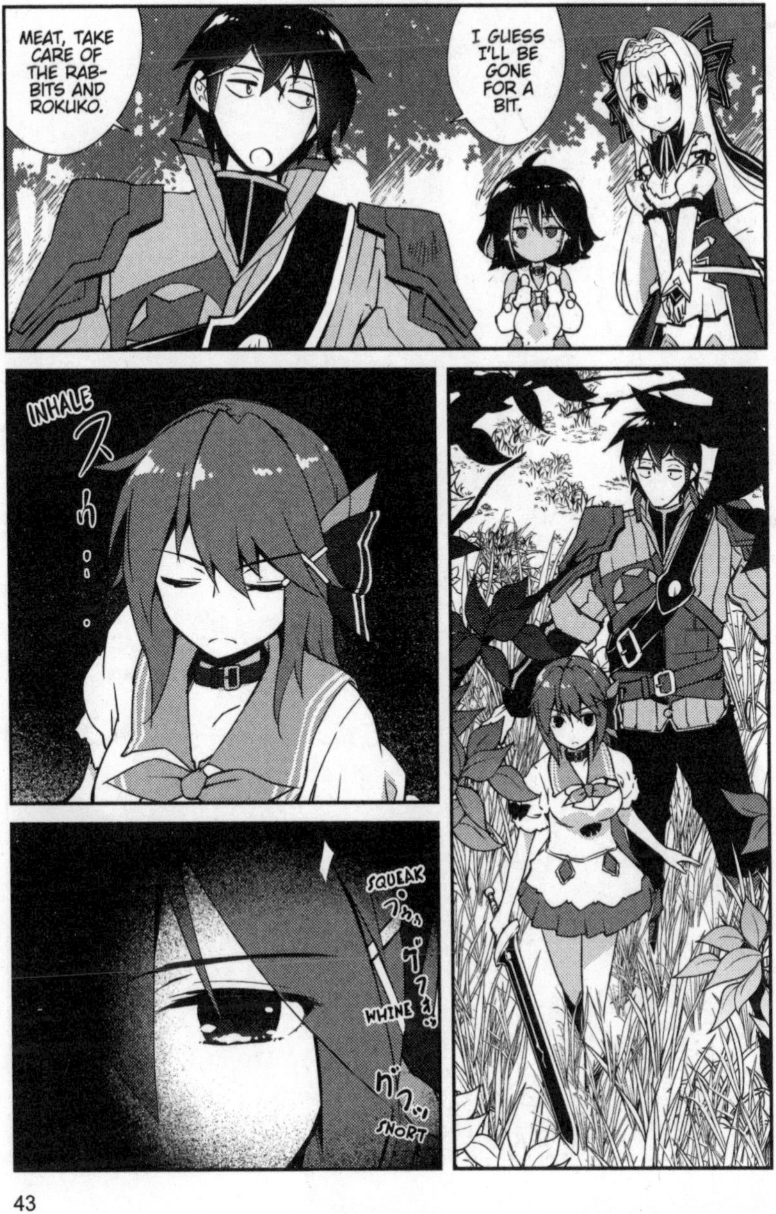
I GUESS I'LL BE GONE FOR A BIT.
MEAT, TAKE CARE OF THE RAB-BITS AND ROKUKO.
INHALE
SQUEAK
WHINE
SNORT

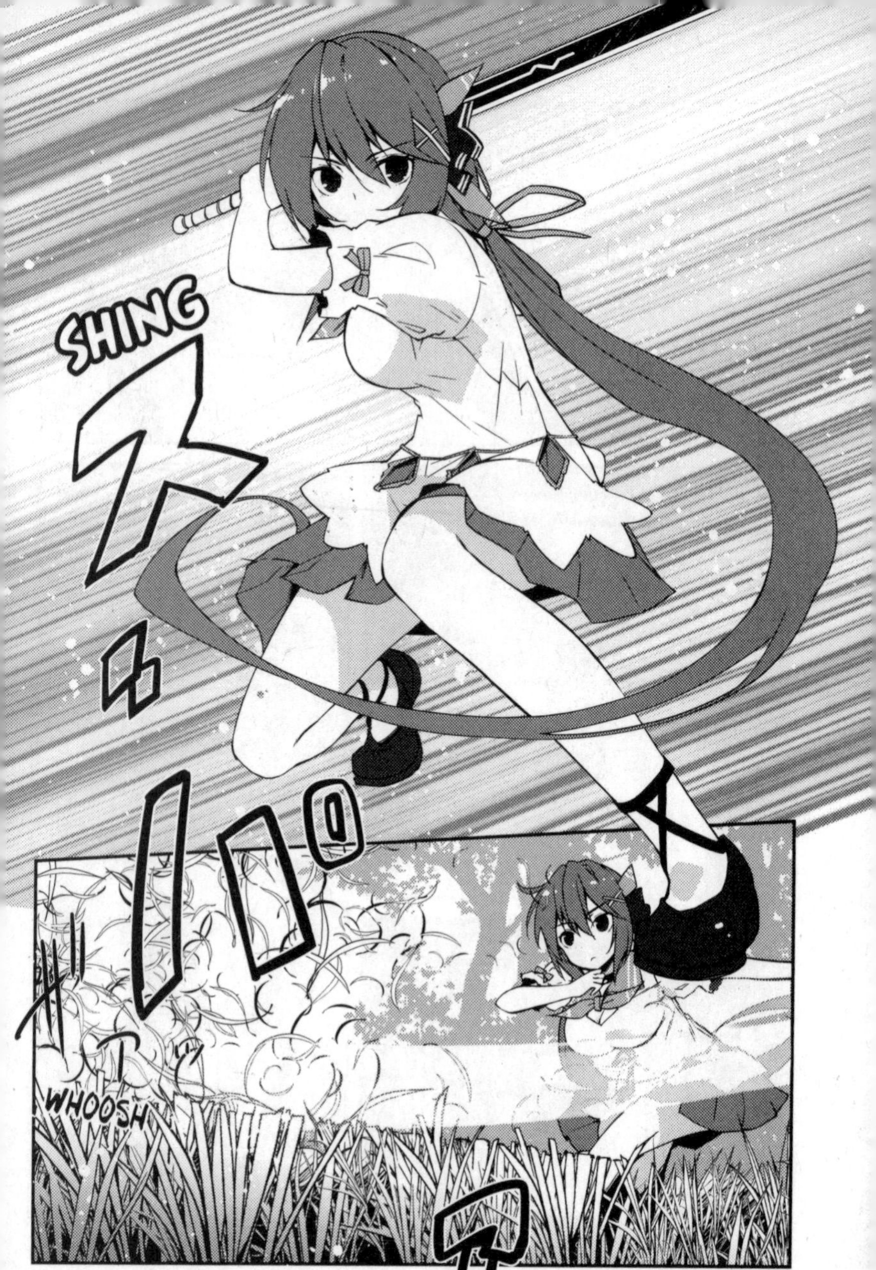
SHING
WHOOSH

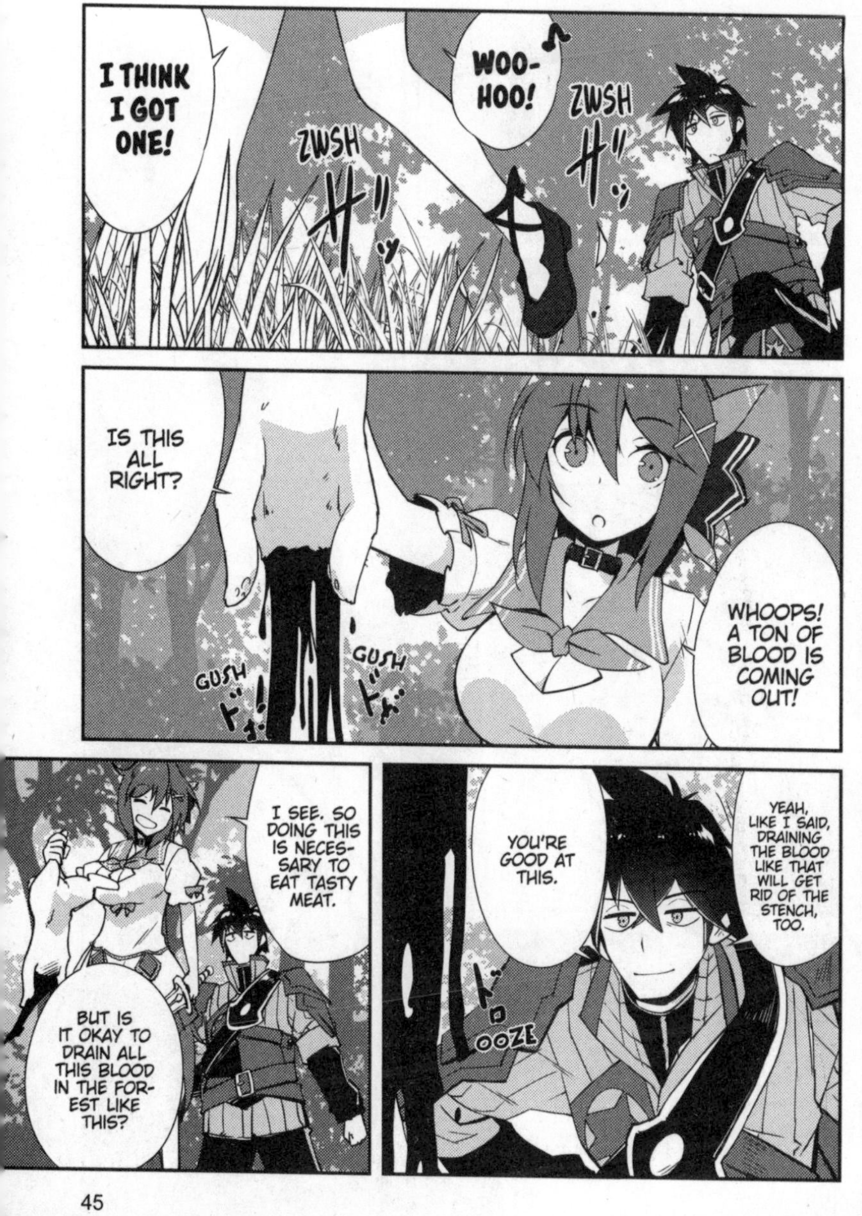

WOO-HOO! ♪
ZWSH
I THINK I GOT ONE!
ZWSH
WHOOPS! A TON OF BLOOD IS COMING OUT!
IS THIS ALL RIGHT?
GUSH
GUSH
YEAH, LIKE I SAID, DRAINING THE BLOOD LIKE THAT WILL GET RID OF THE STENCH, TOO.
YOU'RE GOOD AT THIS.
OOZE
I SEE. SO DOING THIS IS NECES-SARY TO EAT TASTY MEAT.
BUT IS IT OKAY TO DRAIN ALL THIS BLOOD IN THE FOR-EST LIKE THIS?

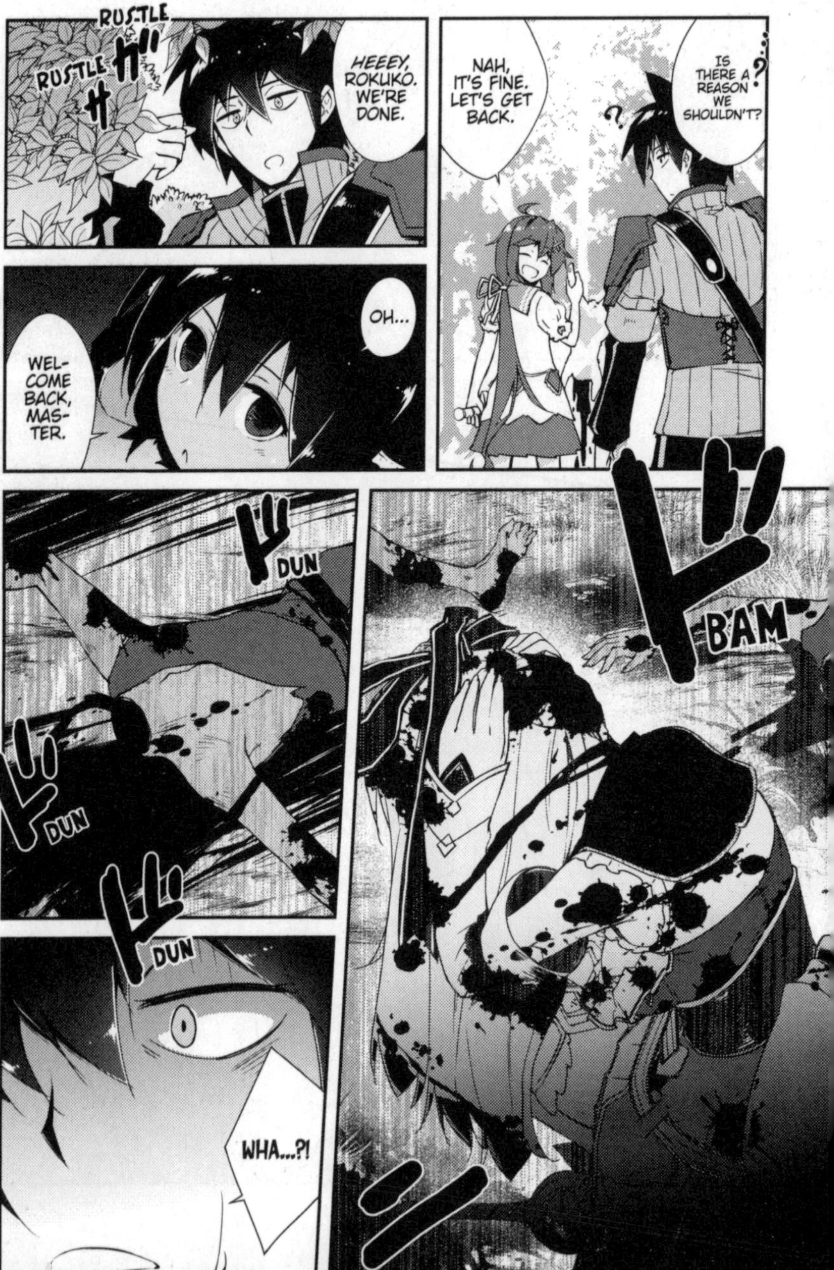
IS THERE A REASON WE SHOULDN'T?
NAH, IT'S FINE. LET'S GET BACK.
RUSTLE
RUSTLE
HEEEY, ROKUKO. WE'RE DONE.
OH...
WEL-COME BACK, MAS-TER.
BAM
DUN
DUN
DUN
WHA...?!

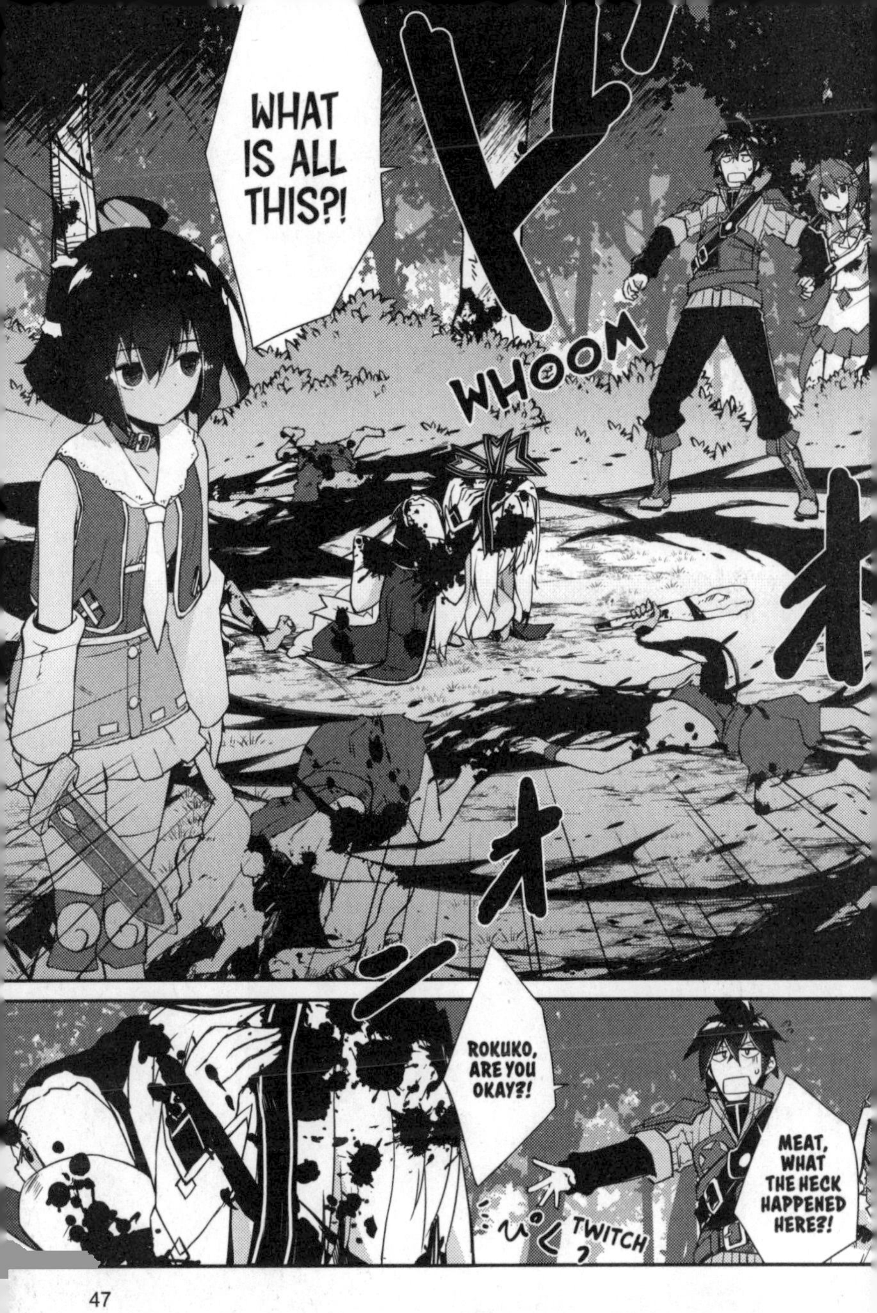
WHOOM
WHAT IS ALL THIS?!
MEAT, WHAT THE HECK HAPPENED HERE?!
ROKUKO, ARE YOU OKAY?!
TWITCH

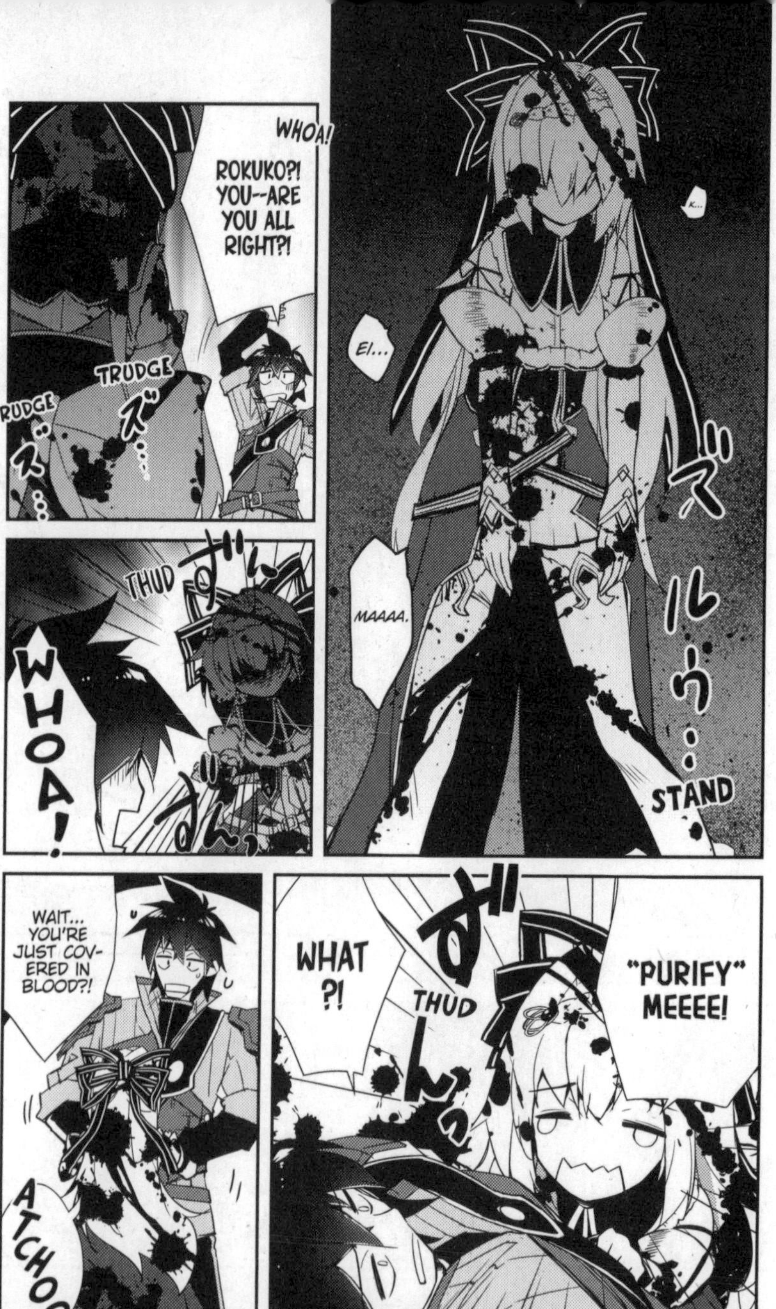
K...
EI...
MAAAA.
STAND
WHOA!
ROKUKO?! YOU--ARE YOU ALL RIGHT?!
TRUDGE
TRUDGE
THUD
WHOA!
"PURIFY" MEEEE!
THUD
WHAT ?!
WAIT... YOU'RE JUST COVERED IN BLOOD?!
ATCHOO!

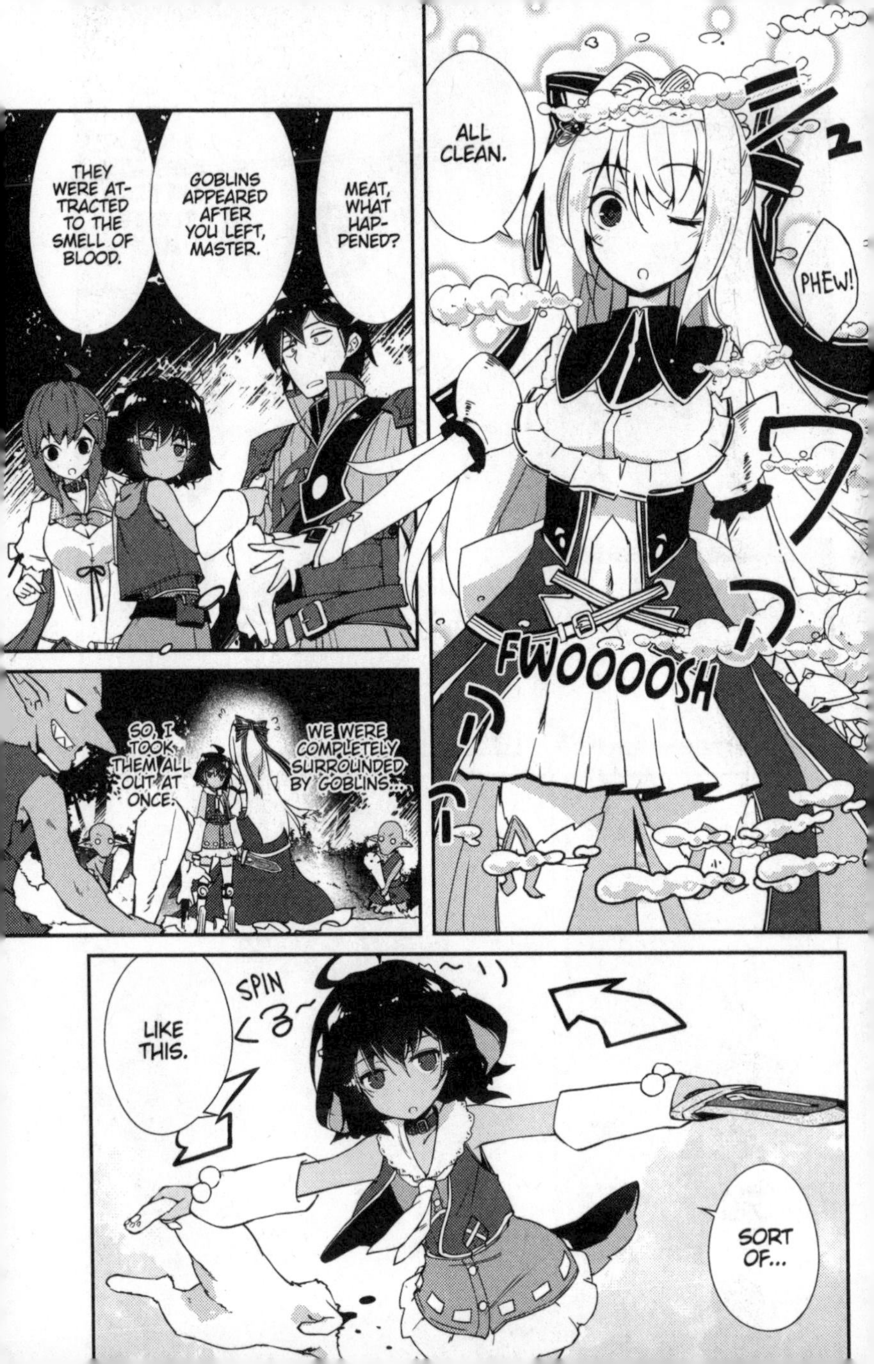
ALL CLEAN.
PHEW!
FWOOOOSH
MEAT, WHAT HAP-PENED?
GOBLINS APPEARED AFTER YOU LEFT, MASTER.
THEY WERE AT-TRACTED TO THE SMELL OF BLOOD.
WE WERE COMPLETELY SURROUNDED BY GOBLINS...
SO, I TOOK THEM ALL OUT AT ONCE.
SPIN
くる~
LIKE THIS.
SORT OF...

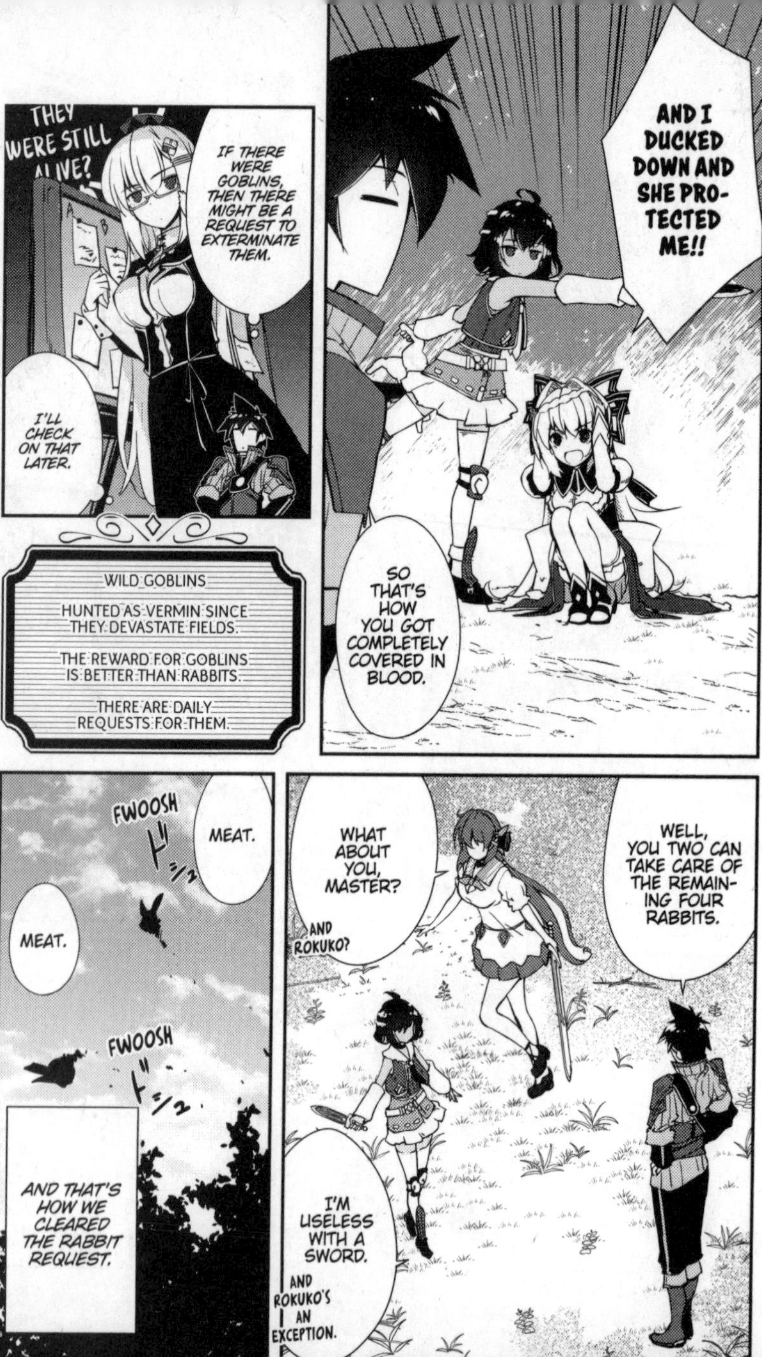
AND I DUCKED DOWN AND SHE PRO-TECTED ME!!
SO THAT'S HOW YOU GOT COMPLETELY COVERED IN BLOOD.
IF THERE WERE GOBLINS, THEN THERE MIGHT BE A REQUEST TO EXTERMINATE THEM.
THEY WERE STILL ALIVE?
I'LL CHECK ON THAT LATER.
WILD GOBLINS
HUNTED AS VERMIN SINCE THEY DEVASTATE FIELDS.
THE REWARD FOR GOBLINS IS BETTER THAN RABBITS.
THERE ARE DAILY REQUESTS FOR THEM.
WELL, YOU TWO CAN TAKE CARE OF THE REMAIN-ING FOUR RABBITS.
WHAT ABOUT YOU, MASTER?
AND ROKUKO?
I'M USELESS WITH A SWORD.
AND ROKUKO'S AN EXCEPTION.
FWOOSH
MEAT.
MEAT.
FWOOSH
AND THAT'S HOW WE CLEARED THE RABBIT REQUEST.

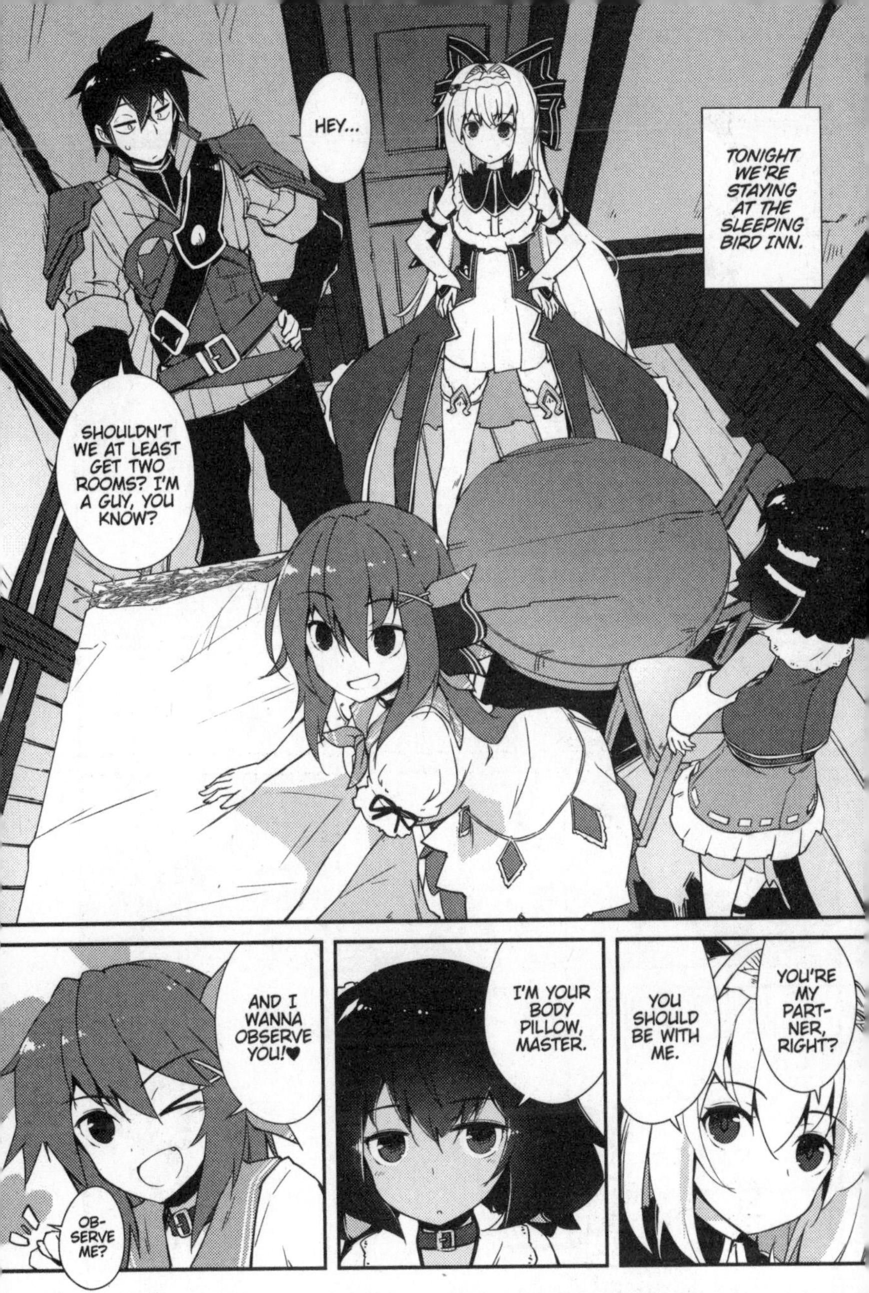
TONIGHT WE'RE STAYING AT THE SLEEPING BIRD INN.
HEY...
SHOULDN'T WE AT LEAST GET TWO ROOMS? I'M A GUY, YOU KNOW?
YOU'RE MY PART-NER, RIGHT?
YOU SHOULD BE WITH ME.
I'M YOUR BODY PILLOW, MASTER.
AND I WANNA OBSERVE YOU!♥
OB-SERVE ME?

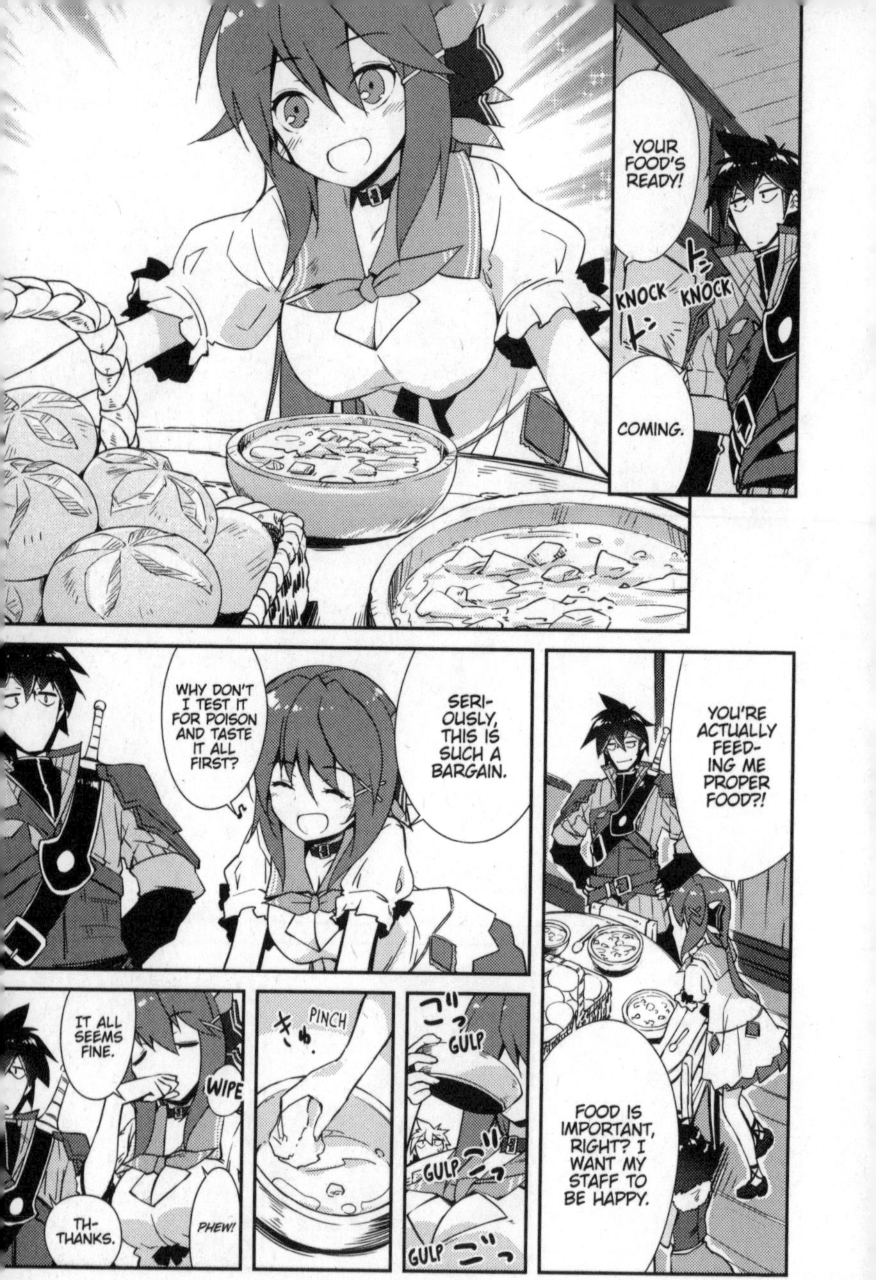
YOUR FOOD'S READY!
KNOCK KNOCK
COMING.
YOU'RE ACTUALLY FEEDING ME PROPER FOOD?!
FOOD IS IMPORTANT, RIGHT? I WANT MY STAFF TO BE HAPPY.
SERIOUSLY, THIS IS SUCH A BARGAIN.
WHY DON'T I TEST IT FOR POISON AND TASTE IT ALL FIRST?
GULP
GULP
GULP
PINCH
IT ALL SEEMS FINE.
WIPE
TH-THANKS.
PHEW!

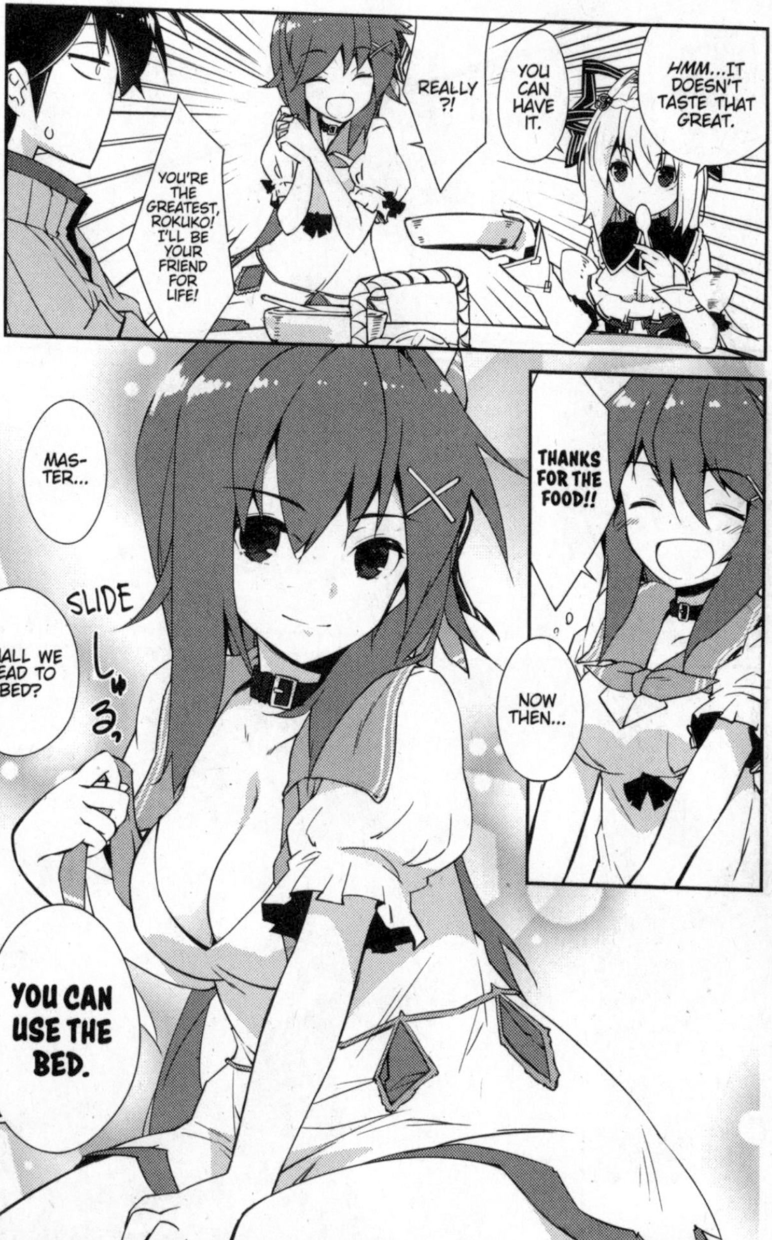
HMM...IT DOESN'T TASTE THAT GREAT.
YOU CAN HAVE IT.
REALLY ?!
YOU'RE THE GREATEST, ROKUKO! I'LL BE YOUR FRIEND FOR LIFE!
THANKS FOR THE FOOD!!
NOW THEN...
MAS- TER...
SLIDE
しゅるっ
SHALL WE HEAD TO BED?
YOU CAN USE THE BED.

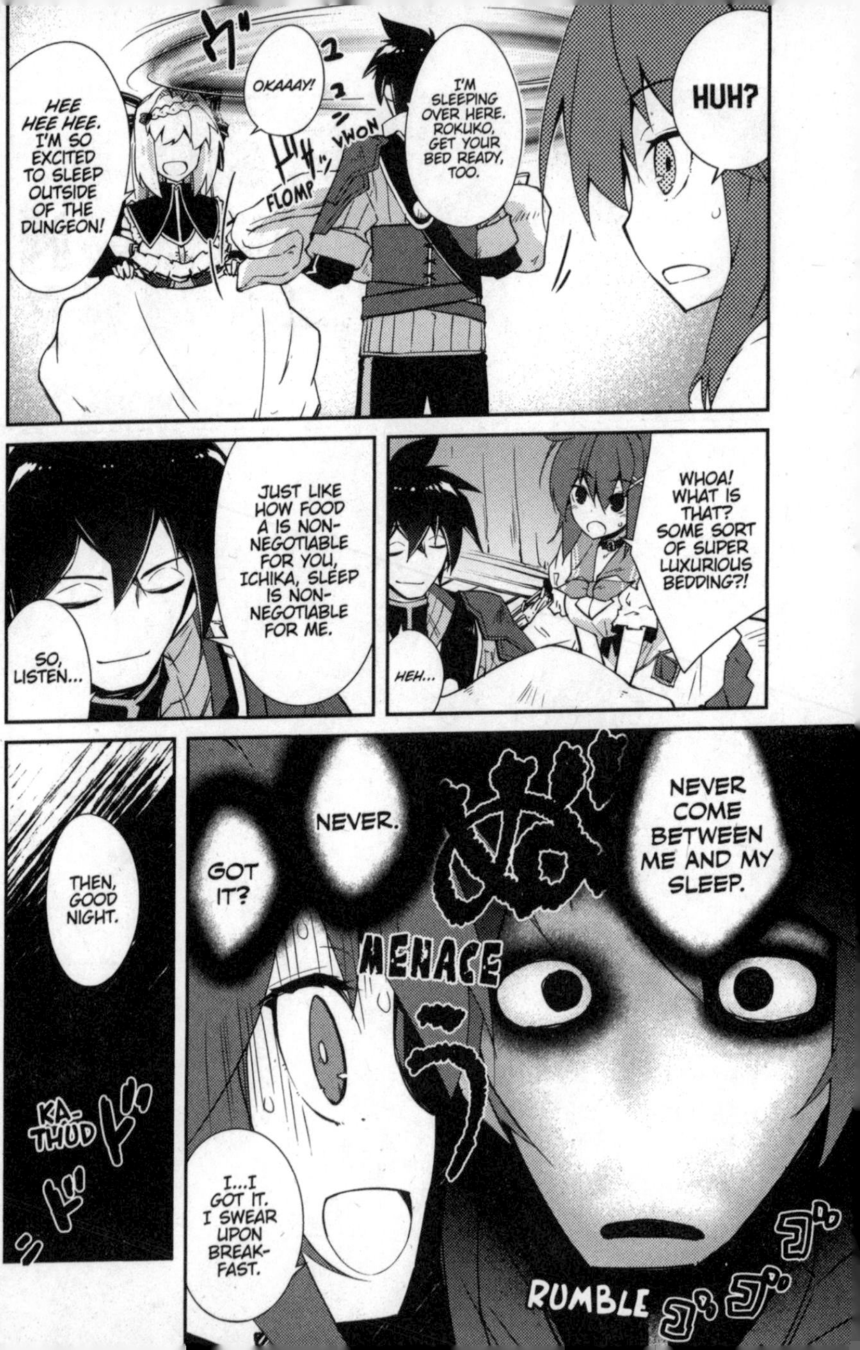
HUH?
I'M SLEEPING OVER HERE. ROKUKO, GET YOUR BED READY, TOO.
VWON
OKAAAY!
FLOMP
HEE HEE HEE. I'M SO EXCITED TO SLEEP OUTSIDE OF THE DUNGEON!
WHOA! WHAT IS THAT? SOME SORT OF SUPER LUXURIOUS BEDDING?!
HEH...
JUST LIKE HOW FOOD A IS NON-NEGOTIABLE FOR YOU, ICHIKA, SLEEP IS NON-NEGOTIABLE FOR ME.
SO, LISTEN...
NEVER COME BETWEEN ME AND MY SLEEP.
NEVER.
GOT IT?
MENACE
I...I GOT IT. I SWEAR UPON BREAK-FAST.
RUMBLE
THEN, GOOD NIGHT.
KA-THUD

LAZY DUNGEON MASTER

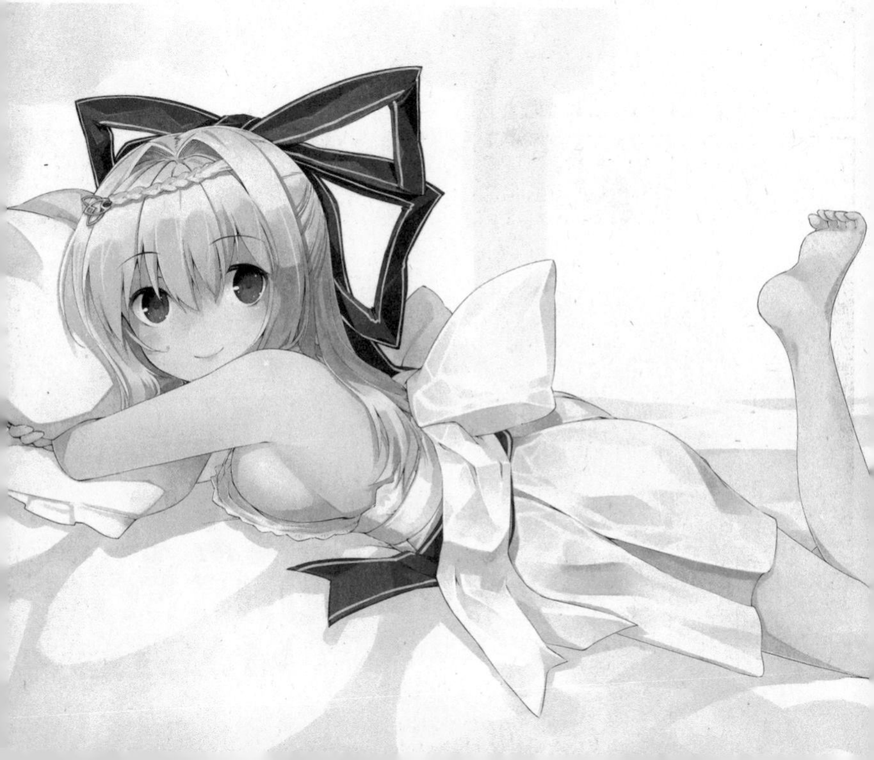

LAZY
DUNGEON
MASTER

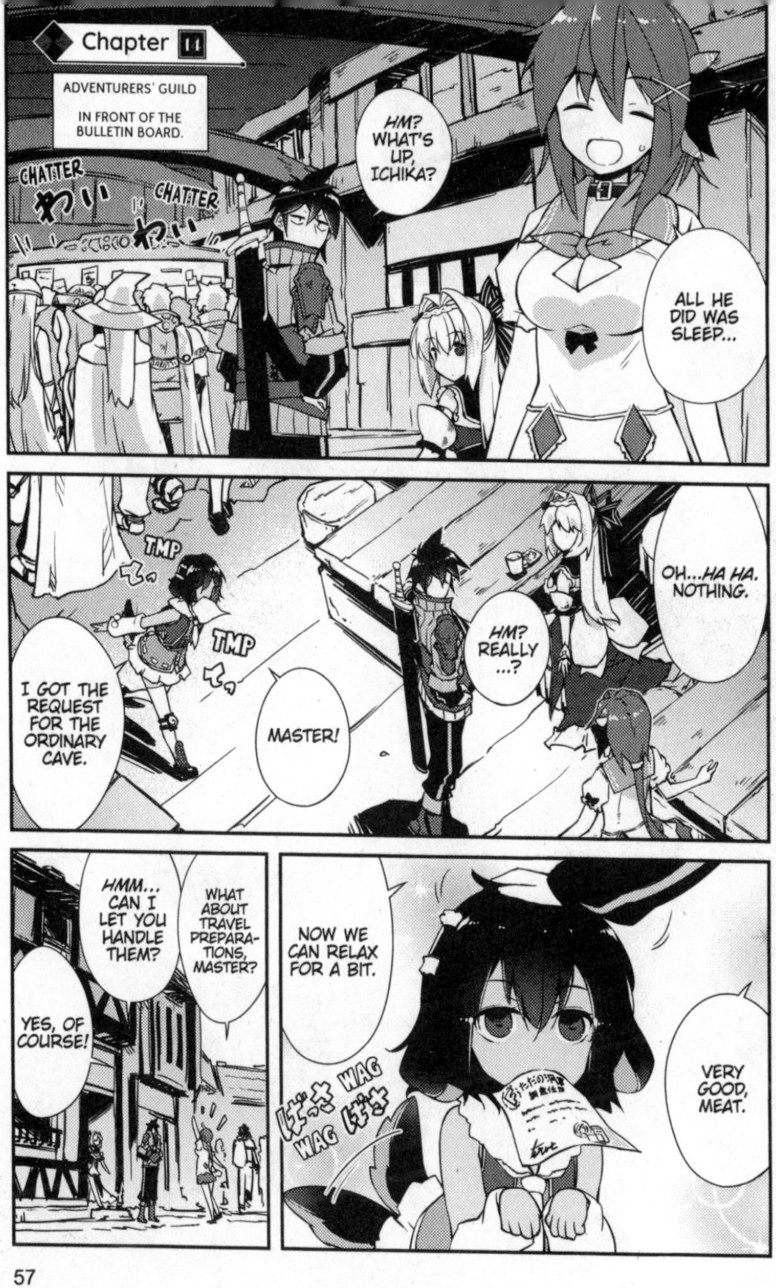
Chapter 14
ADVENTURERS' GUILD
IN FRONT OF THE BULLETIN BOARD.
CHATTER
CHATTER
ALL HE DID WAS SLEEP...
HM? WHAT'S UP, ICHIKA?
OH...HA HA. NOTHING.
HM? REALLY ...?
MASTER!
TMP
TMP
I GOT THE REQUEST FOR THE ORDINARY CAVE.
VERY GOOD, MEAT.
NOW WE CAN RELAX FOR A BIT.
WAG WAG
WHAT ABOUT TRAVEL PREPARATIONS, MASTER?
HMM... CAN I LET YOU HANDLE THEM?
YES, OF COURSE!

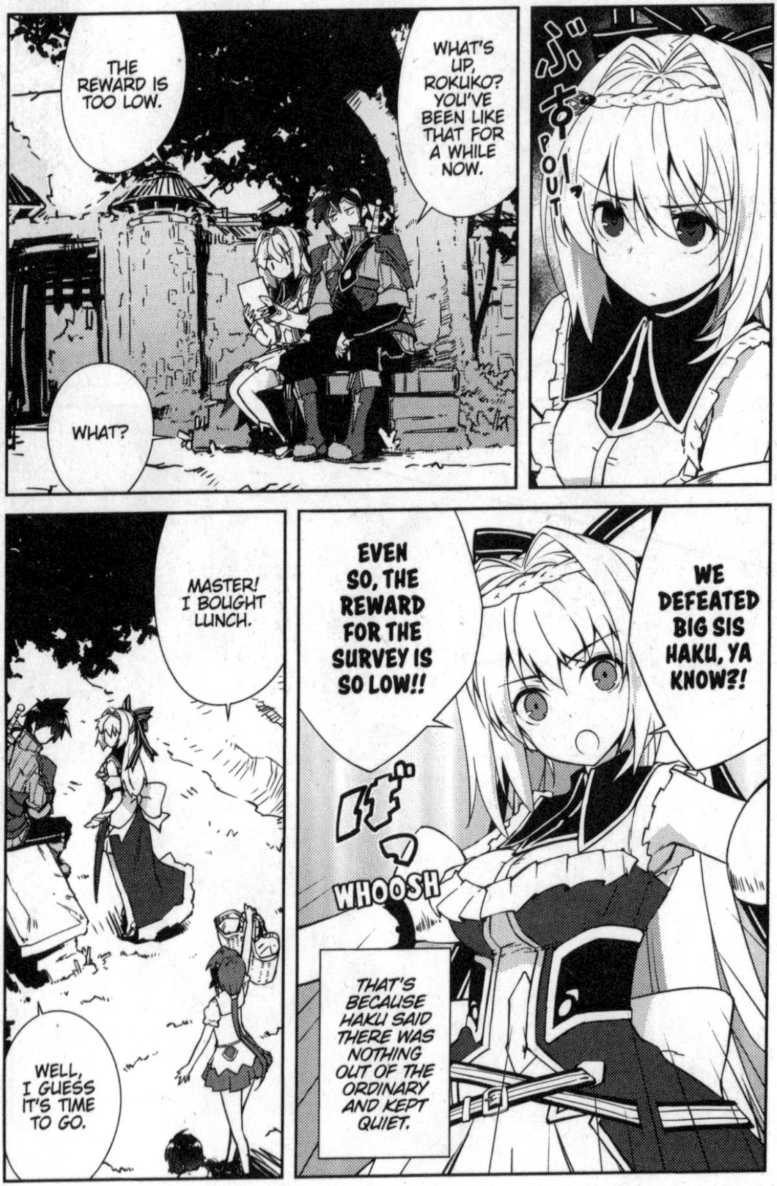
POUT
WHAT'S UP, ROKUKO? YOU'VE BEEN LIKE THAT FOR A WHILE NOW.
THE REWARD IS TOO LOW.
WHAT?
WE DEFEATED BIG SIS HAKU, YA KNOW?!
EVEN SO, THE REWARD FOR THE SURVEY IS SO LOW!!
WHOOSH
THAT'S BECAUSE HAKU SAID THERE WAS NOTHING OUT OF THE ORDINARY AND KEPT QUIET.
MASTER! I BOUGHT LUNCH.
WELL, I GUESS IT'S TIME TO GO.

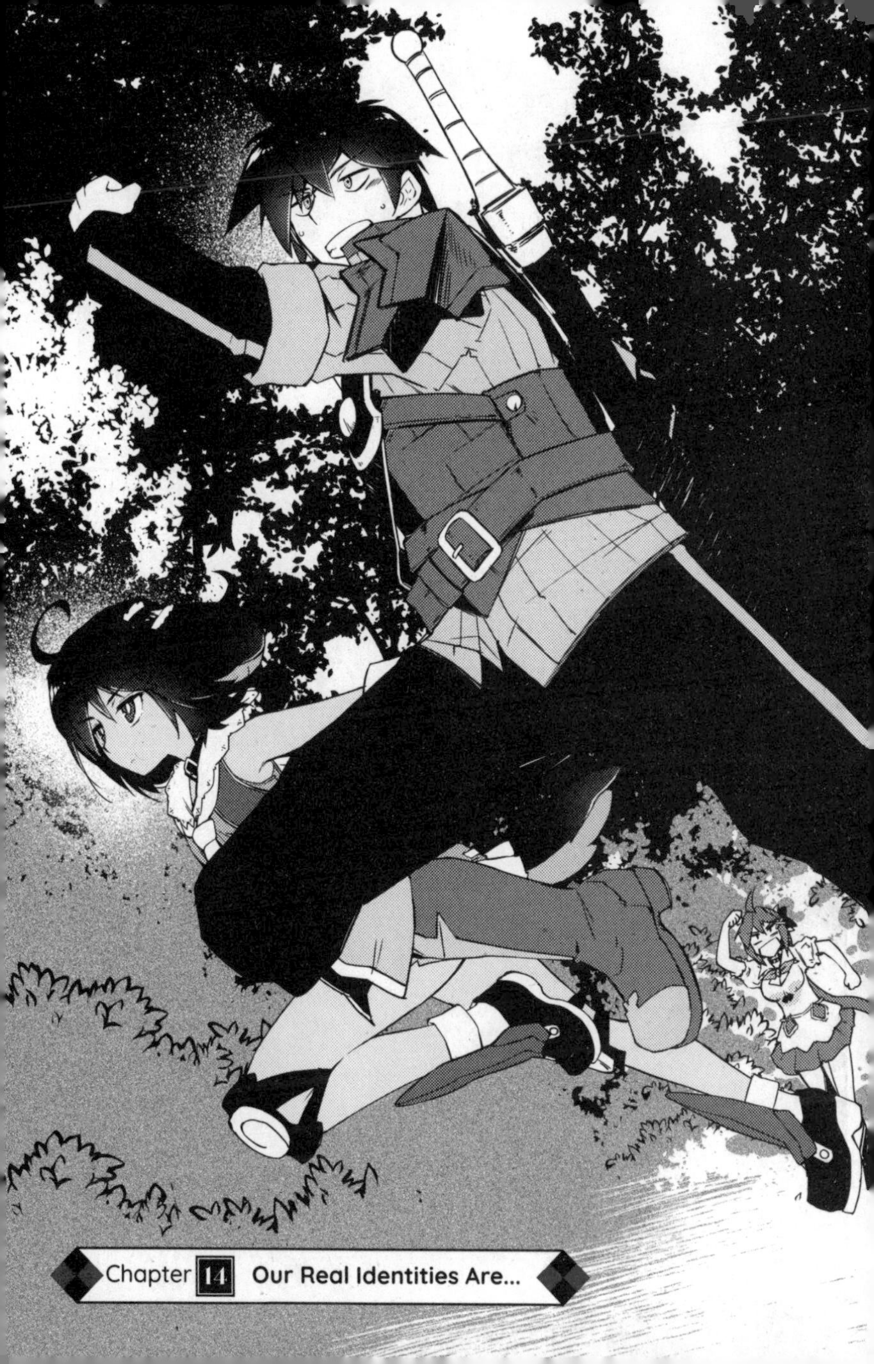
Chapter 14 Our Real Identities Are...

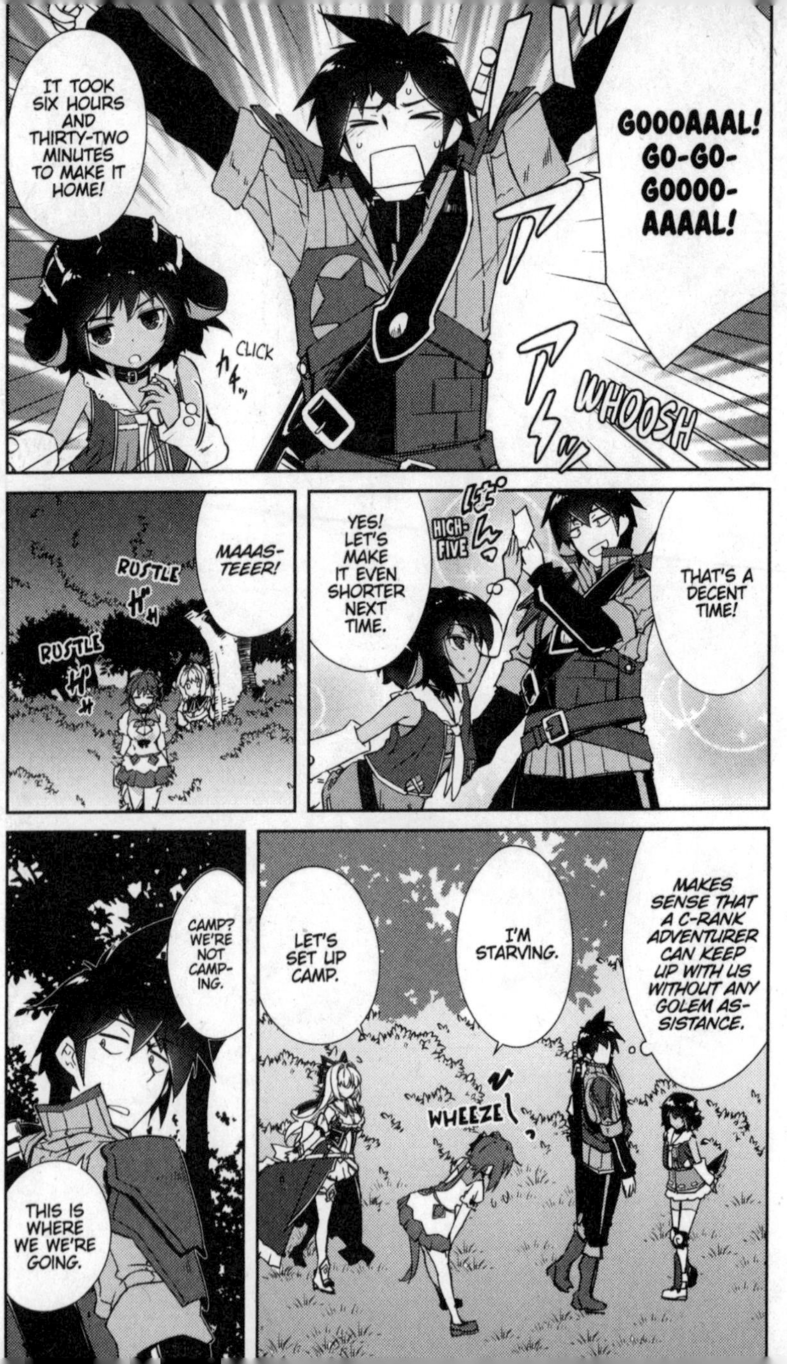
GOOOAAAL! GO-GO-GOOOO-AAAAL!
IT TOOK SIX HOURS AND THIRTY-TWO MINUTES TO MAKE IT HOME!
CLICK
WHOOSH
THAT'S A DECENT TIME!
HIGH-FIVE
YES! LET'S MAKE IT EVEN SHORTER NEXT TIME.
MAAAS-TEEER!
RUSTLE
RUSTLE
MAKES SENSE THAT A C-RANK ADVENTURER CAN KEEP UP WITH US WITHOUT ANY GOLEM AS-SISTANCE.
I'M STARVING.
LET'S SET UP CAMP.
WHEEZE
CAMP? WE'RE NOT CAMP-ING.
THIS IS WHERE WE WE'RE GOING.

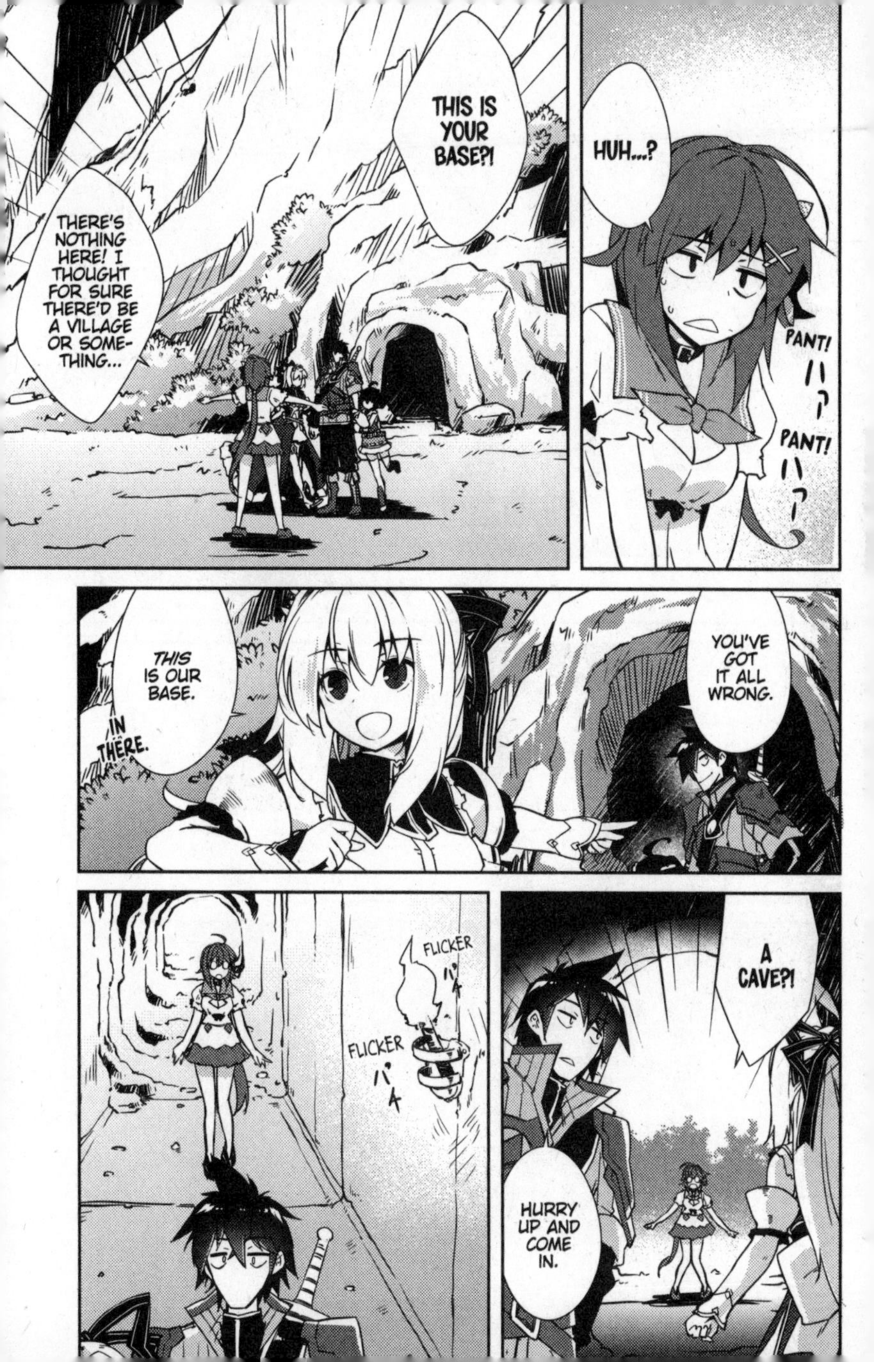
HUH...?
PANT!
ハァ
PANT!
ハァ
THIS IS YOUR BASE?!
THERE'S NOTHING HERE! I THOUGHT FOR SURE THERE'D BE A VILLAGE OR SOME-THING...
YOU'VE GOT IT ALL WRONG.
THIS IS OUR BASE.
IN THERE.
A CAVE?!
HURRY UP AND COME IN.
FLICKER
FLICKER

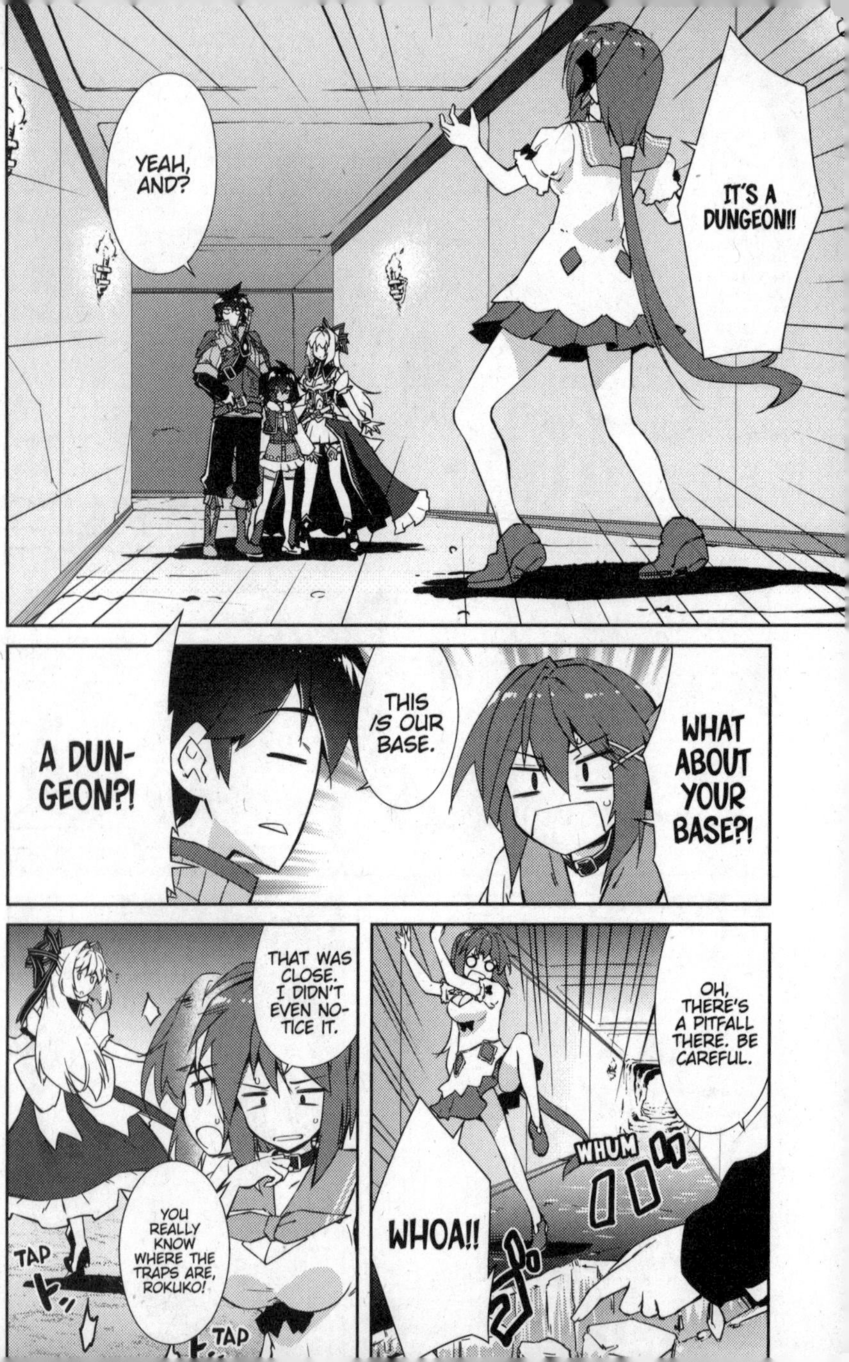
IT'S A DUNGEON!!
YEAH, AND?
WHAT ABOUT YOUR BASE?!
THIS IS OUR BASE.
A DUN-GEON?!
OH, THERE'S A PITFALL THERE. BE CAREFUL.
WHUM
WHOA!!
THAT WAS CLOSE. I DIDN'T EVEN NO-TICE IT.
YOU REALLY KNOW WHERE THE TRAPS ARE, ROKUKO!
TAP
TAP

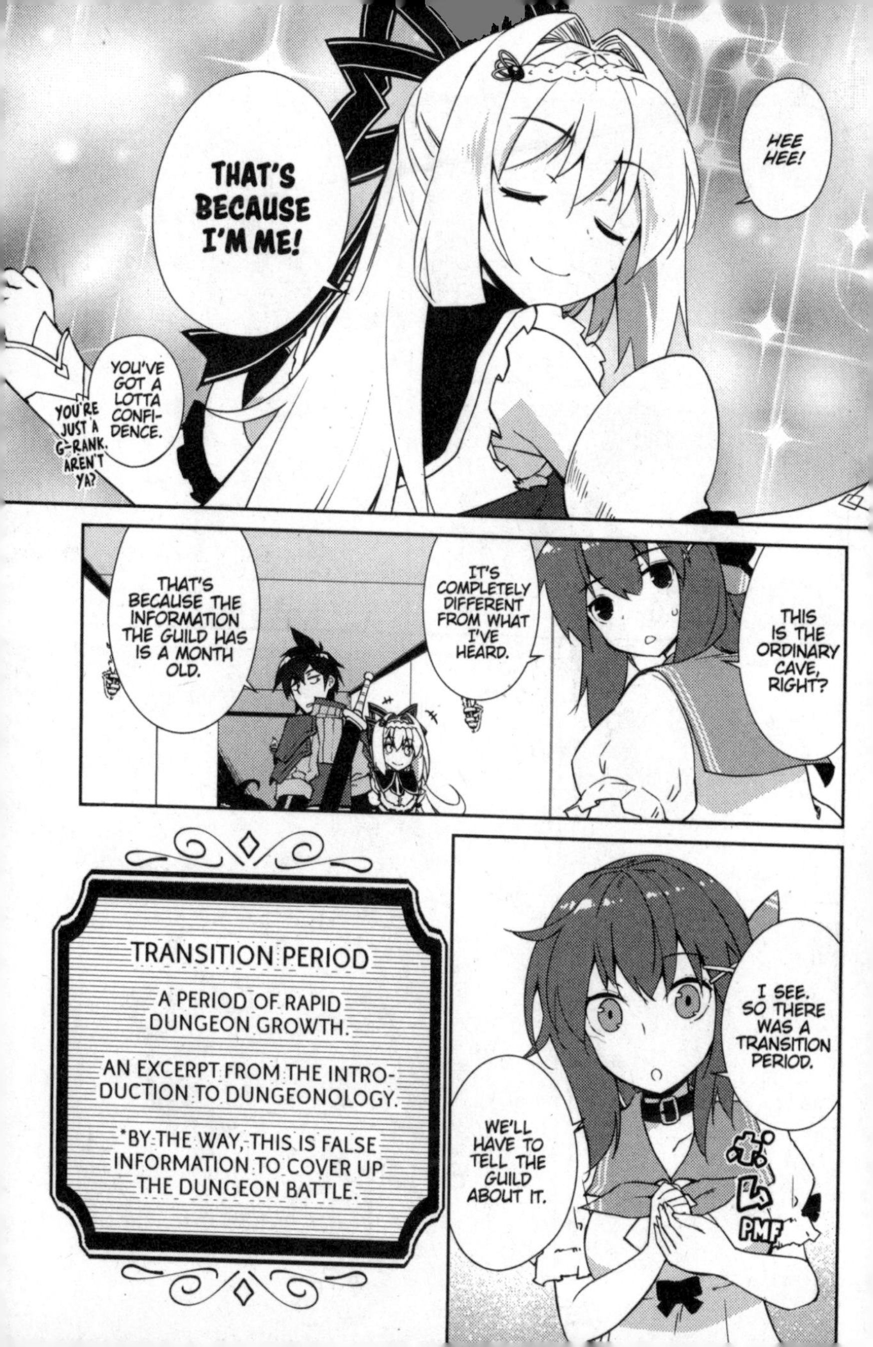
HEE HEE!
THAT'S BECAUSE I'M ME!
YOU'VE GOT A LOTTA CONFI-DENCE.
YOU'RE JUST A G-RANK, AREN'T YA?
THIS IS THE ORDINARY CAVE, RIGHT?
IT'S COMPLETELY DIFFERENT FROM WHAT I'VE HEARD.
THAT'S BECAUSE THE INFORMATION THE GUILD HAS IS A MONTH OLD.
I SEE. SO THERE WAS A TRANSITION PERIOD.
WE'LL HAVE TO TELL THE GUILD ABOUT IT.
PMF
TRANSITION PERIOD
A PERIOD OF RAPID DUNGEON GROWTH.
AN EXCERPT FROM THE INTRO-DUCTION TO DUNGEONOLOGY.
*BY THE WAY, THIS IS FALSE INFORMATION TO COVER UP THE DUNGEON BATTLE.

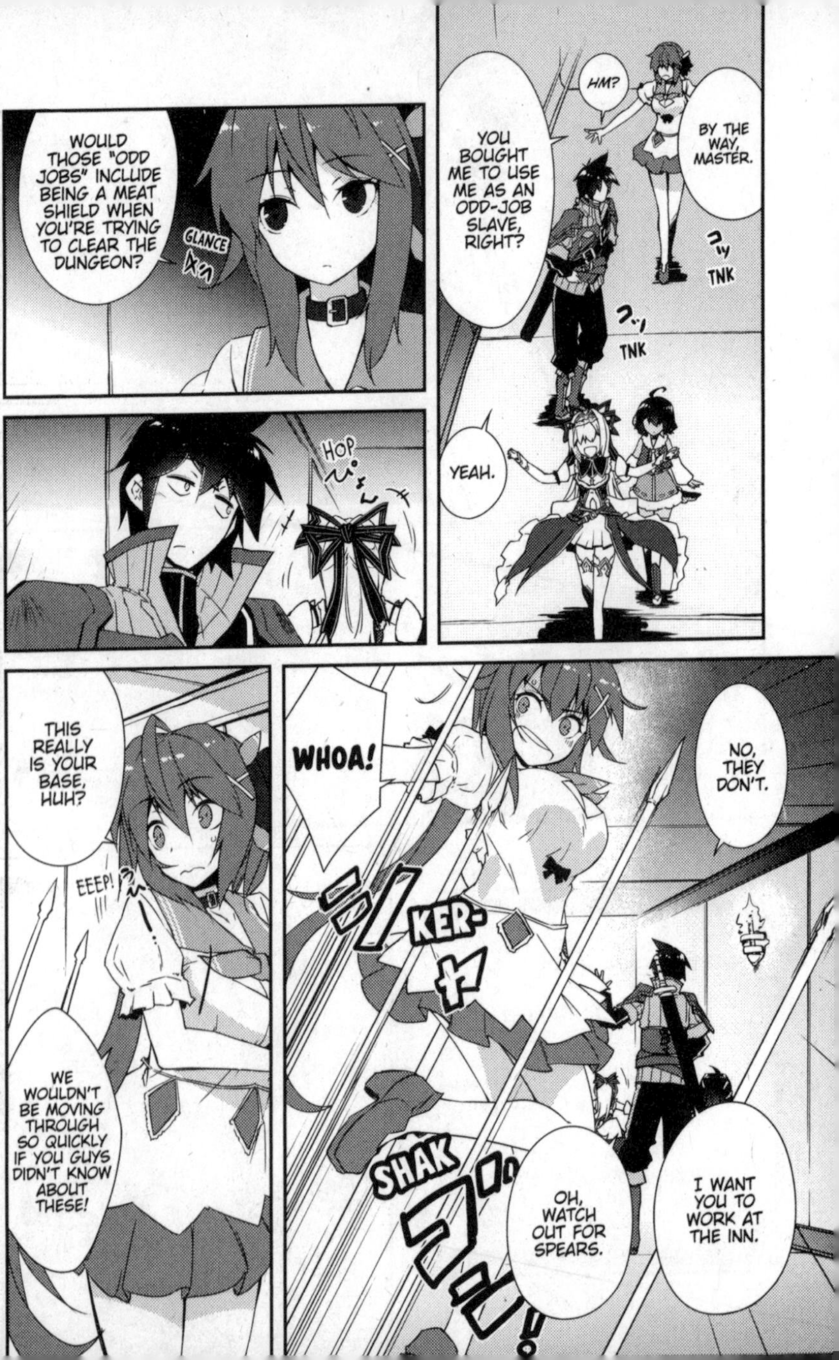
BY THE WAY, MASTER.
HM?
YOU BOUGHT ME TO USE ME AS AN ODD-JOB SLAVE, RIGHT?
TNK
TNK
YEAH.
WOULD THOSE "ODD JOBS" INCLUDE BEING A MEAT SHIELD WHEN YOU'RE TRYING TO CLEAR THE DUNGEON?
GLANCE
HOP
NO, THEY DON'T.
I WANT YOU TO WORK AT THE INN.
WHOA!
KER-
OH, WATCH OUT FOR SPEARS.
SHAK
THIS REALLY IS YOUR BASE, HUH?
EEEP!
WE WOULDN'T BE MOVING THROUGH SO QUICKLY IF YOU GUYS DIDN'T KNOW ABOUT THESE!

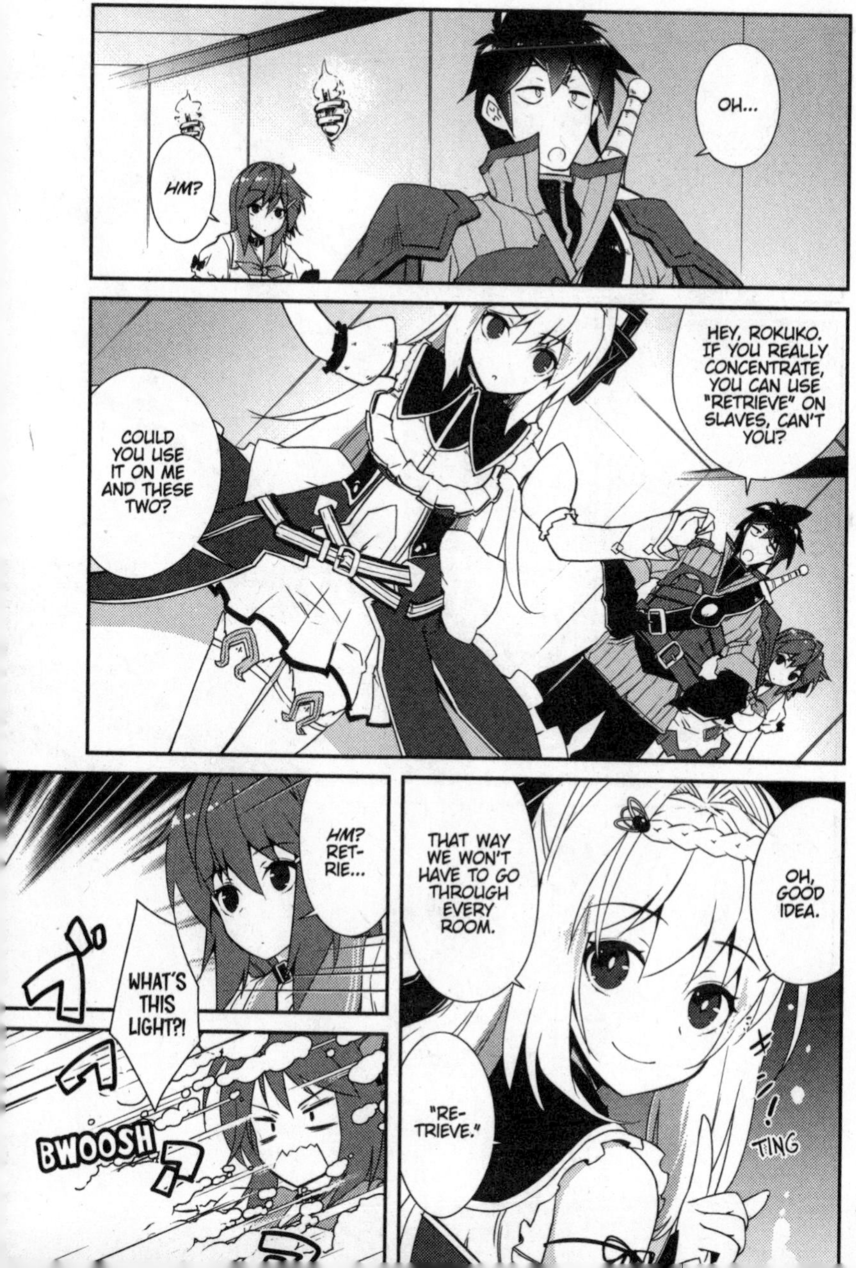
OH...
HM?
HEY, ROKUKO. IF YOU REALLY CONCENTRATE, YOU CAN USE "RETRIEVE" ON SLAVES, CAN'T YOU?
COULD YOU USE IT ON ME AND THESE TWO?
OH, GOOD IDEA.
THAT WAY WE WON'T HAVE TO GO THROUGH EVERY ROOM.
TING
"RE-TRIEVE."
HM? RET-RIE...
WHAT'S THIS LIGHT?!
BWOOSH

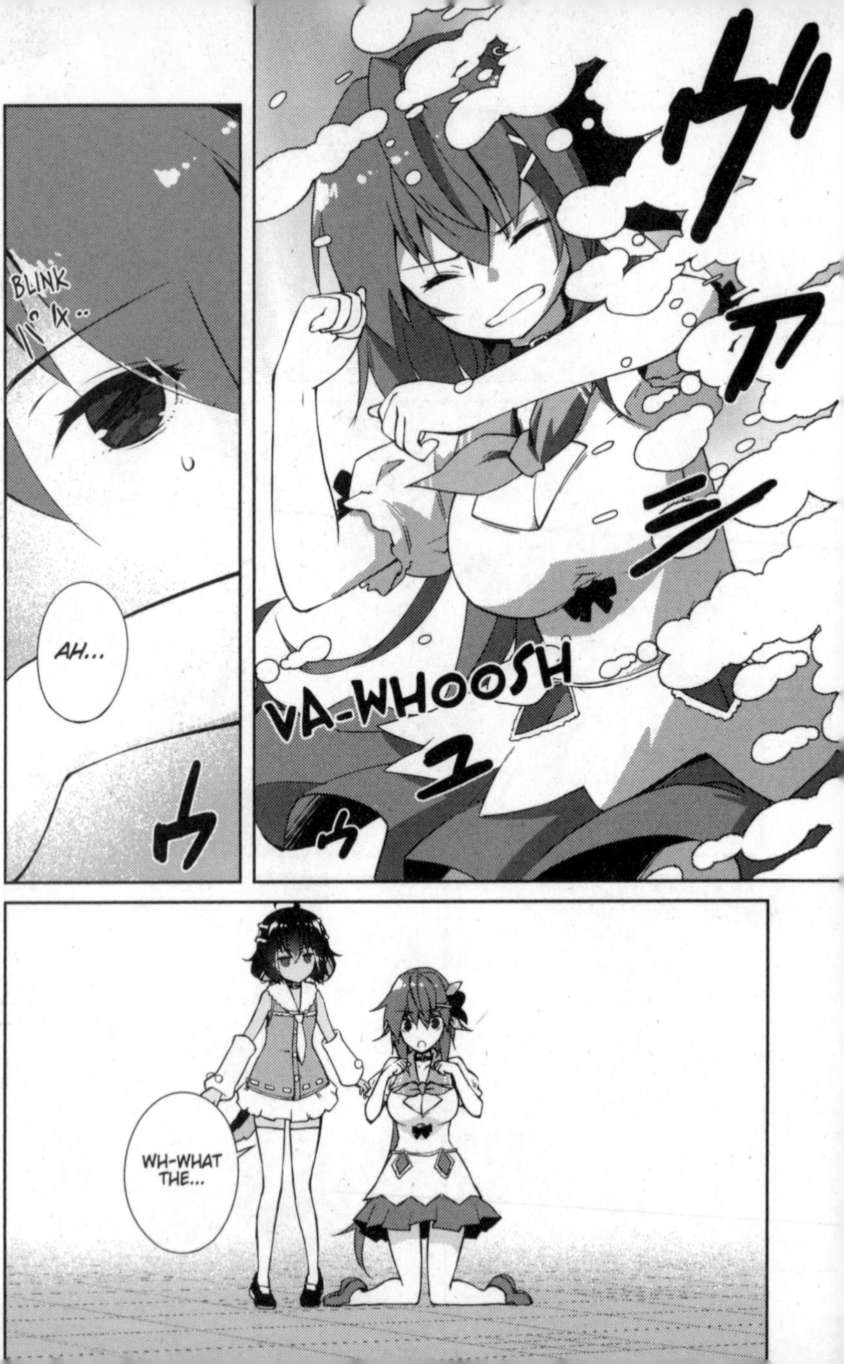
VA-WHOOSH
BLINK
AH...
WH-WHAT THE...

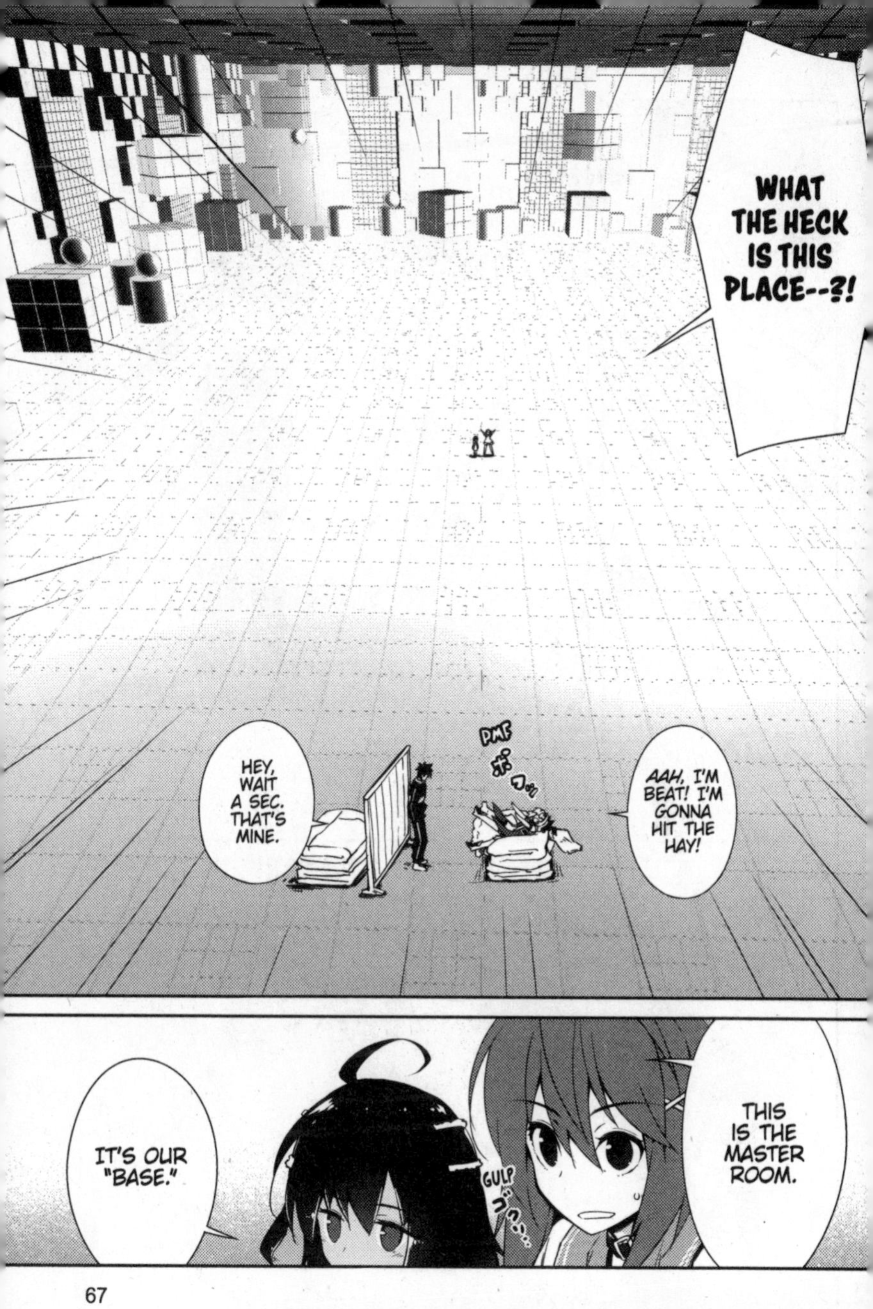
WHAT THE HECK IS THIS PLACE--?!
AAH, I'M BEAT! I'M GONNA HIT THE HAY!
PMF
HEY, WAIT A SEC. THAT'S MINE.
THIS IS THE MASTER ROOM.
GULP
IT'S OUR "BASE."

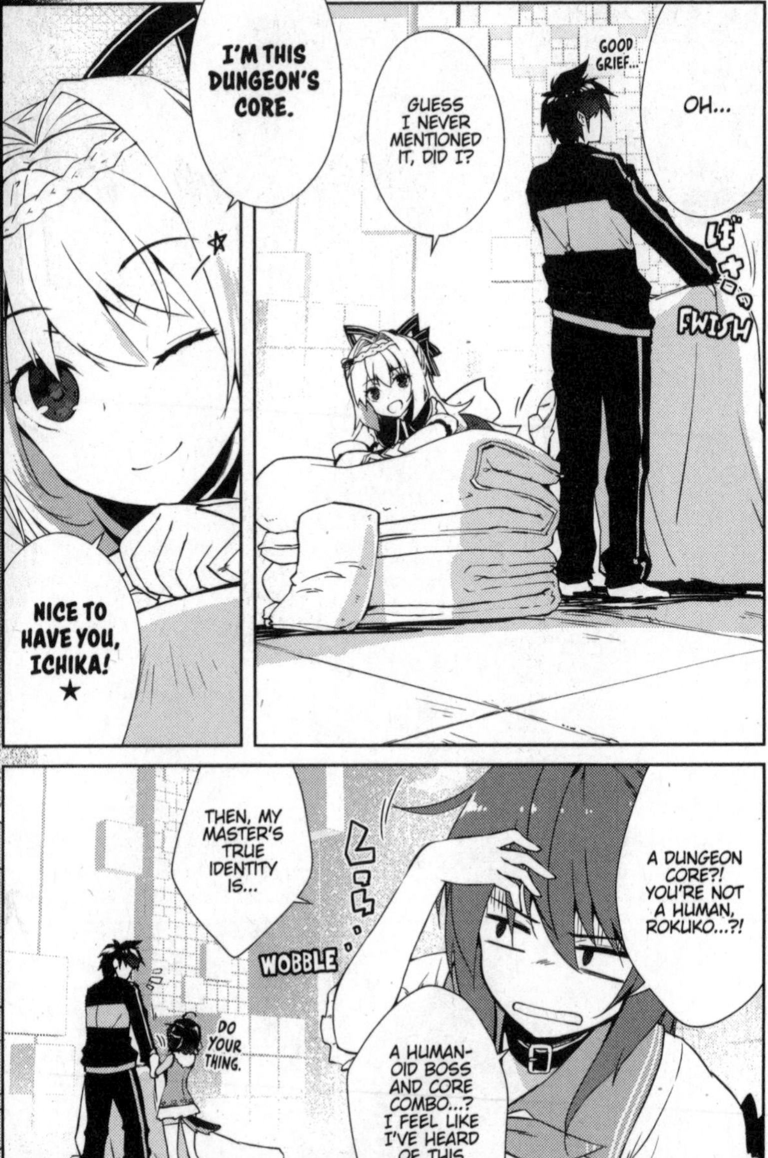
OH...
GOOD GRIEF...
GUESS I NEVER MENTIONED IT, DID I?
FWISH
I'M THIS DUNGEON'S CORE.
NICE TO HAVE YOU, ICHIKA! ★
A DUNGEON CORE?! YOU'RE NOT A HUMAN, ROKUKO...?!
THEN, MY MASTER'S TRUE IDENTITY IS...
WOBBLE
A HUMAN-OID BOSS AND CORE COMBO...? I FEEL LIKE I'VE HEARD OF THIS BEFORE...
DO YOUR THING.

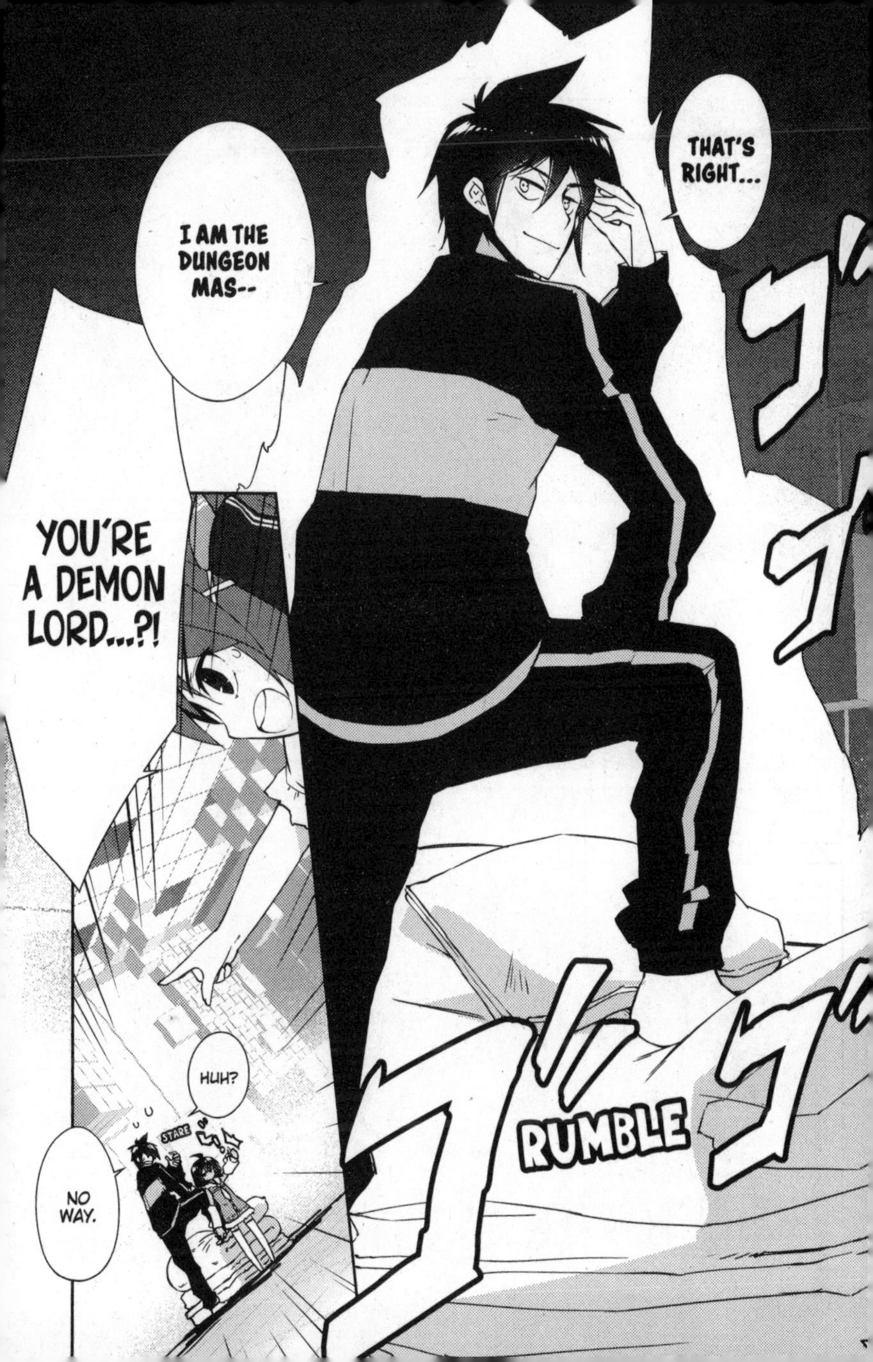
THAT'S RIGHT...
I AM THE DUNGEON MAS--
YOU'RE A DEMON LORD...?!
RUMBLE
HUH?
STARE
NO WAY.

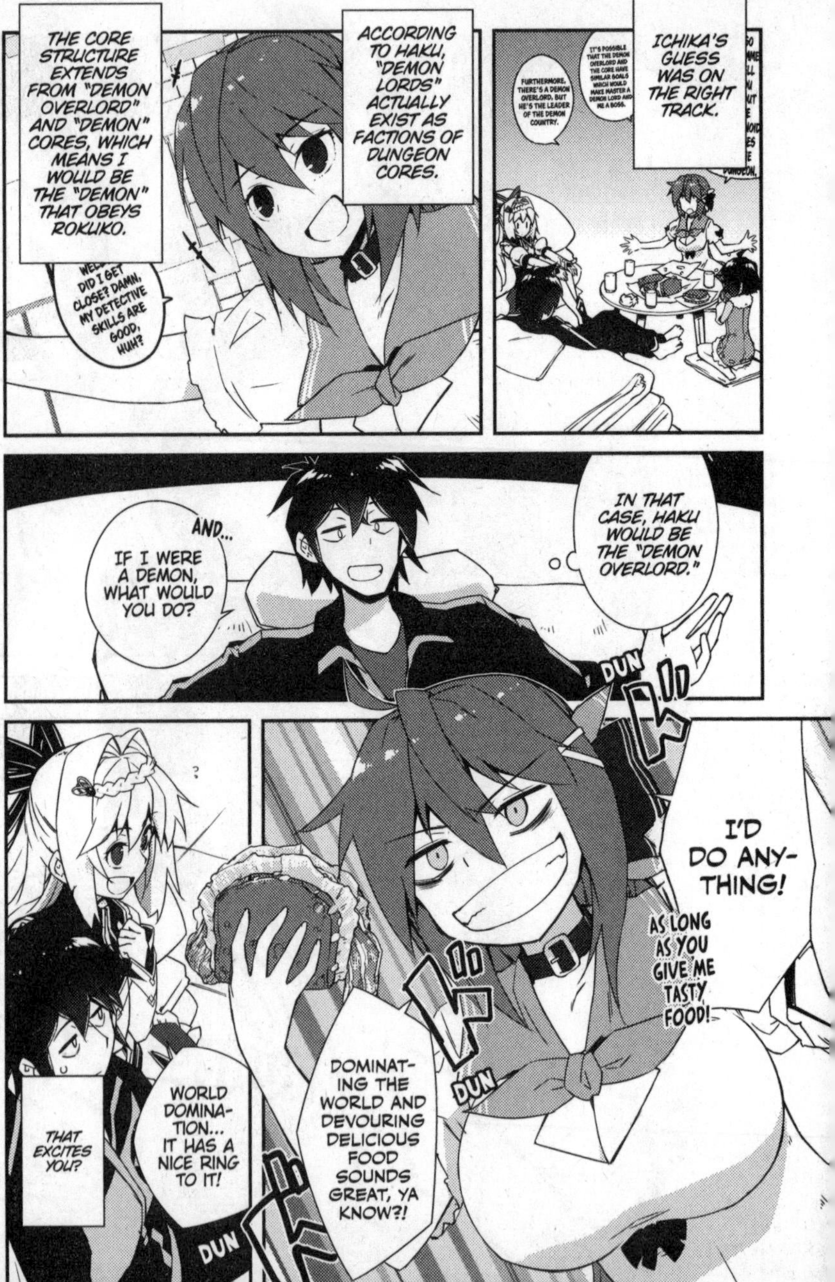
ICHIKA'S GUESS WAS ON THE RIGHT TRACK.
IT'S POSSIBLE THAT THE DEMON OVERLORD AND THE CORE HAVE SIMILAR GOALS WHICH WOULD MAKE MASTER A DEMON LORD AND ME A BOSS.
FURTHERMORE, THERE'S A DEMON OVERLORD, BUT HE'S THE LEADER OF THE DEMON COUNTRY.
ACCORDING TO HAKU, "DEMON LORDS" ACTUALLY EXIST AS FACTIONS OF DUNGEON CORES.
THE CORE STRUCTURE EXTENDS FROM "DEMON OVERLORD" AND "DEMON" CORES, WHICH MEANS I WOULD BE THE "DEMON" THAT OBEYS ROKUKO.
WELL? DID I GET CLOSE? DAMN, MY DETECTIVE SKILLS ARE GOOD, HUH?
IN THAT CASE, HAKU WOULD BE THE "DEMON OVERLORD."
AND...
IF I WERE A DEMON, WHAT WOULD YOU DO?
DUN
I'D DO ANYTHING!
AS LONG AS YOU GIVE ME TASTY FOOD!
DOMINATING THE WORLD AND DEVOURING DELICIOUS FOOD SOUNDS GREAT, YA KNOW?!
DUN
WORLD DOMINATION... IT HAS A NICE RING TO IT!
THAT EXCITES YOU?
DUN

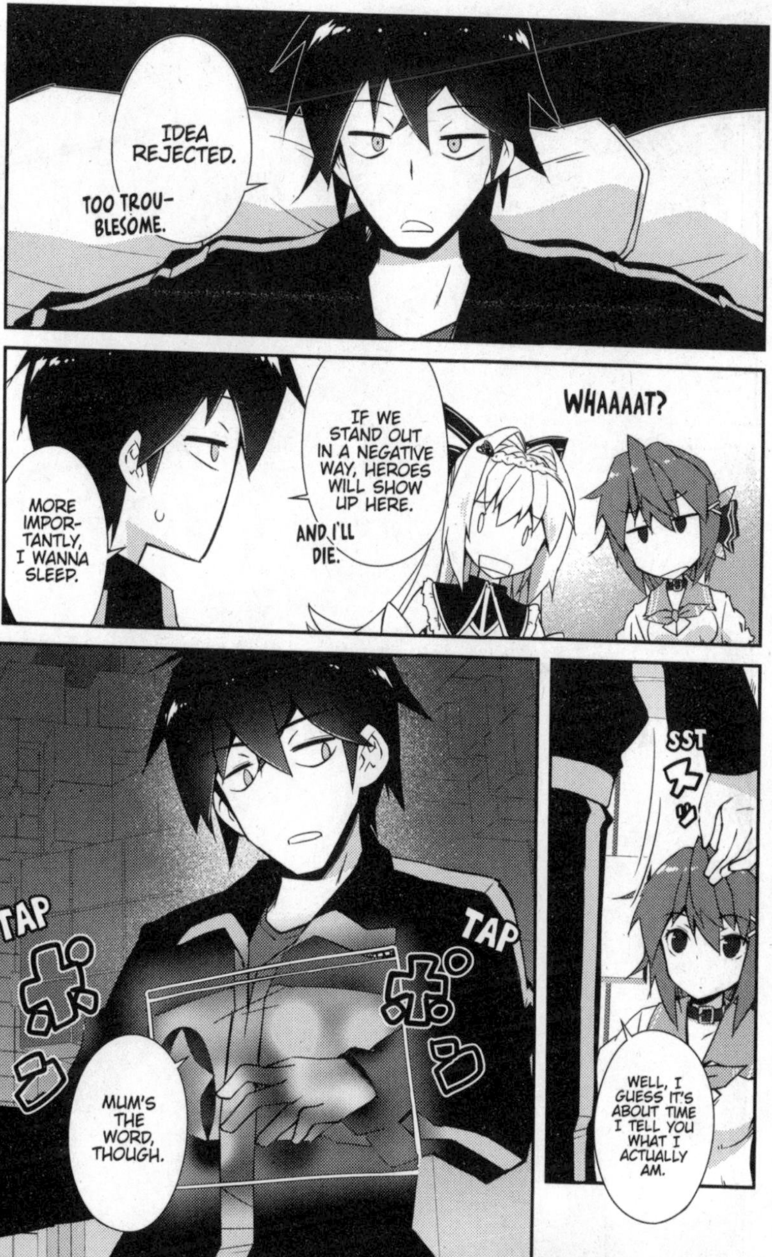
IDEA REJECTED.
TOO TROUBLESOME.
WHAAAAT?
IF WE STAND OUT IN A NEGATIVE WAY, HEROES WILL SHOW UP HERE.
AND I'LL DIE.
MORE IMPORTANTLY, I WANNA SLEEP.
SST
WELL, I GUESS IT'S ABOUT TIME I TELL YOU WHAT I ACTUALLY AM.
TAP
TAP
MUM'S THE WORD, THOUGH.

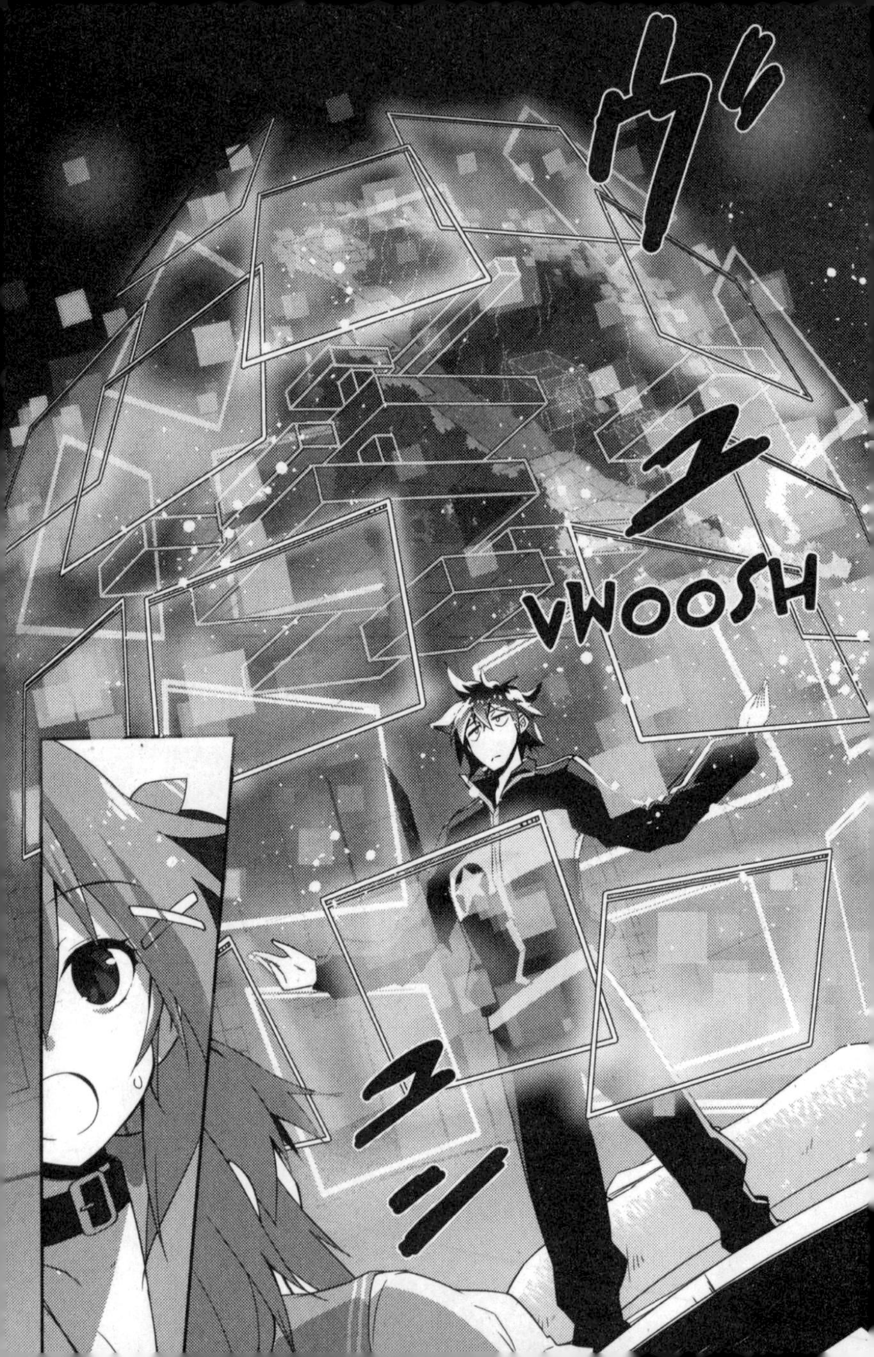
ヴ
ン
VWOOSH
ン

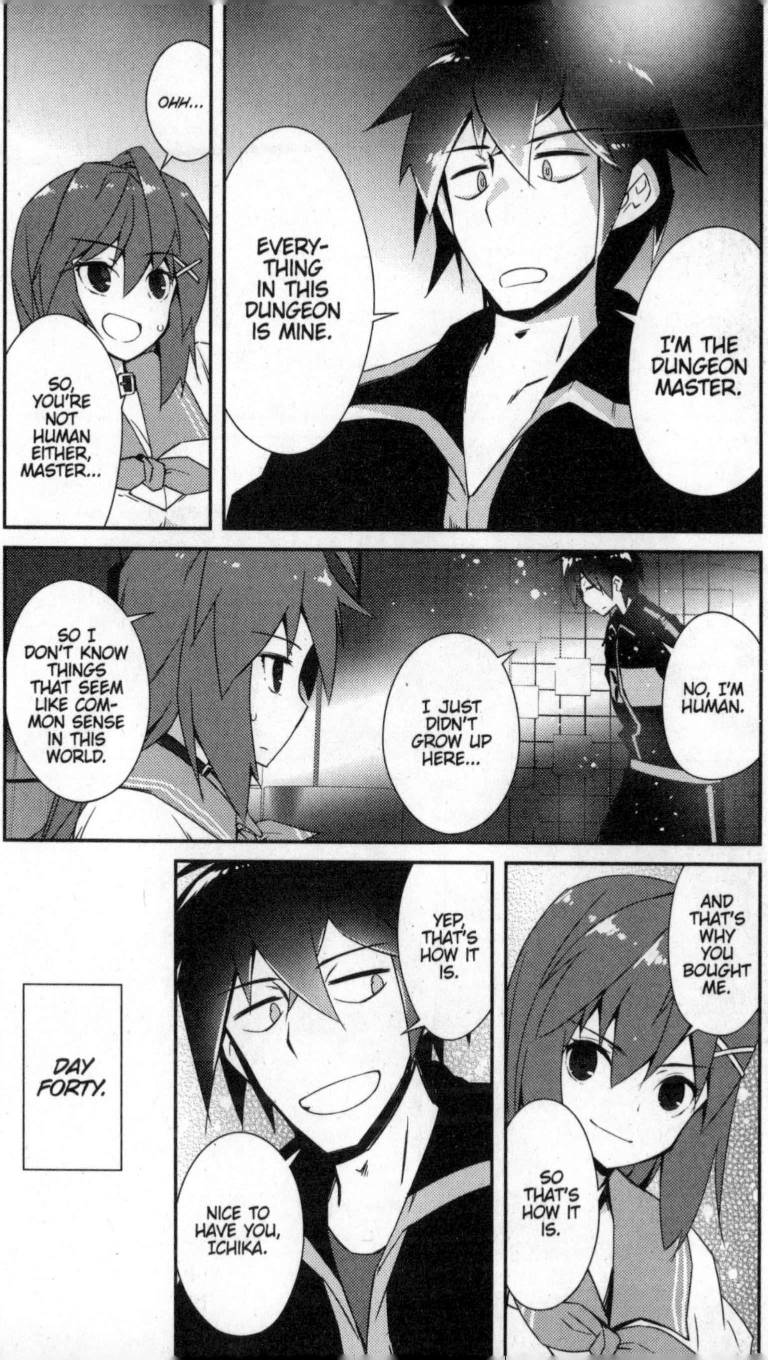

I'M THE DUNGEON MASTER.
EVERYTHING IN THIS DUNGEON IS MINE.
OHH...
SO, YOU'RE NOT HUMAN EITHER, MASTER...
NO, I'M HUMAN.
I JUST DIDN'T GROW UP HERE...
SO I DON'T KNOW THINGS THAT SEEM LIKE COMMON SENSE IN THIS WORLD.
AND THAT'S WHY YOU BOUGHT ME.
SO THAT'S HOW IT IS.
YEP, THAT'S HOW IT IS.
NICE TO HAVE YOU, ICHIKA.
DAY FORTY.

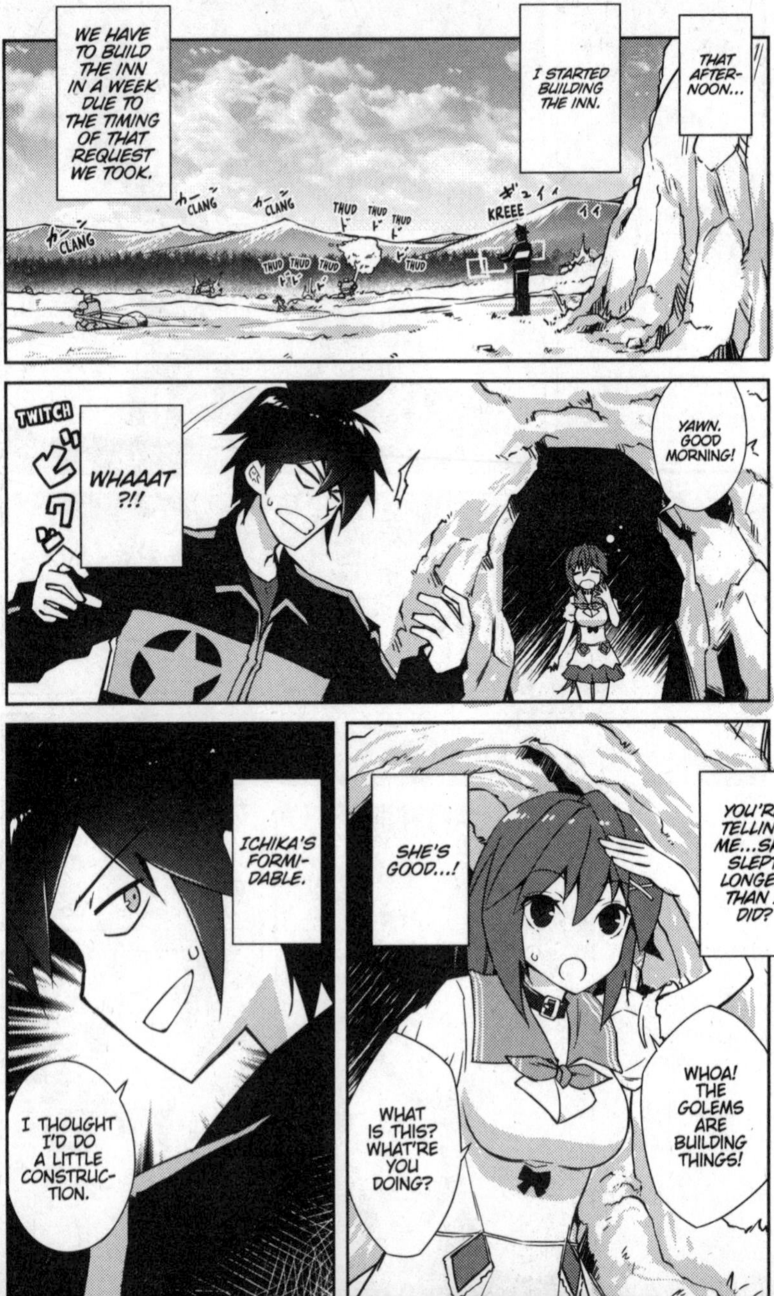
THAT AFTER-NOON...
I STARTED BUILDING THE INN.
WE HAVE TO BUILD THE INN IN A WEEK DUE TO THE TIMING OF THAT REQUEST WE TOOK.
KREEE
THUD
THUD THUD THUD
THUD THUD THUD
CLANG
CLANG
CLANG
YAWN. GOOD MORNING!
WHAAAT?!!
TWITCH
YOU'RE TELLING ME...SHE SLEPT LONGER THAN I DID?
SHE'S GOOD...!
WHOA! THE GOLEMS ARE BUILDING THINGS!
WHAT IS THIS? WHAT'RE YOU DOING?
ICHIKA'S FORMIDABLE.
I THOUGHT I'D DO A LITTLE CONSTRUCTION.

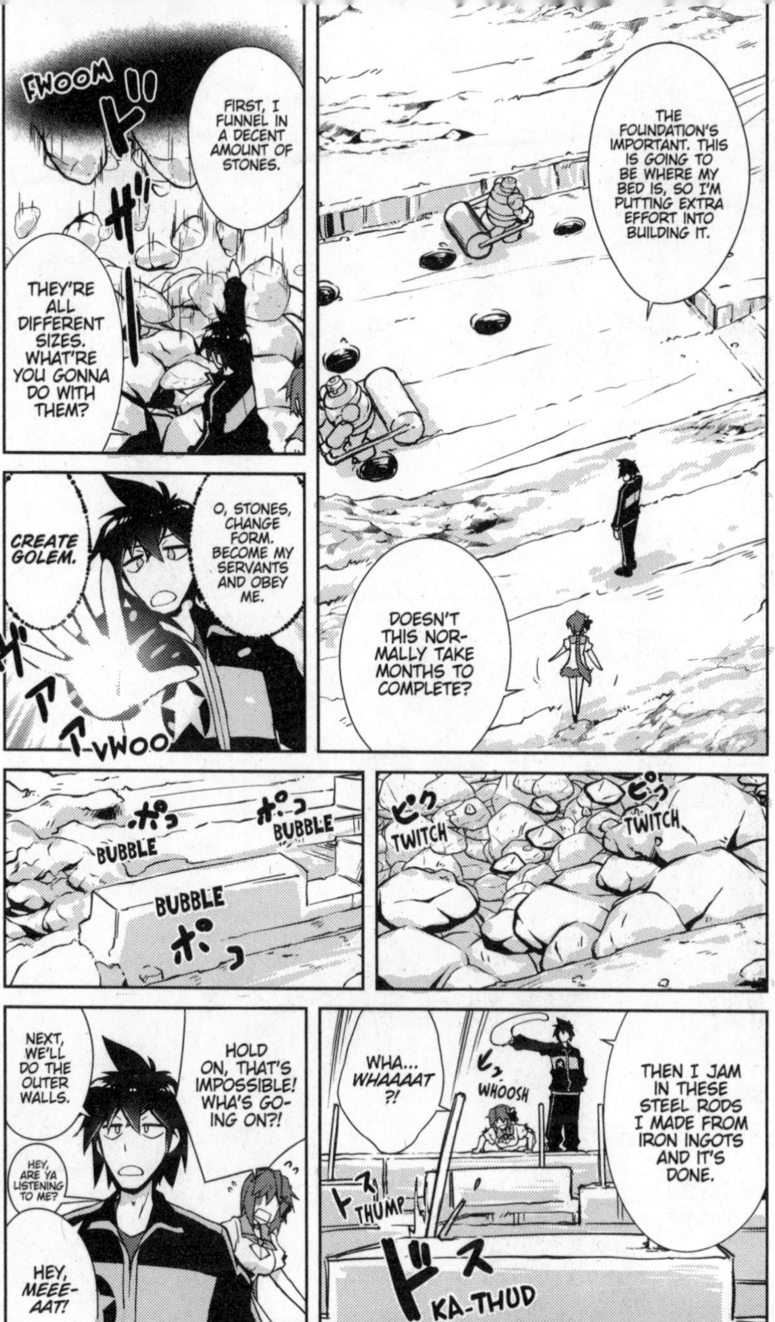
THE FOUNDATION'S IMPORTANT. THIS IS GOING TO BE WHERE MY BED IS, SO I'M PUTTING EXTRA EFFORT INTO BUILDING IT.
DOESN'T THIS NORMALLY TAKE MONTHS TO COMPLETE?
FWOOM
FIRST, I FUNNEL IN A DECENT AMOUNT OF STONES.
THEY'RE ALL DIFFERENT SIZES. WHAT'RE YOU GONNA DO WITH THEM?
O, STONES, CHANGE FORM. BECOME MY SERVANTS AND OBEY ME.
CREATE GOLEM.
VWOO
TWITCH
TWITCH
BUBBLE
BUBBLE
BUBBLE
THEN I JAM IN THESE STEEL RODS I MADE FROM IRON INGOTS AND IT'S DONE.
WHOOSH
WHA... WHAAAAT?!
THUMP
KA-THUD
HOLD ON, THAT'S IMPOSSIBLE! WHA'S GO-ING ON?!
NEXT, WE'LL DO THE OUTER WALLS.
HEY, ARE YA LISTENING TO ME?
HEY, MEEE-AAT!

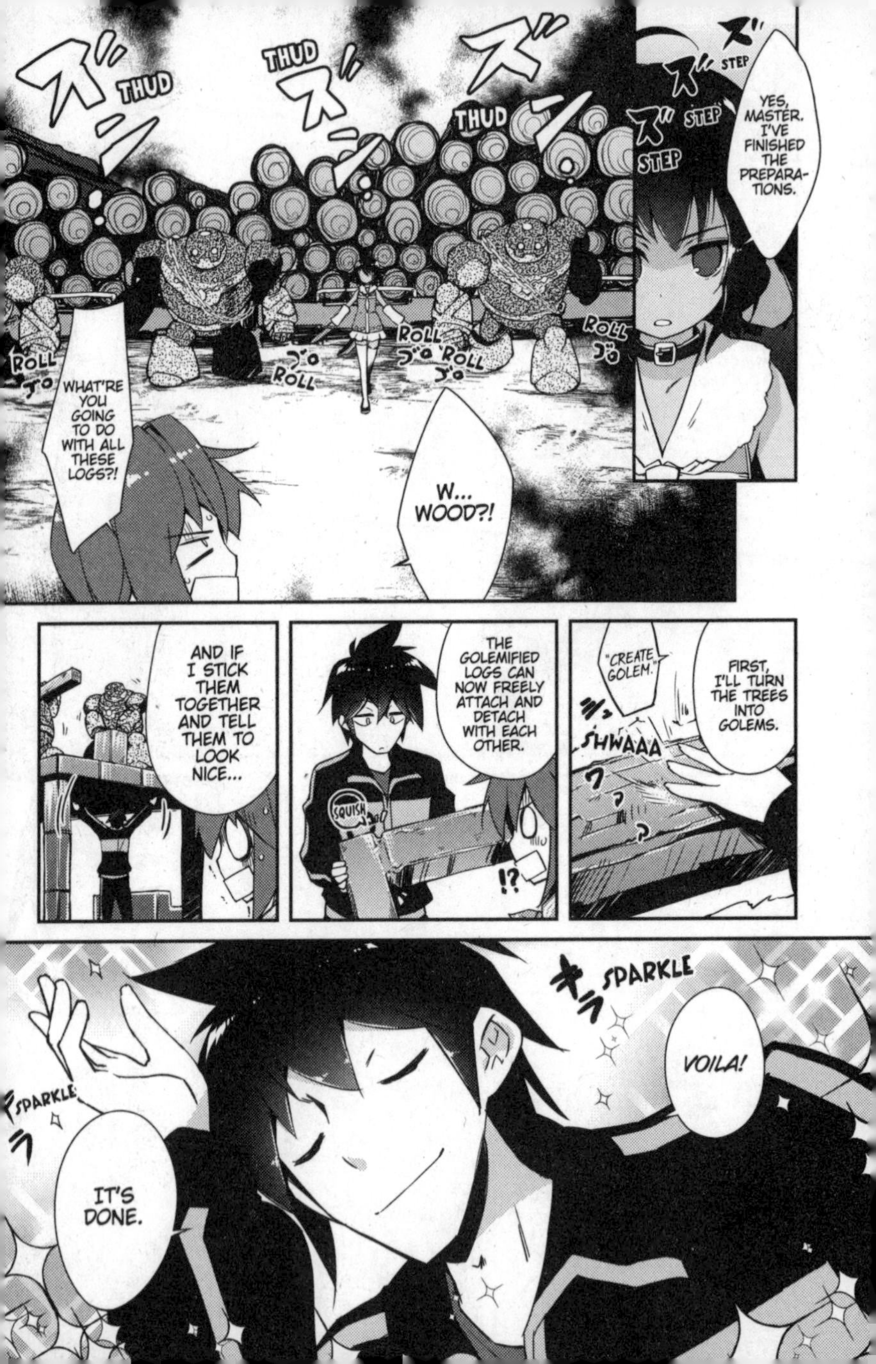
STEP
STEP
STEP
YES, MASTER. I'VE FINISHED THE PREPARATIONS.
THUD
THUD
THUD
ROLL
ROLL
ROLL
ROLL
W... WOOD?!
WHAT'RE YOU GOING TO DO WITH ALL THESE LOGS?!
FIRST, I'LL TURN THE TREES INTO GOLEMS.
"CREATE GOLEM."
SHWAAA
THE GOLEMIFIED LOGS CAN NOW FREELY ATTACH AND DETACH WITH EACH OTHER.
SQUISH
!?
AND IF I STICK THEM TOGETHER AND TELL THEM TO LOOK NICE...
SPARKLE
VOILA!
SPARKLE
IT'S DONE.

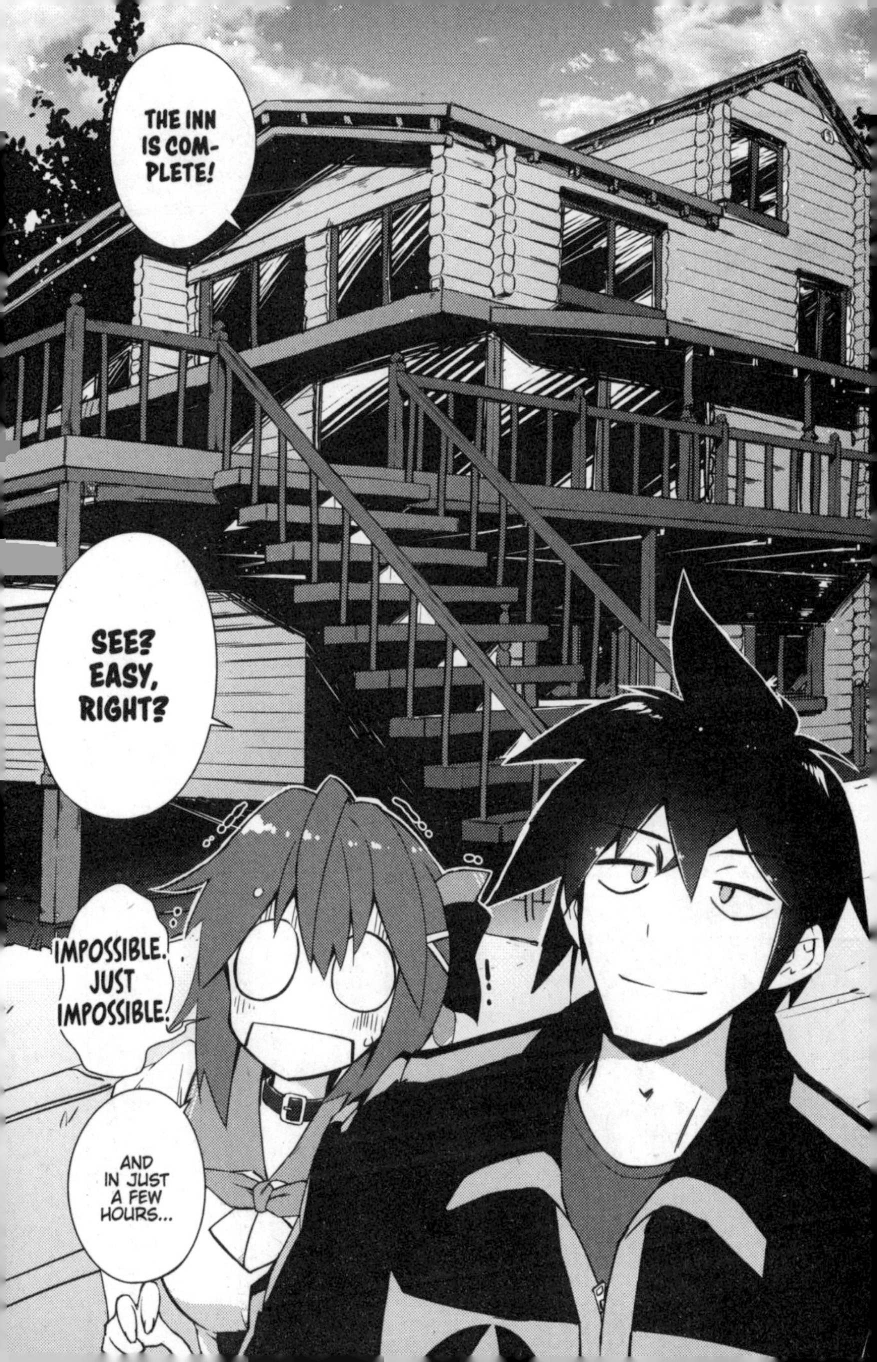
THE INN IS COM- PLETE!
SEE? EASY, RIGHT?
IMPOSSIBLE. JUST IMPOSSIBLE.
!
AND IN JUST A FEW HOURS...

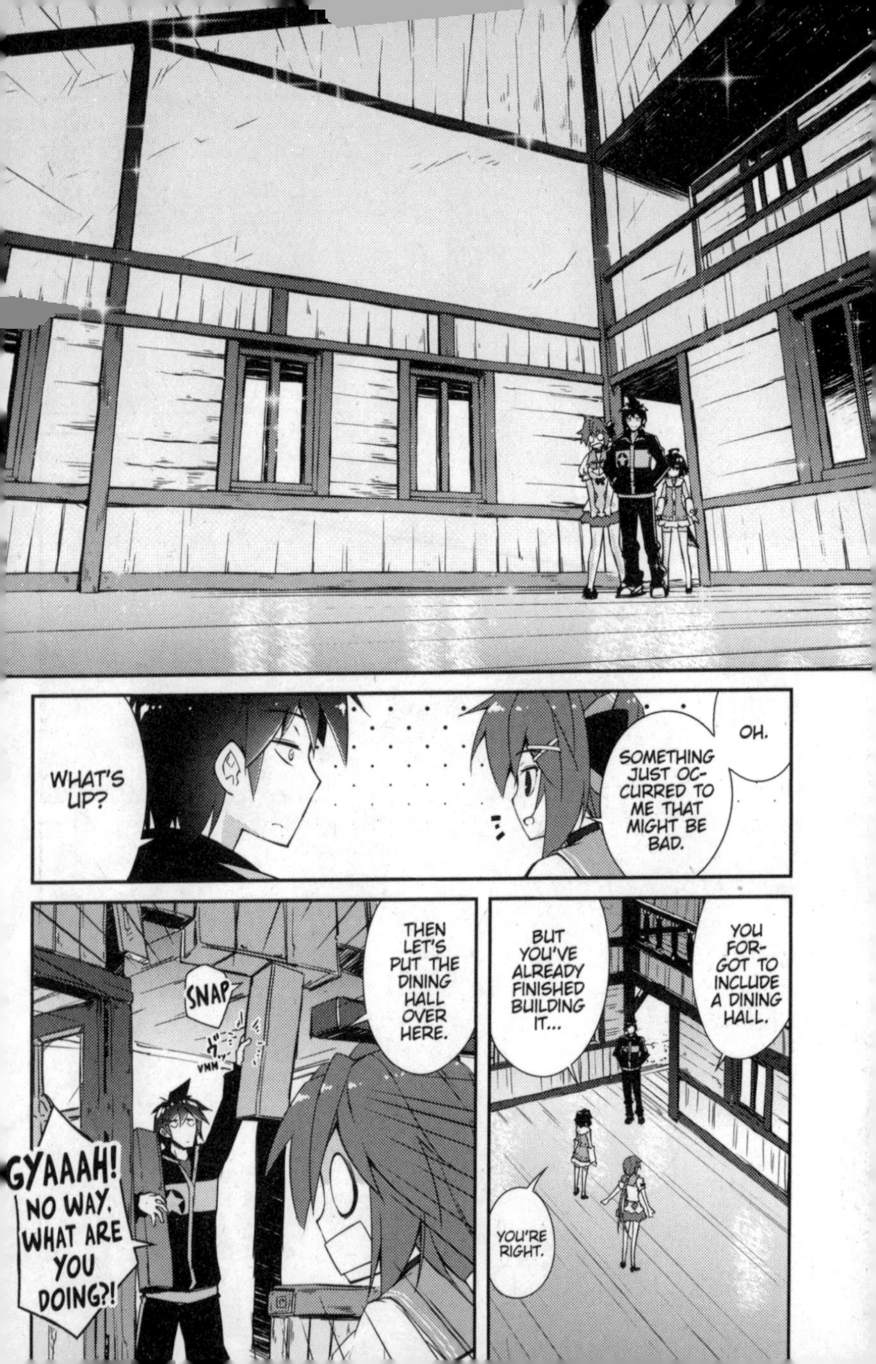
OH.
SOMETHING JUST OC-CURRED TO ME THAT MIGHT BE BAD.
WHAT'S UP?
YOU FOR-GOT TO INCLUDE A DINING HALL.
BUT YOU'VE ALREADY FINISHED BUILDING IT...
YOU'RE RIGHT.
THEN LET'S PUT THE DINING HALL OVER HERE.
SNAP
VMM
GYAAAH! NO WAY. WHAT ARE YOU DOING?!

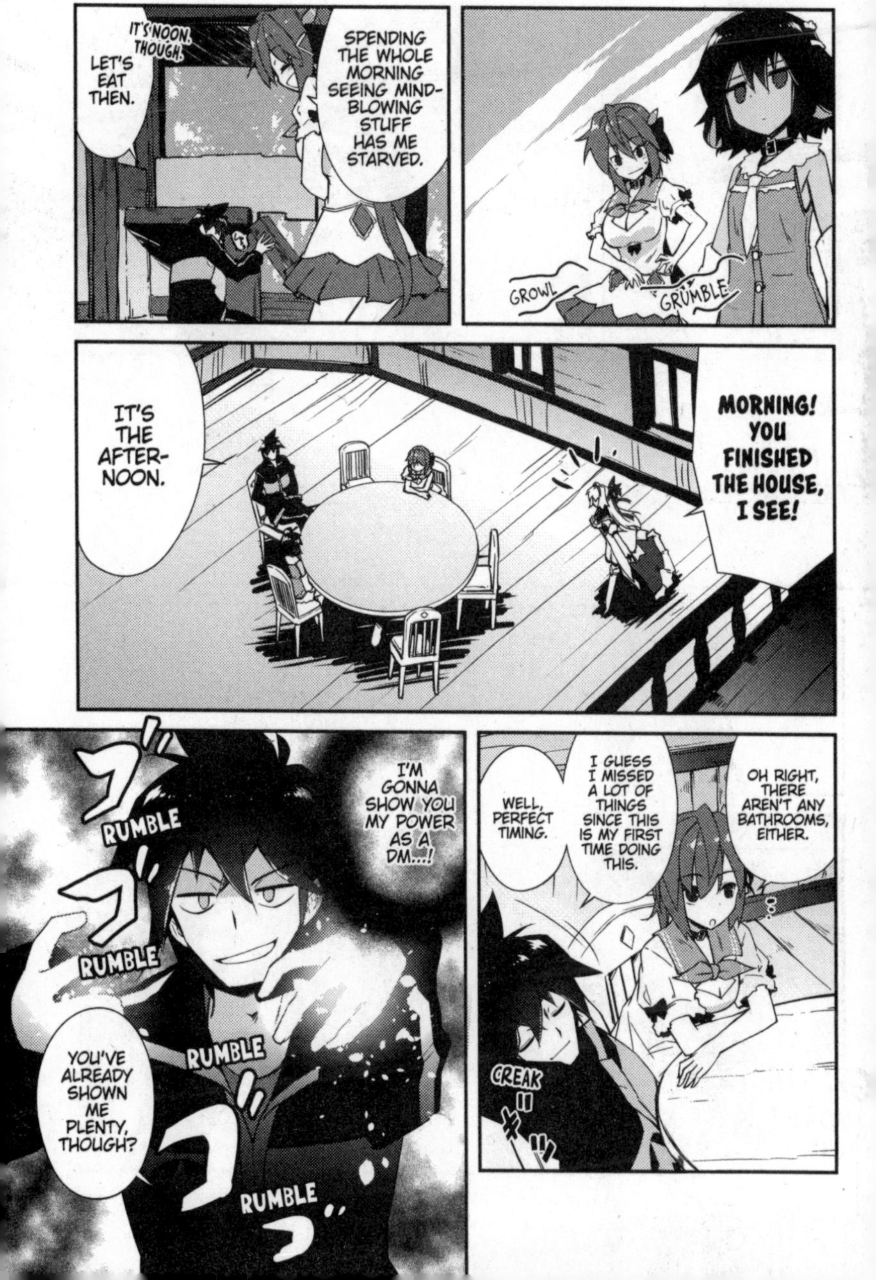
GROWL
GRUMBLE
SPENDING THE WHOLE MORNING SEEING MIND-BLOWING STUFF HAS ME STARVED.
IT'S NOON, THOUGH.
LET'S EAT THEN.
MORNING! YOU FINISHED THE HOUSE, I SEE!
IT'S THE AFTERNOON.
OH RIGHT, THERE AREN'T ANY BATHROOMS, EITHER.
I GUESS I MISSED A LOT OF THINGS SINCE THIS IS MY FIRST TIME DOING THIS.
WELL, PERFECT TIMING.
CREAK
I'M GONNA SHOW YOU MY POWER AS A DM...!
RUMBLE
RUMBLE
RUMBLE
YOU'VE ALREADY SHOWN ME PLENTY, THOUGH?
RUMBLE

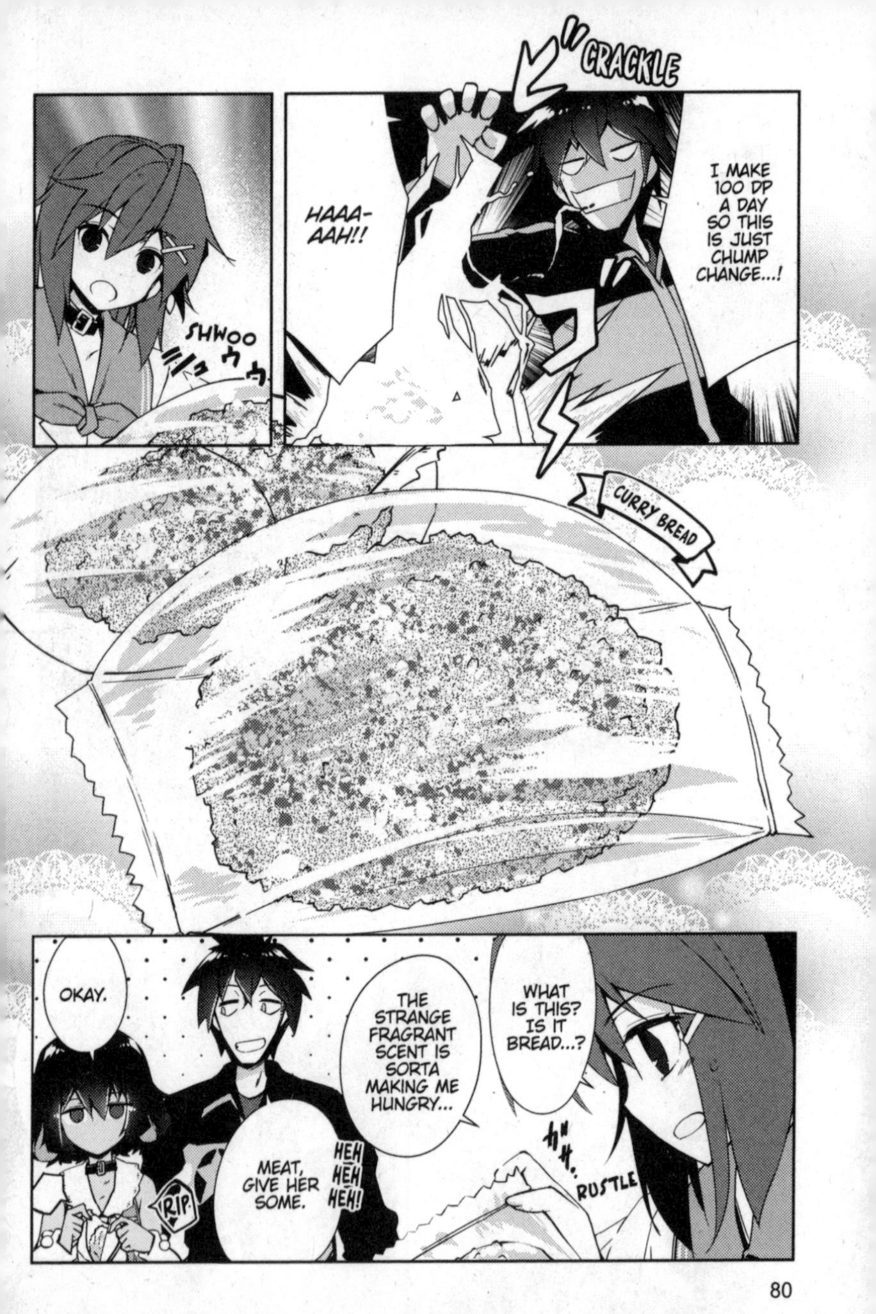
CRACKLE
I MAKE 100 DP A DAY SO THIS IS JUST CHUMP CHANGE...!
HAAAA-AAH!!
SHWOO
CURRY BREAD
WHAT IS THIS? IS IT BREAD...?
RUSTLE
THE STRANGE FRAGRANT SCENT IS SORTA MAKING ME HUNGRY...
HEH HEH HEH!
MEAT, GIVE HER SOME.
RIP
OKAY.

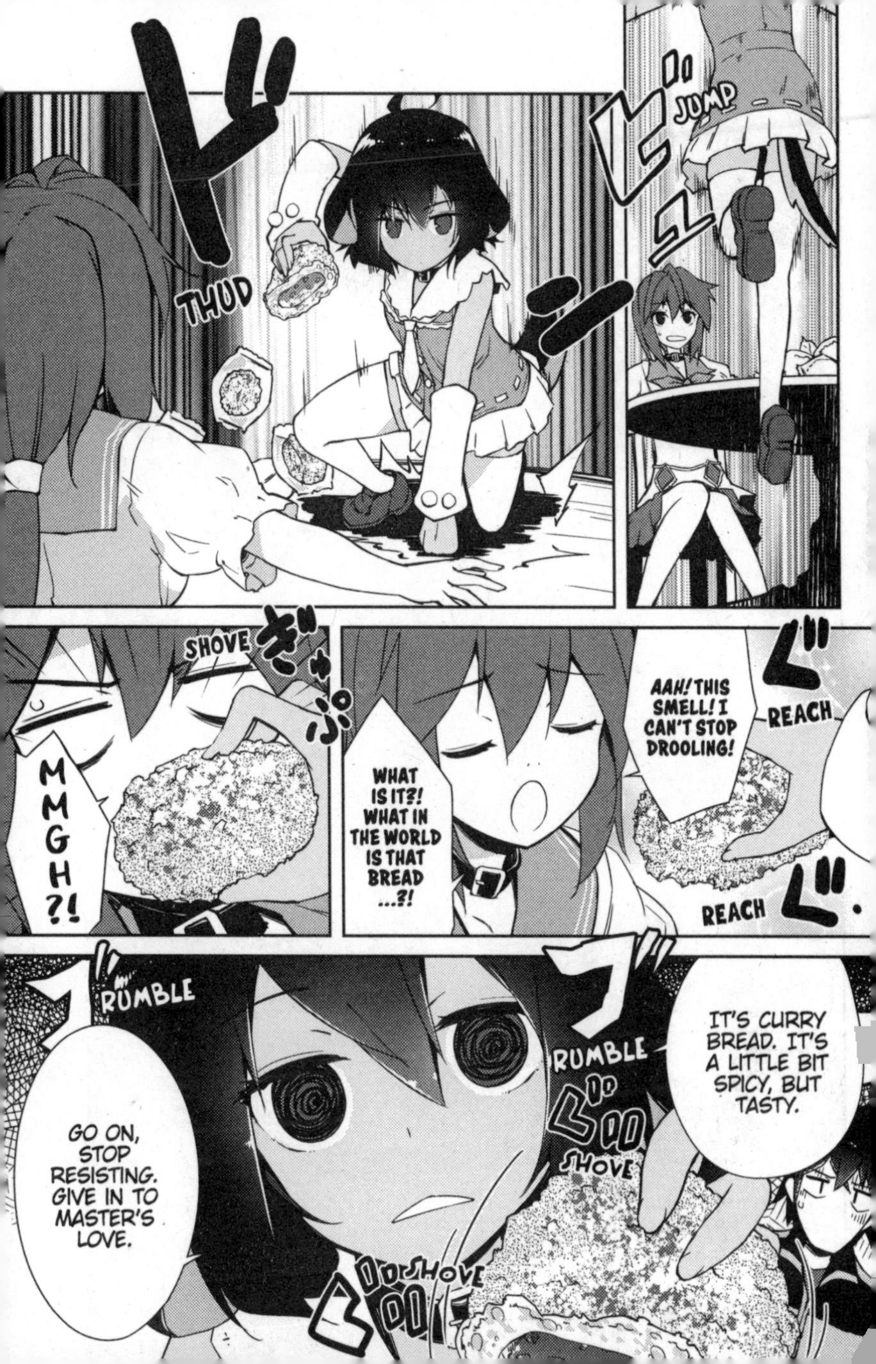
JUMP
THUD
AAH! THIS SMELL! I CAN'T STOP DROOLING!
REACH
REACH
WHAT IS IT?! WHAT IN THE WORLD IS THAT BREAD ...?!
SHOVE
MMGH ?!
IT'S CURRY BREAD. IT'S A LITTLE BIT SPICY, BUT TASTY.
RUMBLE
SHOVE
RUMBLE
GO ON, STOP RESISTING. GIVE IN TO MASTER'S LOVE.
SHOVE

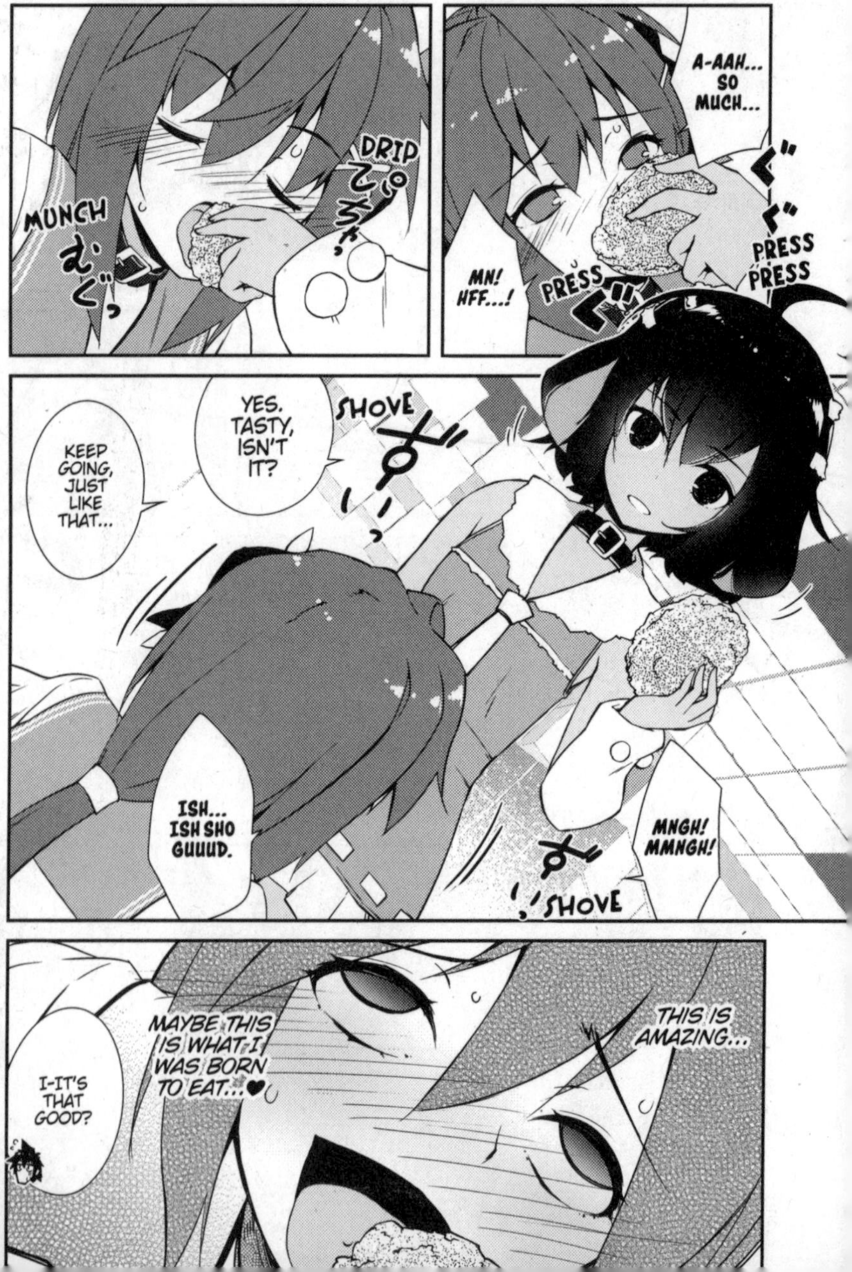
A-AAH... SO MUCH...
PRESS PRESS
MN! HFF...!
PRESS
DRIP
MUNCH
むぐっ
SHOVE
YES. TASTY, ISN'T IT?
KEEP GOING, JUST LIKE THAT...
MNGH! MMNGH!
ISH... ISH SHO GUUUD.
SHOVE
THIS IS AMAZING...
MAYBE THIS IS WHAT I WAS BORN TO EAT...♥
I-IT'S THAT GOOD?

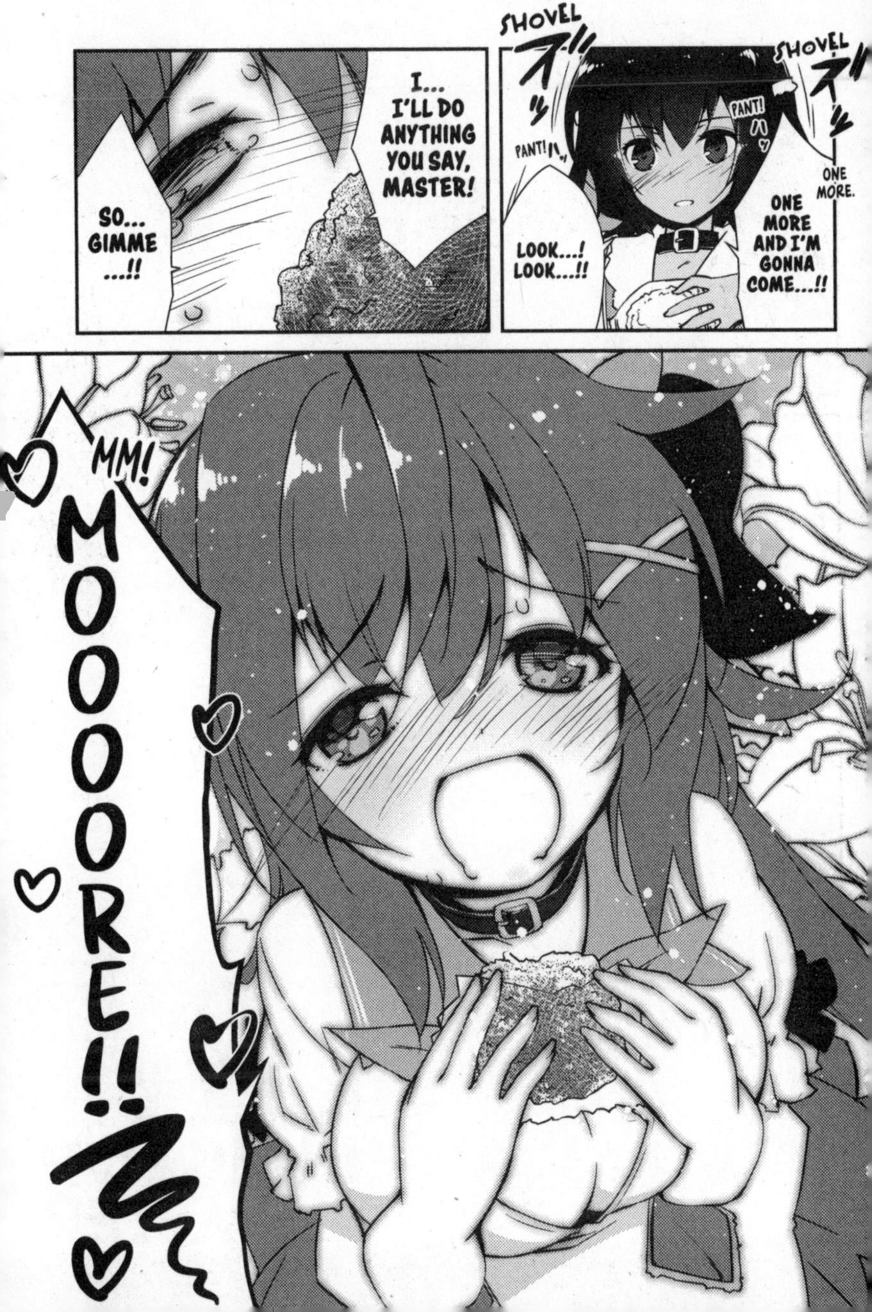
SHOVEL
SHOVEL
PANT!
ONE MORE.
ONE MORE AND I'M GONNA COME...!!
PANT!
LOOK...! LOOK...!!
I... I'LL DO ANYTHING YOU SAY, MASTER!
SO... GIMME ...!!
MM!
MOOOOORE!!

LAZY
DUNGEON
MASTER

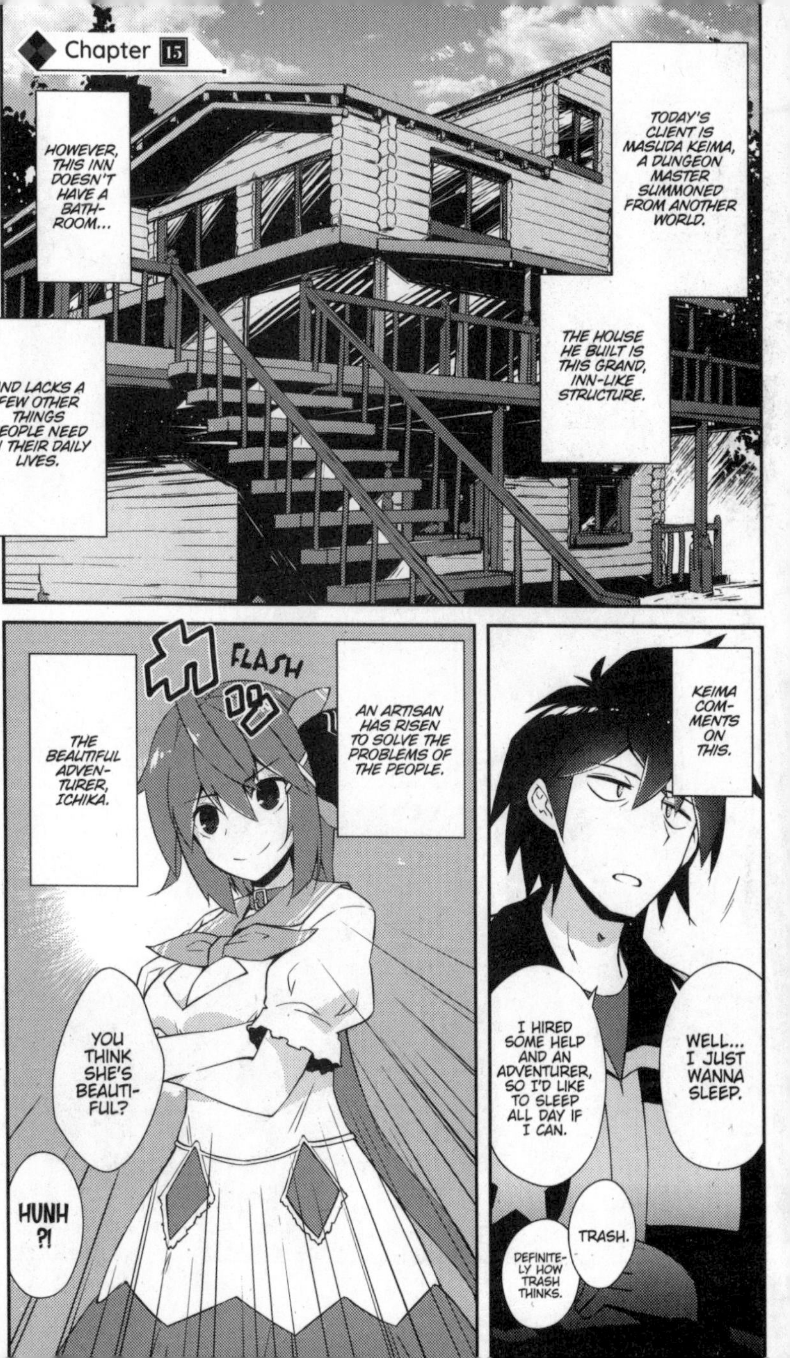
Chapter 15
TODAY'S CLIENT IS MASUDA KEIMA, A DUNGEON MASTER SUMMONED FROM ANOTHER WORLD.
THE HOUSE HE BUILT IS THIS GRAND, INN-LIKE STRUCTURE.
HOWEVER, THIS INN DOESN'T HAVE A BATH-ROOM...
AND LACKS A FEW OTHER THINGS PEOPLE NEED IN THEIR DAILY LIVES.
KEIMA COM-MENTS ON THIS.
WELL... I JUST WANNA SLEEP.
I HIRED SOME HELP AND AN ADVENTURER, SO I'D LIKE TO SLEEP ALL DAY IF I CAN.
TRASH.
DEFINITE-LY HOW TRASH THINKS.
AN ARTISAN HAS RISEN TO SOLVE THE PROBLEMS OF THE PEOPLE.
FLASH
THE BEAUTIFUL ADVEN-TURER, ICHIKA.
YOU THINK SHE'S BEAUTI-FUL?
HUNH ?!

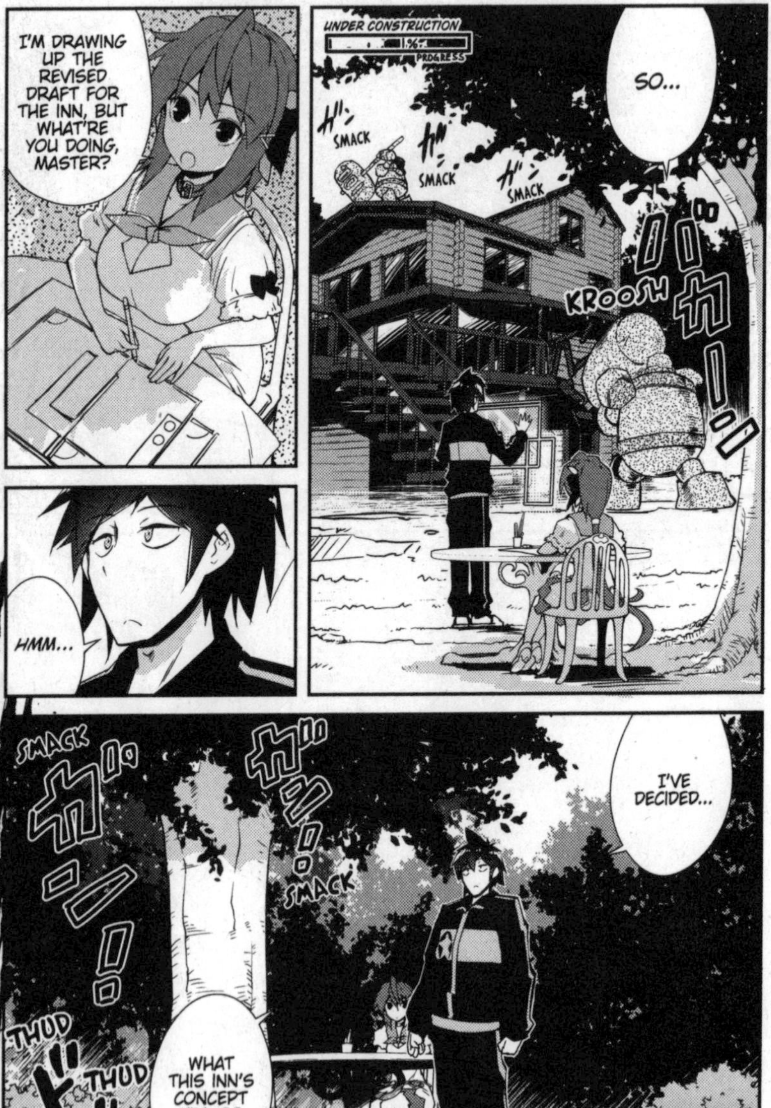
UNDER CONSTRUCTION
PROGRESS
SO...
SMACK
SMACK
SMACK
KROOSH
I'M DRAWING UP THE REVISED DRAFT FOR THE INN, BUT WHAT'RE YOU DOING, MASTER?
HMM...
I'VE DECIDED...
SMACK
SMACK
WHAT THIS INN'S CONCEPT WILL BE.
THUD
THUD

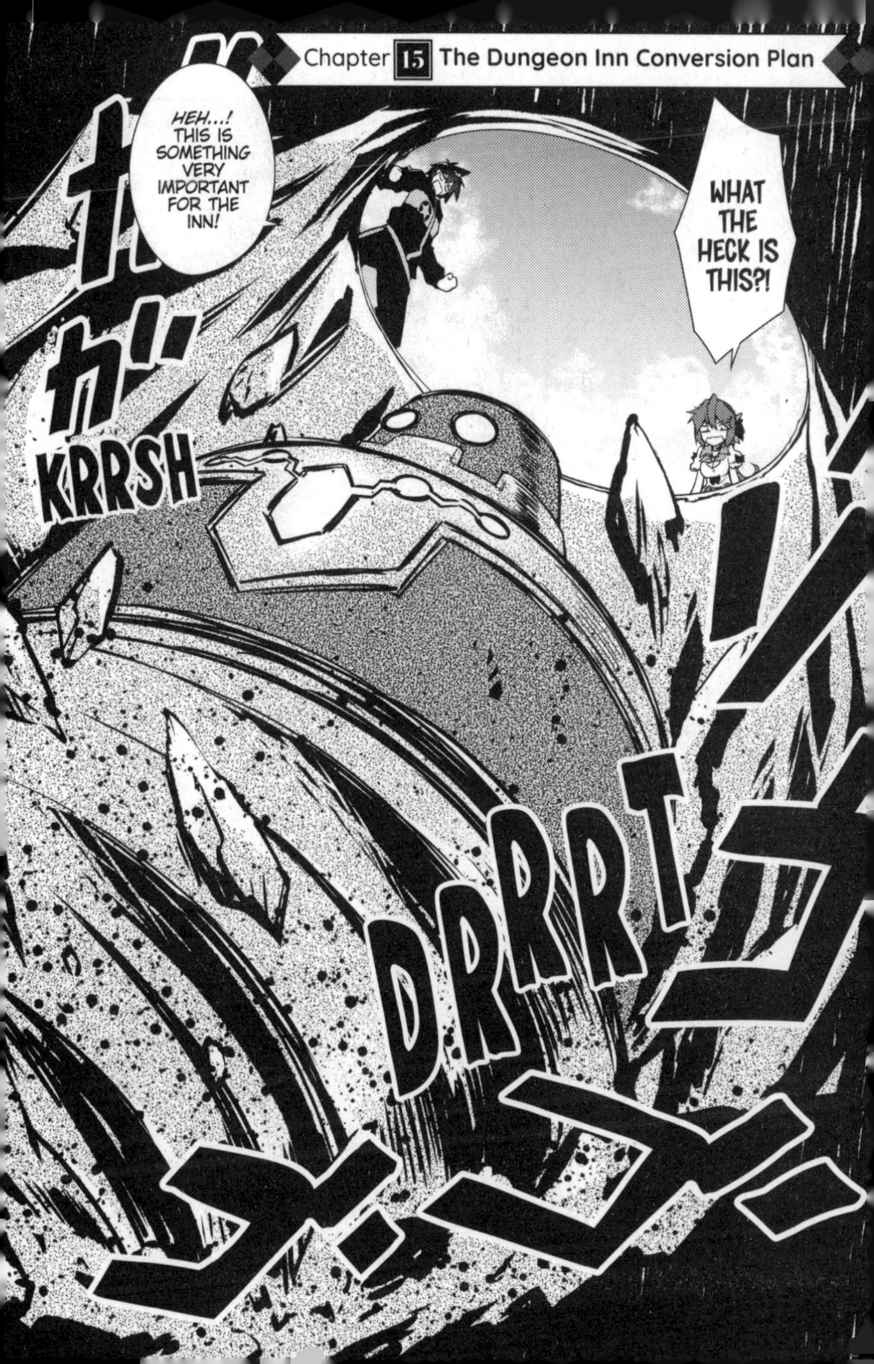
Chapter 15 The Dungeon Inn Conversion Plan
WHAT THE HECK IS THIS?!
HEH...! THIS IS SOMETHING VERY IMPORTANT FOR THE INN!
KRRSH
DRRRT

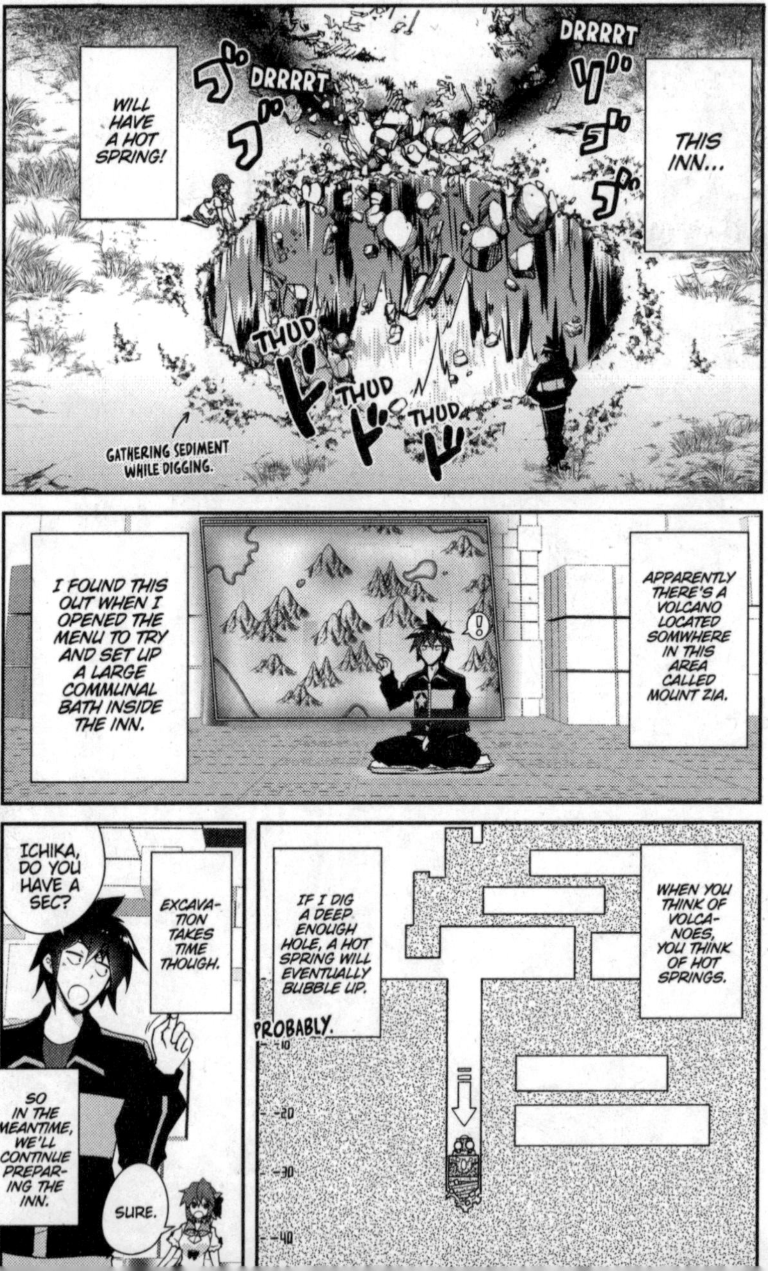
THIS INN...
WILL HAVE A HOT SPRING!
DRRRRT
DRRRRT
THUD
THUD
THUD
GATHERING SEDIMENT WHILE DIGGING.
APPARENTLY THERE'S A VOLCANO LOCATED SOMWHERE IN THIS AREA CALLED MOUNT ZIA.
I FOUND THIS OUT WHEN I OPENED THE MENU TO TRY AND SET UP A LARGE COMMUNAL BATH INSIDE THE INN.
!
WHEN YOU THINK OF VOLCA-NOES, YOU THINK OF HOT SPRINGS.
IF I DIG A DEEP ENOUGH HOLE, A HOT SPRING WILL EVENTUALLY BUBBLE UP.
PROBABLY.
-10
-20
-30
-40
EXCAVA-TION TAKES TIME THOUGH.
ICHIKA, DO YOU HAVE A SEC?
SO IN THE MEANTIME, WE'LL CONTINUE PREPAR-ING THE INN.
SURE.

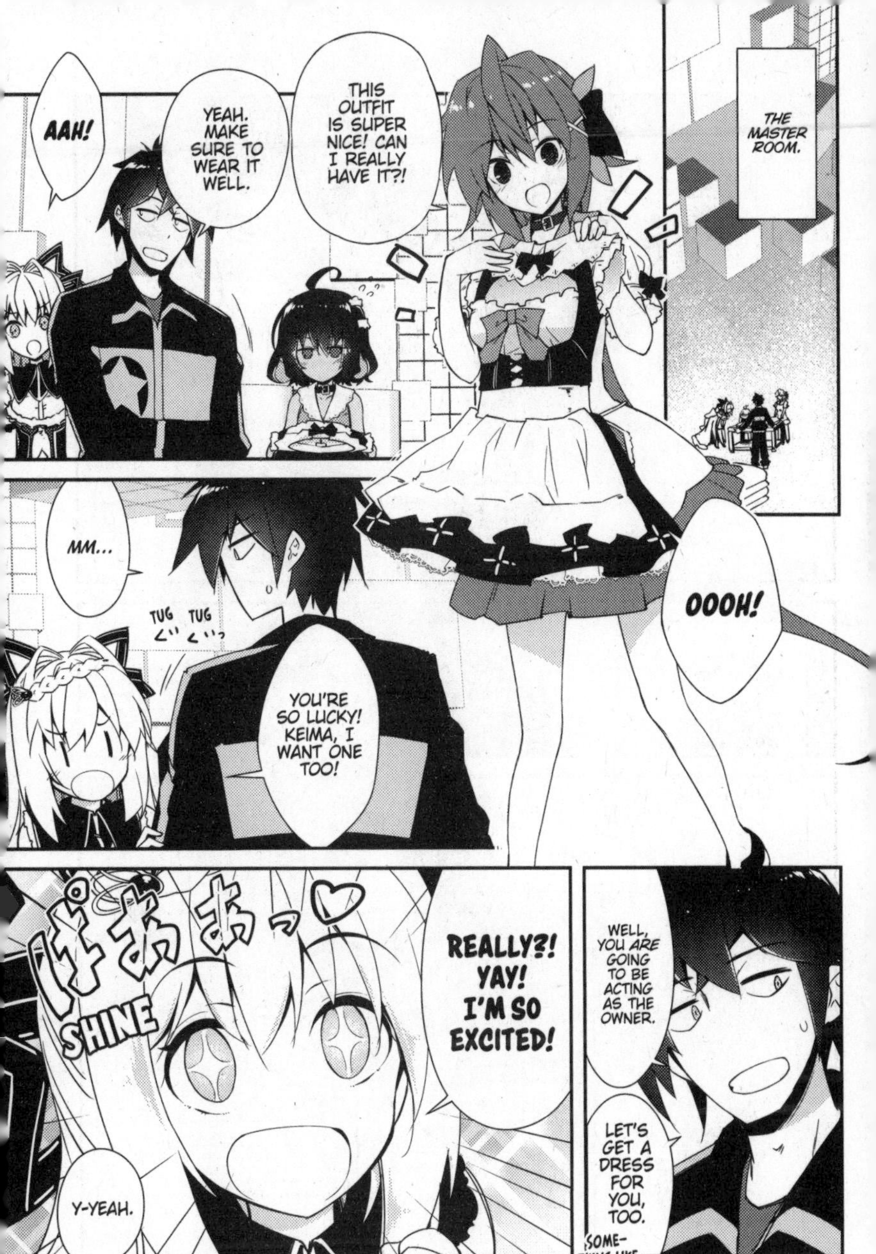
THE MASTER ROOM.
THIS OUTFIT IS SUPER NICE! CAN I REALLY HAVE IT?!
YEAH. MAKE SURE TO WEAR IT WELL.
AAH!
OOOH!
MM...
TUG TUG
ぐい ぐいっ
YOU'RE SO LUCKY! KEIMA, I WANT ONE TOO!
WELL, YOU *ARE* GOING TO BE ACTING AS THE OWNER.
LET'S GET A DRESS FOR YOU, TOO.
SOMETHING LIKE HAKU'S.
REALLY?! YAY! I'M SO EXCITED!
ぱああっ
SHINE
Y-YEAH.

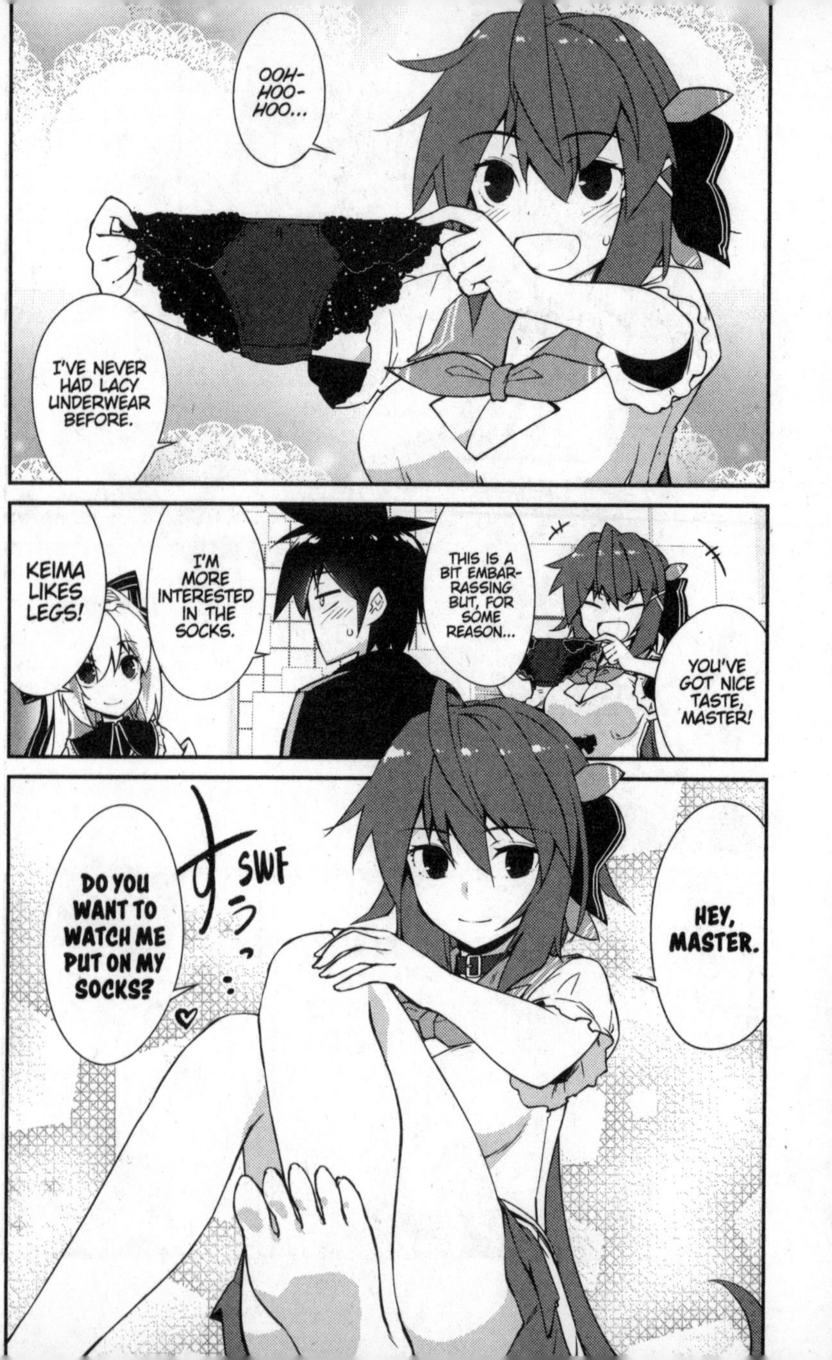
OOH-HOO-HOO...
I'VE NEVER HAD LACY UNDERWEAR BEFORE.
THIS IS A BIT EMBARRASSING BUT, FOR SOME REASON...
YOU'VE GOT NICE TASTE, MASTER!
I'M MORE INTERESTED IN THE SOCKS.
KEIMA LIKES LEGS!
HEY, MASTER.
SWF
DO YOU WANT TO WATCH ME PUT ON MY SOCKS?

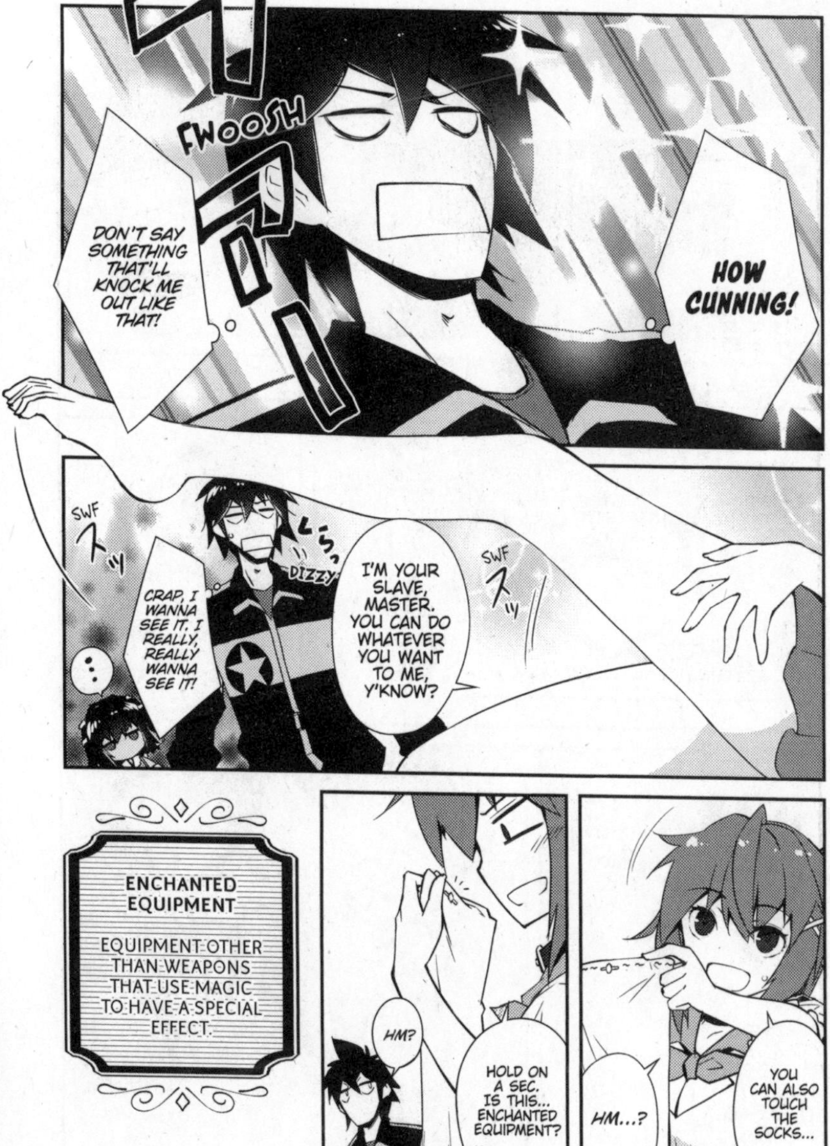
HOW CUNNING!
FWOOSH
DON'T SAY SOMETHING THAT'LL KNOCK ME OUT LIKE THAT!
SWF
I'M YOUR SLAVE, MASTER. YOU CAN DO WHATEVER YOU WANT TO ME, Y'KNOW?
DIZZY
CRAP, I WANNA SEE IT. I REALLY, REALLY WANNA SEE IT!
SWF
...
YOU CAN ALSO TOUCH THE SOCKS...
HM...?
HOLD ON A SEC. IS THIS... ENCHANTED EQUIPMENT?
HM?
THERE'S A MAGIC STONE ON IT...

ENCHANTED EQUIPMENT

EQUIPMENT OTHER THAN WEAPONS THAT USE MAGIC TO HAVE A SPECIAL EFFECT.

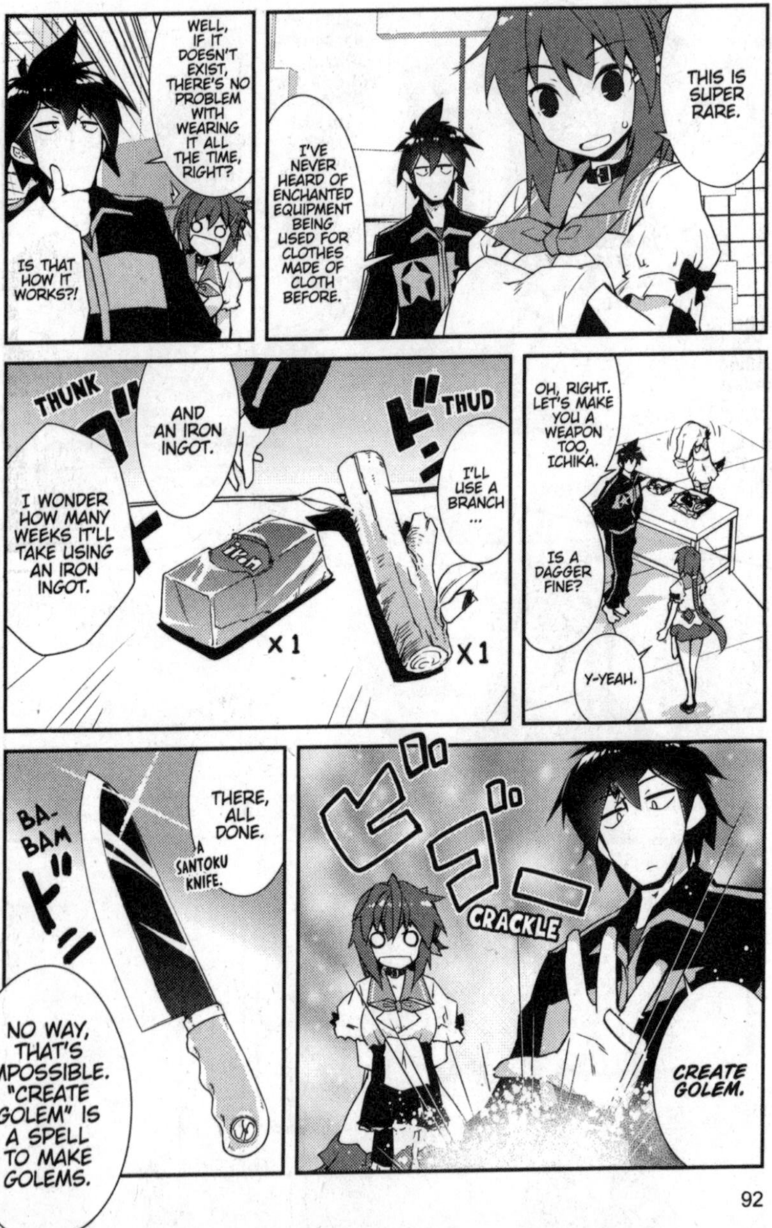
THIS IS SUPER RARE.
I'VE NEVER HEARD OF ENCHANTED EQUIPMENT BEING USED FOR CLOTHES MADE OF CLOTH BEFORE.
WELL, IF IT DOESN'T EXIST, THERE'S NO PROBLEM WITH WEARING IT ALL THE TIME, RIGHT?
IS THAT HOW IT WORKS?!
OH, RIGHT. LET'S MAKE YOU A WEAPON TOO, ICHIKA.
IS A DAGGER FINE?
Y-YEAH.
THUD
I'LL USE A BRANCH ...
AND AN IRON INGOT.
THUNK
I WONDER HOW MANY WEEKS IT'LL TAKE USING AN IRON INGOT.
X 1
X 1
CREATE GOLEM.
CRACKLE
THERE, ALL DONE.
A SANTOKU KNIFE.
BA-BAM
NO WAY, THAT'S IMPOSSIBLE. "CREATE GOLEM" IS A SPELL TO MAKE GOLEMS.

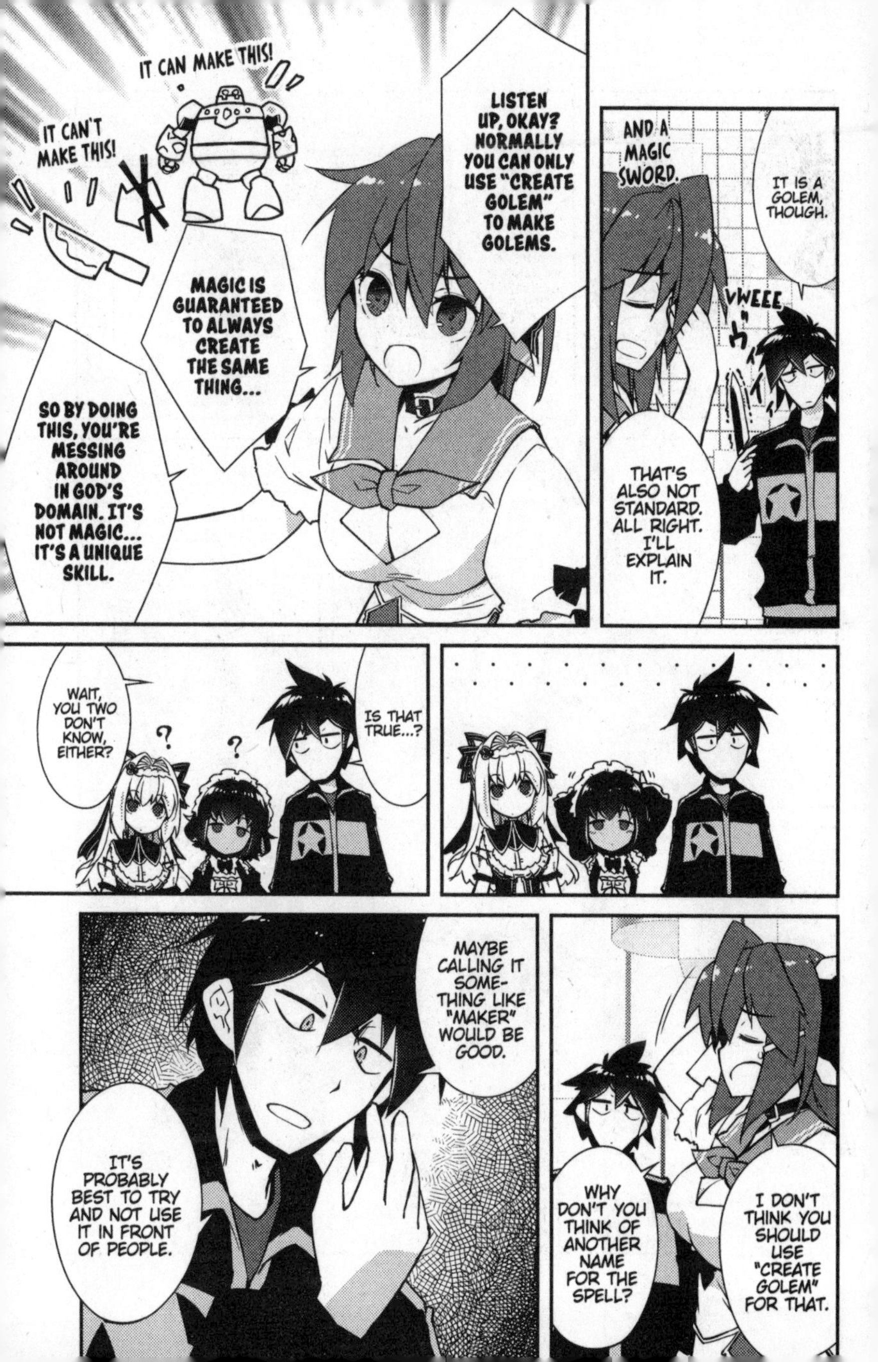
IT IS A GOLEM, THOUGH.
VWEEE
AND A MAGIC SWORD.
THAT'S ALSO NOT STANDARD. ALL RIGHT. I'LL EXPLAIN IT.
LISTEN UP, OKAY? NORMALLY YOU CAN ONLY USE "CREATE GOLEM" TO MAKE GOLEMS.
IT CAN MAKE THIS!
IT CAN'T MAKE THIS!
MAGIC IS GUARANTEED TO ALWAYS CREATE THE SAME THING...
SO BY DOING THIS, YOU'RE MESSING AROUND IN GOD'S DOMAIN. IT'S NOT MAGIC... IT'S A UNIQUE SKILL.
IS THAT TRUE...?
?
?
WAIT, YOU TWO DON'T KNOW, EITHER?
I DON'T THINK YOU SHOULD USE "CREATE GOLEM" FOR THAT.
WHY DON'T YOU THINK OF ANOTHER NAME FOR THE SPELL?
MAYBE CALLING IT SOME-THING LIKE "MAKER" WOULD BE GOOD.
IT'S PROBABLY BEST TO TRY AND NOT USE IT IN FRONT OF PEOPLE.

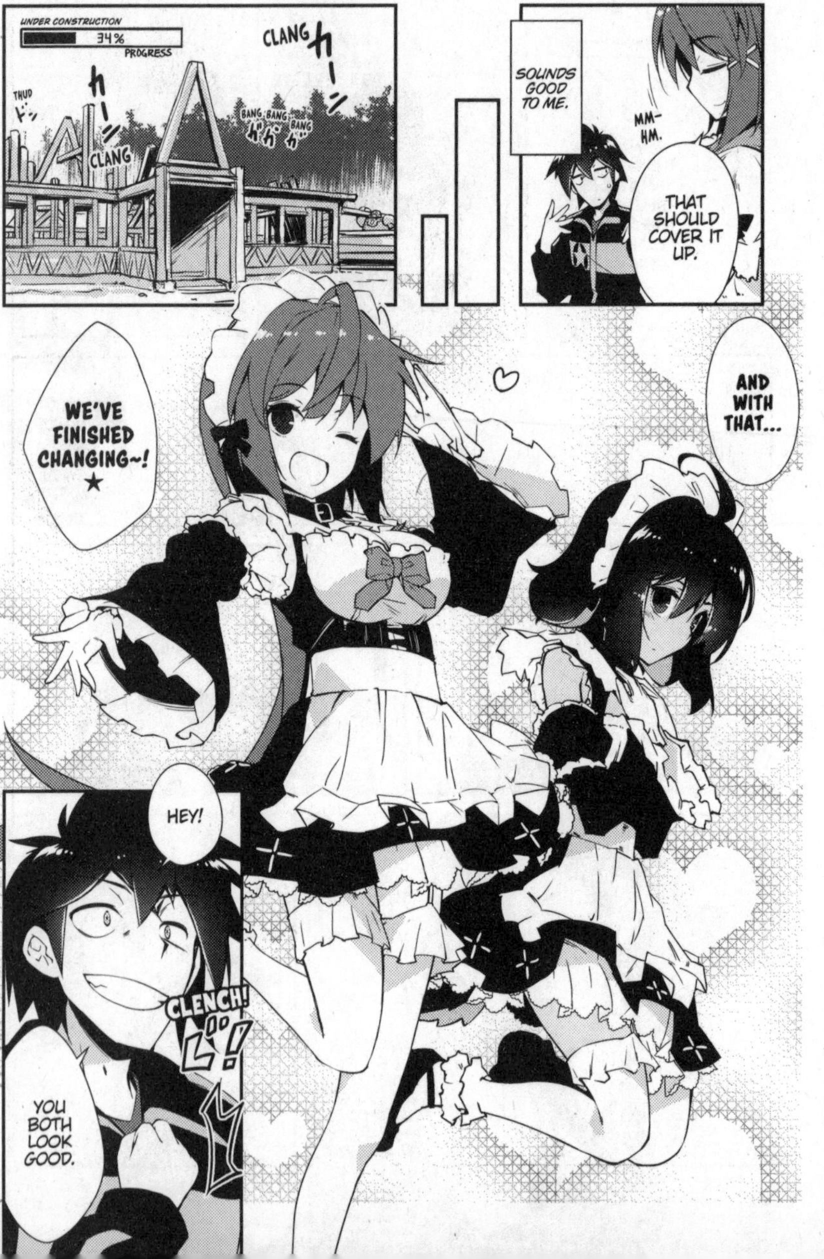
THAT SHOULD COVER IT UP.
MM-HM.
SOUNDS GOOD TO ME.
UNDER CONSTRUCTION
34%
PROGRESS
CLANG
THUD
CLANG
BANG BANG BANG
AND WITH THAT...
WE'VE FINISHED CHANGING~! ★
HEY!
CLENCH!
YOU BOTH LOOK GOOD.

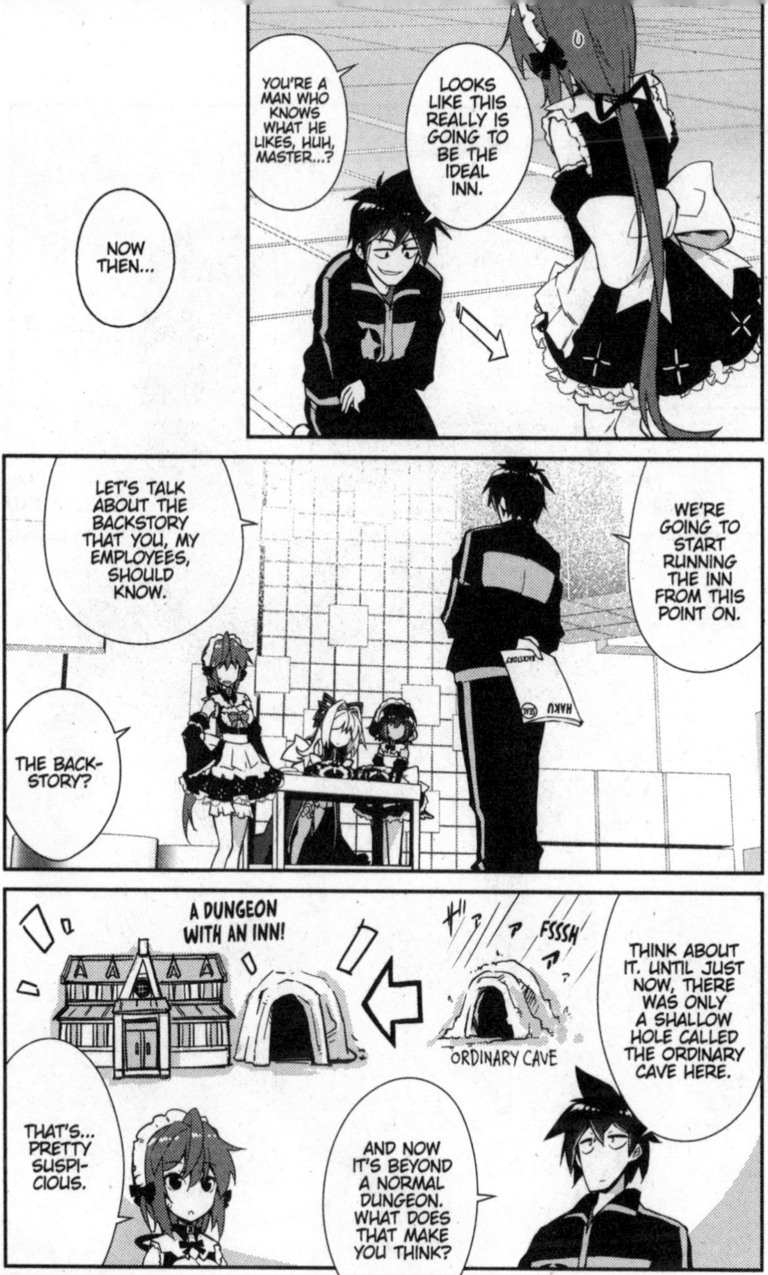
LOOKS LIKE THIS REALLY IS GOING TO BE THE IDEAL INN.
YOU'RE A MAN WHO KNOWS WHAT HE LIKES, HUH, MASTER...?
NOW THEN...
WE'RE GOING TO START RUNNING THE INN FROM THIS POINT ON.
LET'S TALK ABOUT THE BACKSTORY THAT YOU, MY EMPLOYEES, SHOULD KNOW.
THE BACK-STORY?
THINK ABOUT IT. UNTIL JUST NOW, THERE WAS ONLY A SHALLOW HOLE CALLED THE ORDINARY CAVE HERE.
FSSSH
ORDINARY CAVE
A DUNGEON WITH AN INN!
AND NOW IT'S BEYOND A NORMAL DUNGEON. WHAT DOES THAT MAKE YOU THINK?
THAT'S... PRETTY SUSPI-CIOUS.

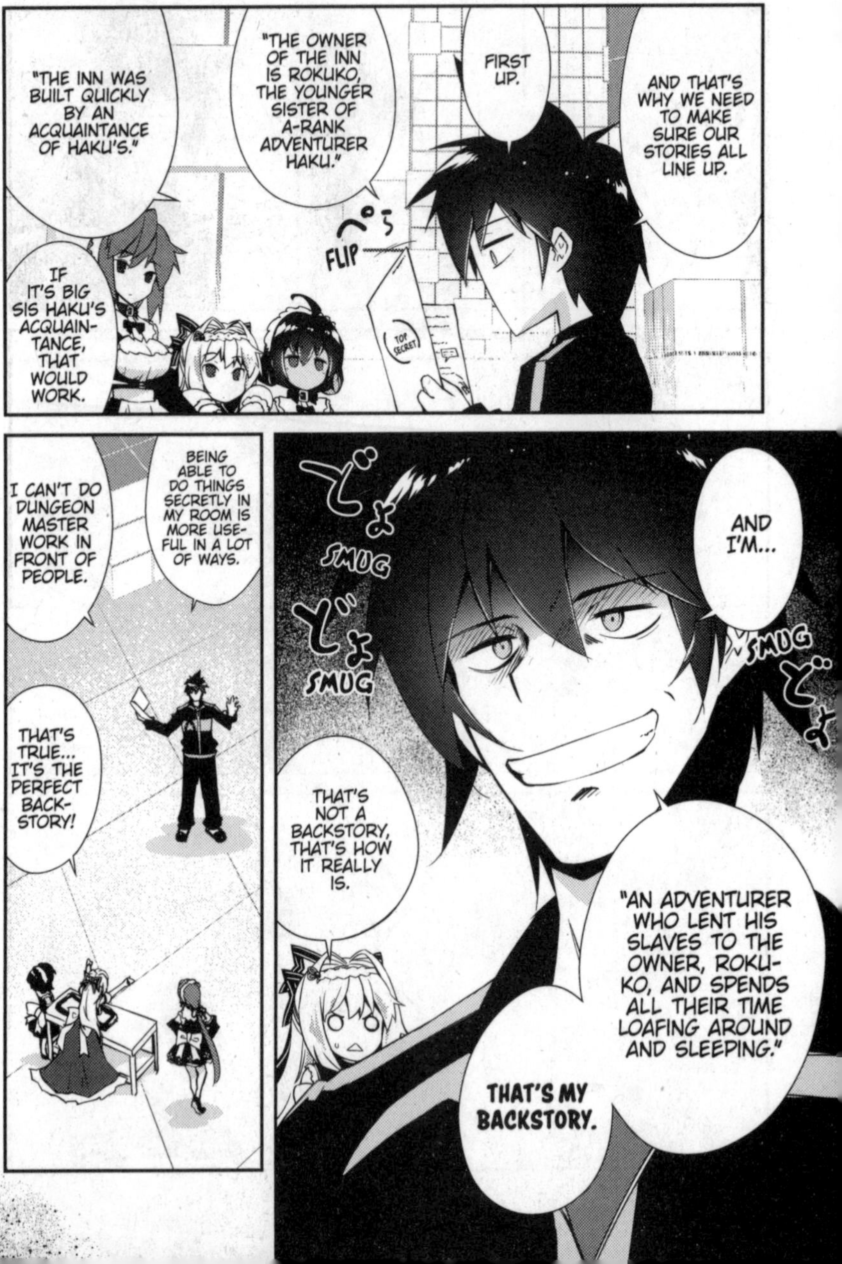
AND THAT'S WHY WE NEED TO MAKE SURE OUR STORIES ALL LINE UP.
FIRST UP.
"THE OWNER OF THE INN IS ROKUKO, THE YOUNGER SISTER OF A-RANK ADVENTURER HAKU."
"THE INN WAS BUILT QUICKLY BY AN ACQUAINTANCE OF HAKU'S."
ぺら
FLIP
TOP SECRET
IF IT'S BIG SIS HAKU'S ACQUAINTANCE, THAT WOULD WORK.
AND I'M...
SMUG
どよ
どよ
SMUG
どよ
SMUG
"AN ADVENTURER WHO LENT HIS SLAVES TO THE OWNER, ROKUKO, AND SPENDS ALL THEIR TIME LOAFING AROUND AND SLEEPING."
THAT'S MY BACKSTORY.
THAT'S NOT A BACKSTORY, THAT'S HOW IT REALLY IS.
BEING ABLE TO DO THINGS SECRETLY IN MY ROOM IS MORE USEFUL IN A LOT OF WAYS.
I CAN'T DO DUNGEON MASTER WORK IN FRONT OF PEOPLE.
THAT'S TRUE... IT'S THE PERFECT BACKSTORY!

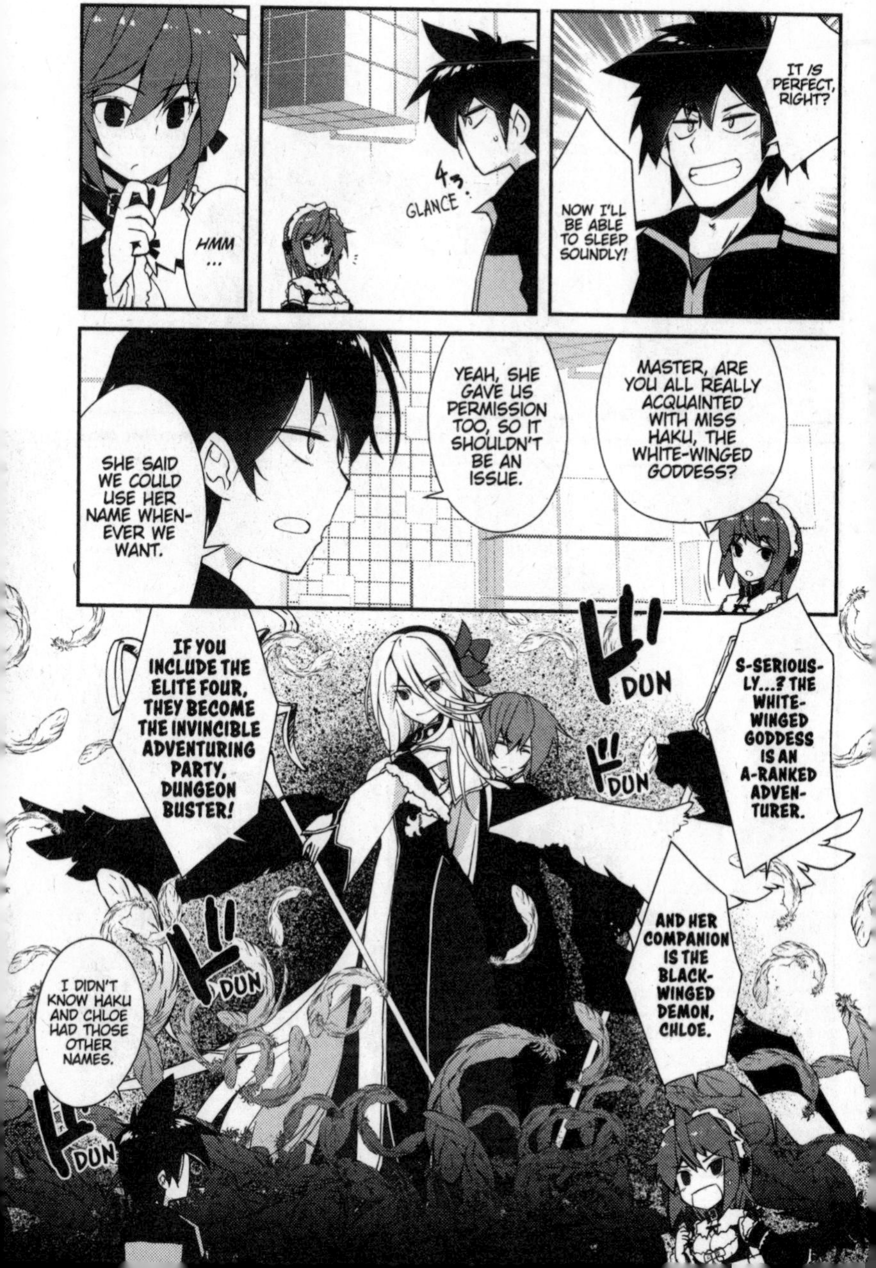
IT IS PERFECT, RIGHT?
NOW I'LL BE ABLE TO SLEEP SOUNDLY!
GLANCE
HMM ...
MASTER, ARE YOU ALL REALLY ACQUAINTED WITH MISS HAKU, THE WHITE-WINGED GODDESS?
YEAH, SHE GAVE US PERMISSION TOO, SO IT SHOULDN'T BE AN ISSUE.
SHE SAID WE COULD USE HER NAME WHENEVER WE WANT.
DUN
S-SERIOUSLY...? THE WHITE-WINGED GODDESS IS AN A-RANKED ADVENTURER.
DUN
AND HER COMPANION IS THE BLACK-WINGED DEMON, CHLOE.
IF YOU INCLUDE THE ELITE FOUR, THEY BECOME THE INVINCIBLE ADVENTURING PARTY, DUNGEON BUSTER!
DUN
I DIDN'T KNOW HAKU AND CHLOE HAD THOSE OTHER NAMES.
DUN

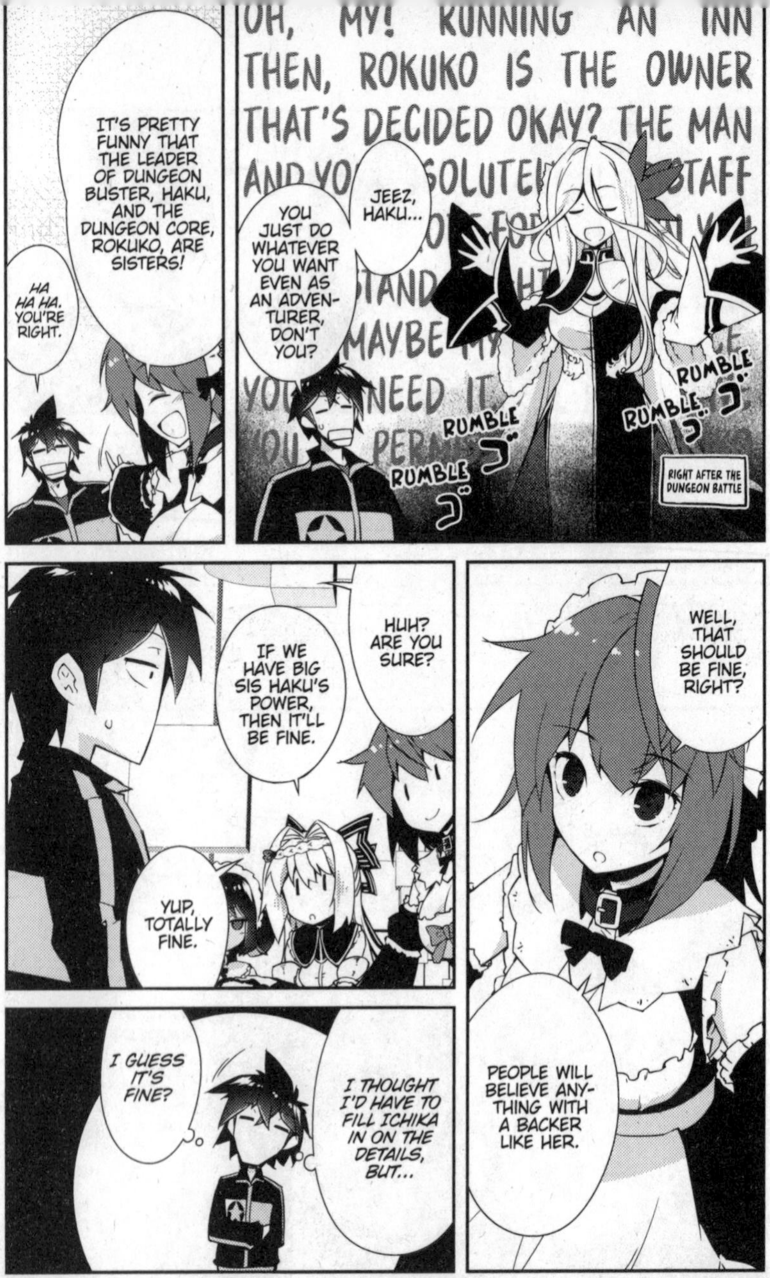

OH, MY! RUNNING AN INN
THEN, ROKUKO IS THE OWNER
THAT'S DECIDED OKAY? THE MAN
JEEZ, HAKU...
YOU JUST DO WHATEVER YOU WANT EVEN AS AN ADVENTURER, DON'T YOU?
RUMBLE RUMBLE
RUMBLE RUMBLE
RIGHT AFTER THE DUNGEON BATTLE
IT'S PRETTY FUNNY THAT THE LEADER OF DUNGEON BUSTER, HAKU, AND THE DUNGEON CORE, ROKUKO, ARE SISTERS!
HA HA HA. YOU'RE RIGHT.
WELL, THAT SHOULD BE FINE, RIGHT?
PEOPLE WILL BELIEVE ANYTHING WITH A BACKER LIKE HER.
HUH? ARE YOU SURE?
IF WE HAVE BIG SIS HAKU'S POWER, THEN IT'LL BE FINE.
YUP, TOTALLY FINE.
I THOUGHT I'D HAVE TO FILL ICHIKA IN ON THE DETAILS, BUT...
I GUESS IT'S FINE?

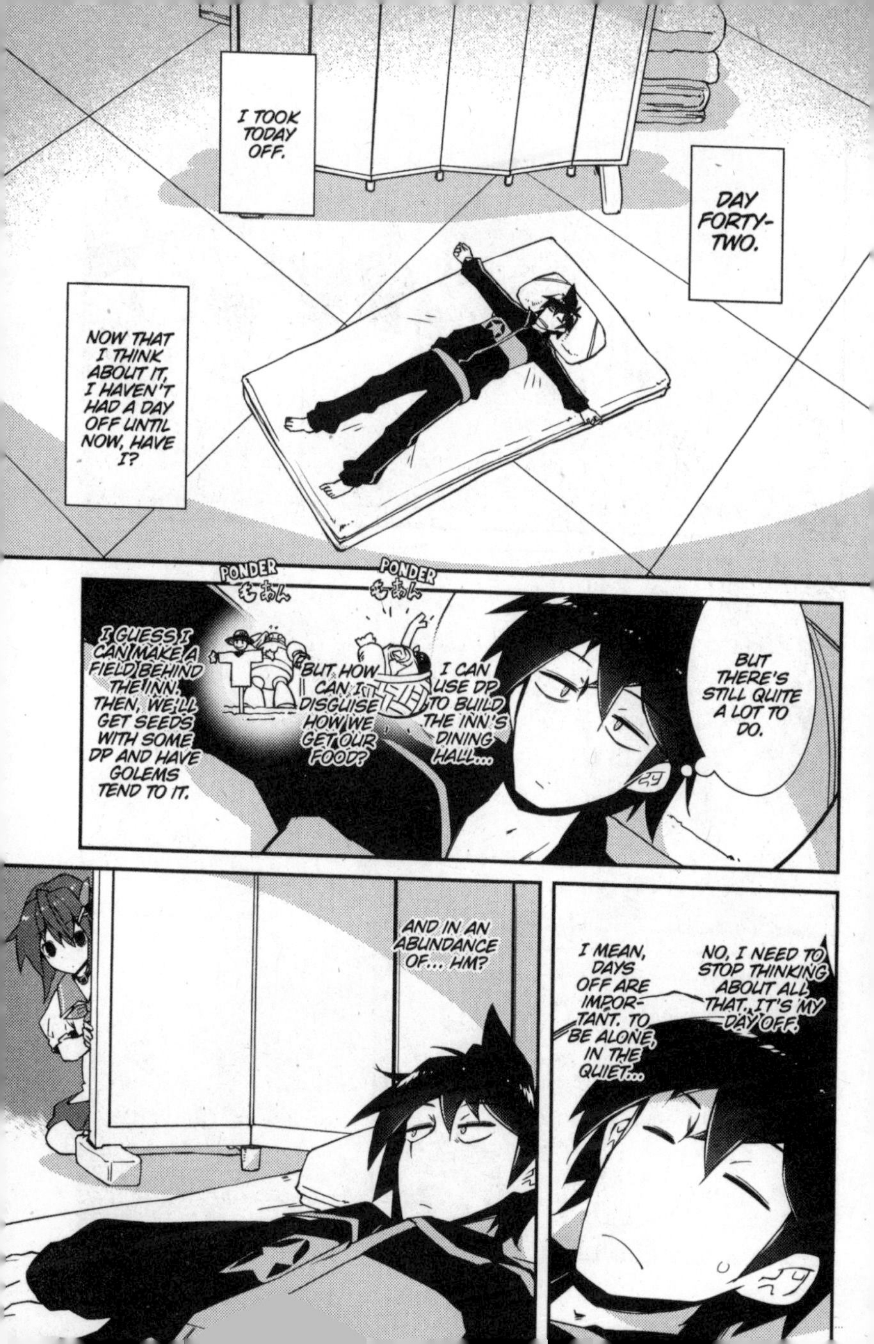

DAY FORTY-TWO.
I TOOK TODAY OFF.
NOW THAT I THINK ABOUT IT, I HAVEN'T HAD A DAY OFF UNTIL NOW, HAVE I?
BUT THERE'S STILL QUITE A LOT TO DO.
I CAN USE DP TO BUILD THE INN'S DINING HALL...
PONDER もあん
BUT HOW CAN I DISGUISE HOW WE GET OUR FOOD?
PONDER もあん
I GUESS I CAN MAKE A FIELD BEHIND THE INN. THEN, WE'LL GET SEEDS WITH SOME DP AND HAVE GOLEMS TEND TO IT.
NO, I NEED TO STOP THINKING ABOUT ALL THAT. IT'S MY DAY OFF.
I MEAN, DAYS OFF ARE IMPORTANT. TO BE ALONE, IN THE QUIET...
AND IN AN ABUNDANCE OF... HM?

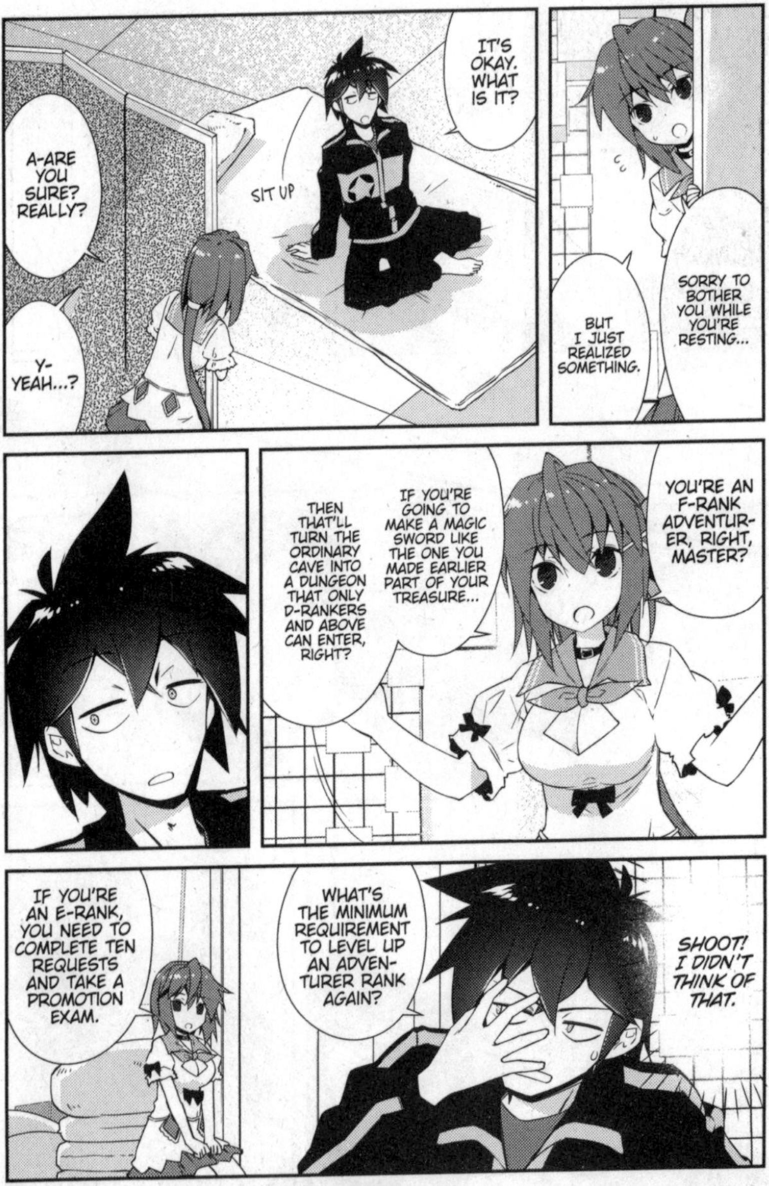
SORRY TO BOTHER YOU WHILE YOU'RE RESTING...
BUT I JUST REALIZED SOMETHING.
IT'S OKAY. WHAT IS IT?
SIT UP
A-ARE YOU SURE? REALLY?
Y-YEAH...?
YOU'RE AN F-RANK ADVENTURER, RIGHT, MASTER?
IF YOU'RE GOING TO MAKE A MAGIC SWORD LIKE THE ONE YOU MADE EARLIER PART OF YOUR TREASURE...
THEN THAT'LL TURN THE ORDINARY CAVE INTO A DUNGEON THAT ONLY D-RANKERS AND ABOVE CAN ENTER, RIGHT?
SHOOT! I DIDN'T THINK OF THAT.
WHAT'S THE MINIMUM REQUIREMENT TO LEVEL UP AN ADVENTURER RANK AGAIN?
IF YOU'RE AN E-RANK, YOU NEED TO COMPLETE TEN REQUESTS AND TAKE A PROMOTION EXAM.

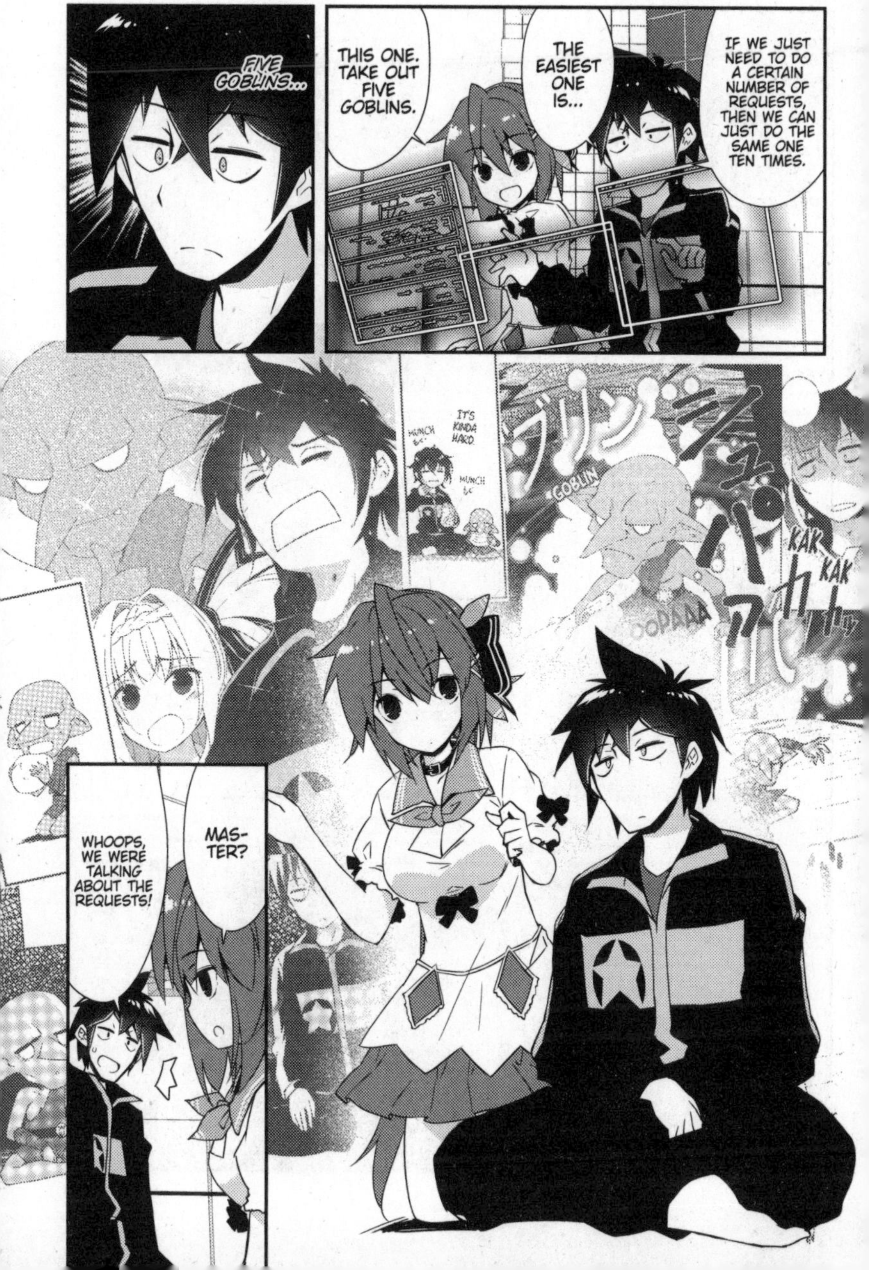
IF WE JUST NEED TO DO A CERTAIN NUMBER OF REQUESTS, THEN WE CAN JUST DO THE SAME ONE TEN TIMES.
THE EASIEST ONE IS...
THIS ONE. TAKE OUT FIVE GOBLINS.
FIVE GOBLINS...
GOBLIN
KAK
KAK
OOPAAA
IT'S KINDA HARD.
MUNCH
MUNCH
MAS-TER?
WHOOPS, WE WERE TALKING ABOUT THE REQUESTS!

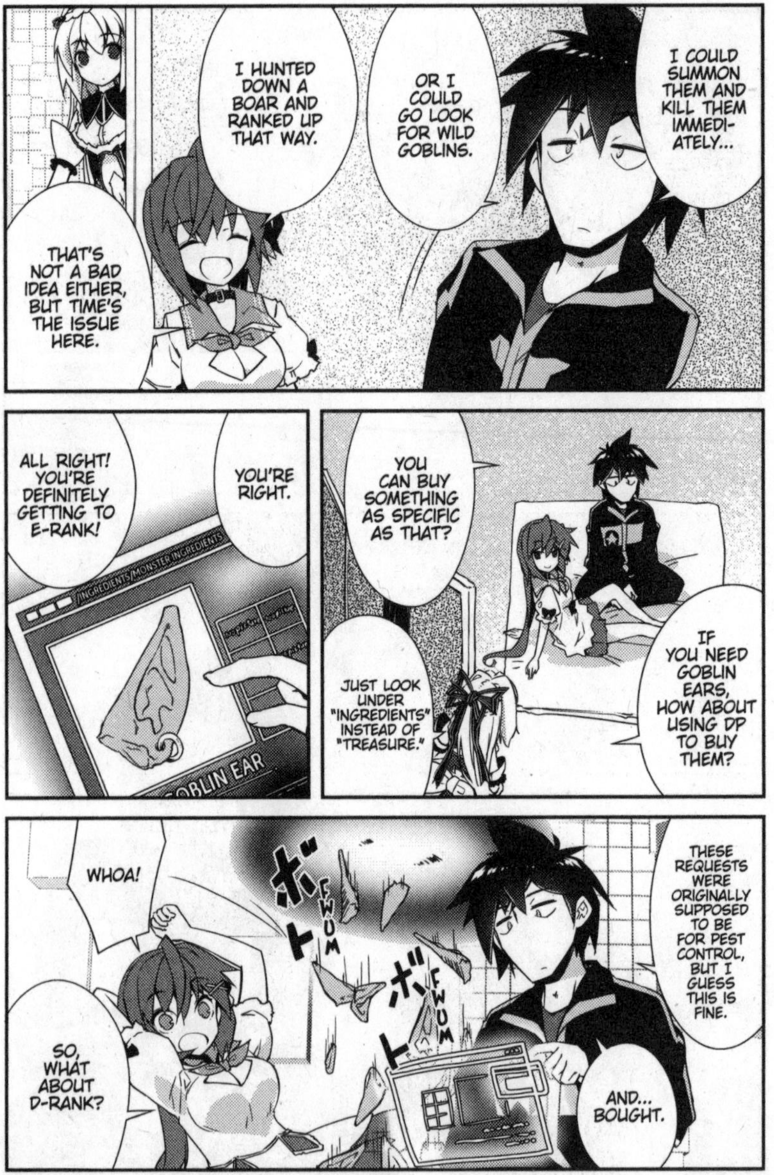
I COULD SUMMON THEM AND KILL THEM IMMEDI-ATELY...
OR I COULD GO LOOK FOR WILD GOBLINS.
I HUNTED DOWN A BOAR AND RANKED UP THAT WAY.
THAT'S NOT A BAD IDEA EITHER, BUT TIME'S THE ISSUE HERE.
IF YOU NEED GOBLIN EARS, HOW ABOUT USING DP TO BUY THEM?
YOU CAN BUY SOMETHING AS SPECIFIC AS THAT?
JUST LOOK UNDER "INGREDIENTS" INSTEAD OF "TREASURE."
YOU'RE RIGHT.
ALL RIGHT! YOU'RE DEFINITELY GETTING TO E-RANK!
/INGREDIENTS/MONSTER INGREDIENTS
GOBLIN EAR
THESE REQUESTS WERE ORIGINALLY SUPPOSED TO BE FOR PEST CONTROL, BUT I GUESS THIS IS FINE.
AND... BOUGHT.
ボト FWUM
ボト FWUM
WHOA!
SO, WHAT ABOUT D-RANK?

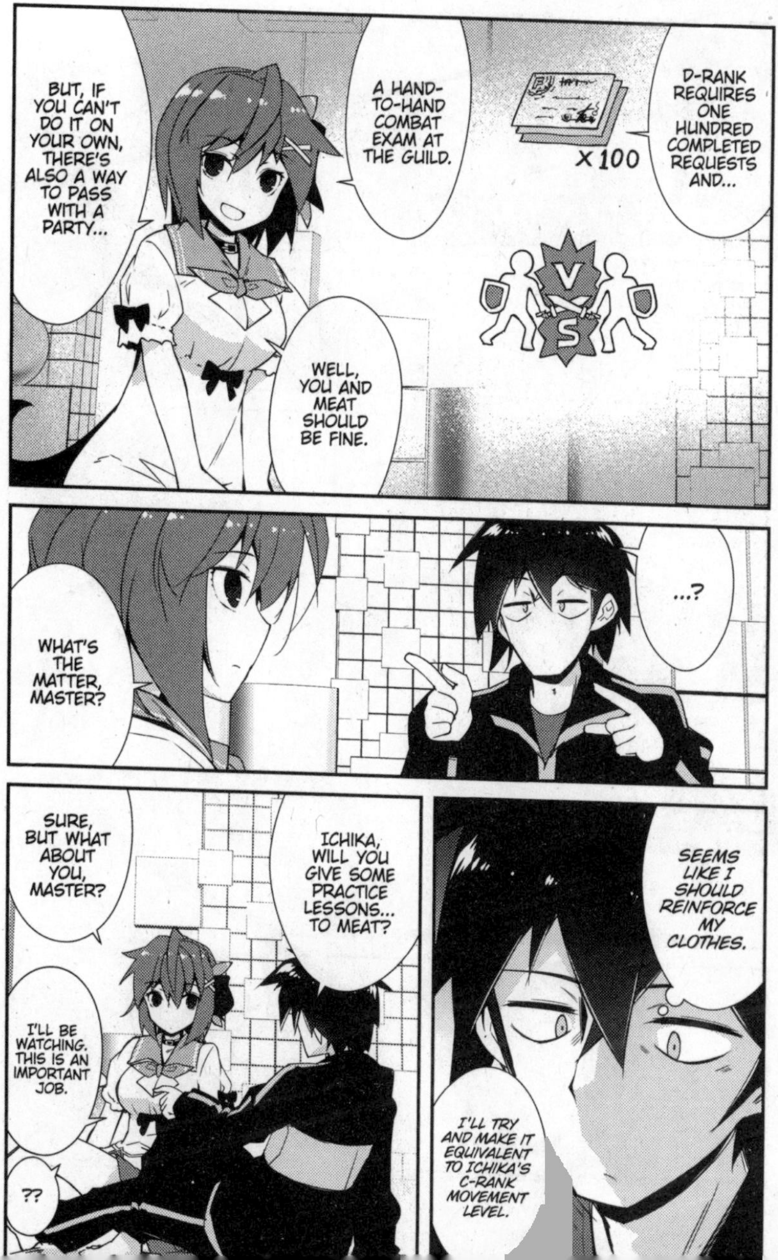
D-RANK REQUIRES ONE HUNDRED COMPLETED REQUESTS AND...
X100
VS
A HAND-TO-HAND COMBAT EXAM AT THE GUILD.
BUT, IF YOU CAN'T DO IT ON YOUR OWN, THERE'S ALSO A WAY TO PASS WITH A PARTY...
WELL, YOU AND MEAT SHOULD BE FINE.
...?
WHAT'S THE MATTER, MASTER?
SEEMS LIKE I SHOULD REINFORCE MY CLOTHES.
I'LL TRY AND MAKE IT EQUIVALENT TO ICHIKA'S C-RANK MOVEMENT LEVEL.
ICHIKA, WILL YOU GIVE SOME PRACTICE LESSONS... TO MEAT?
SURE, BUT WHAT ABOUT YOU, MASTER?
I'LL BE WATCHING. THIS IS AN IMPORTANT JOB.
??

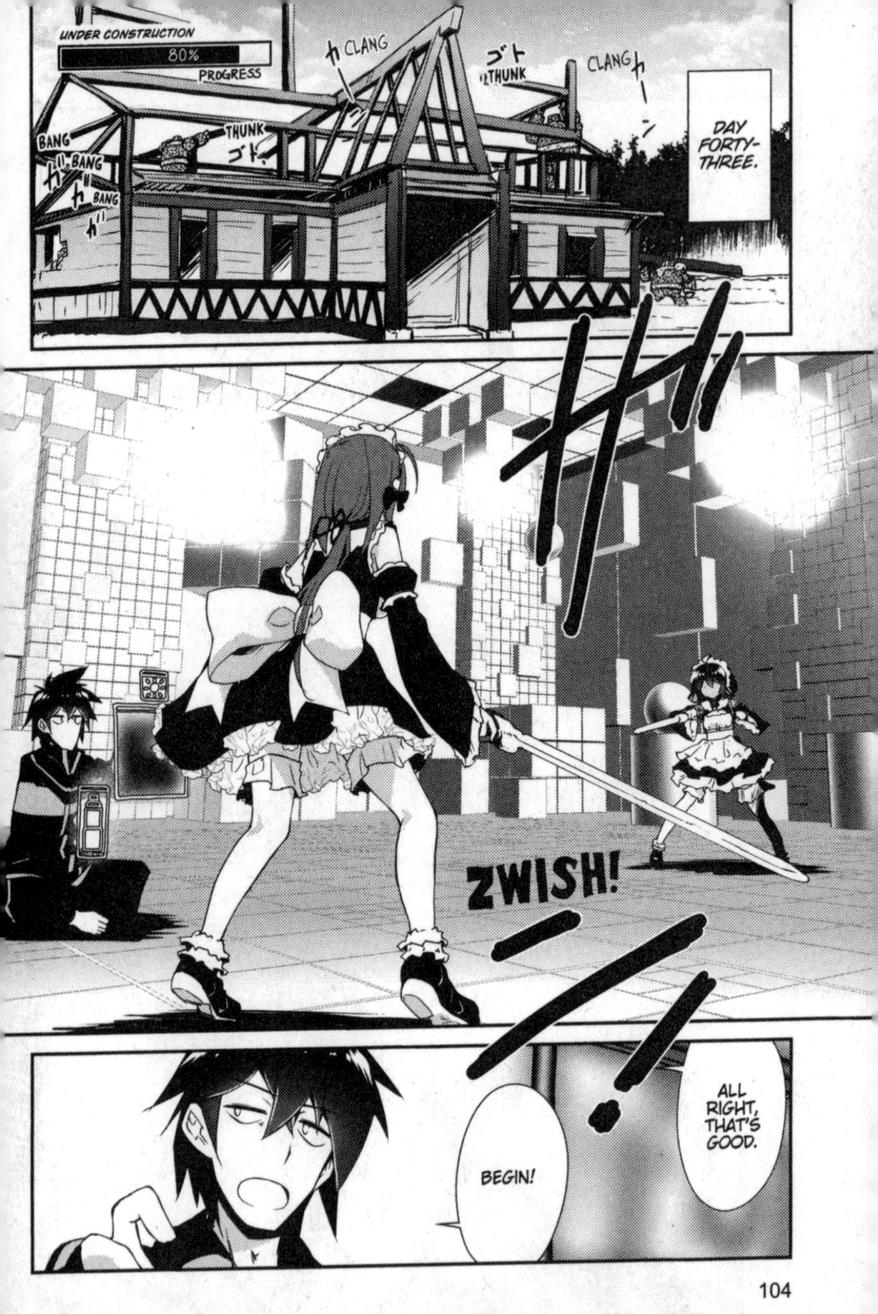
DAY FORTY-THREE.
CLANG
THUNK
CLANG
UNDER CONSTRUCTION
80%
PROGRESS
THUNK
BANG
BANG
BANG
ZWISH!
ALL RIGHT, THAT'S GOOD.
BEGIN!

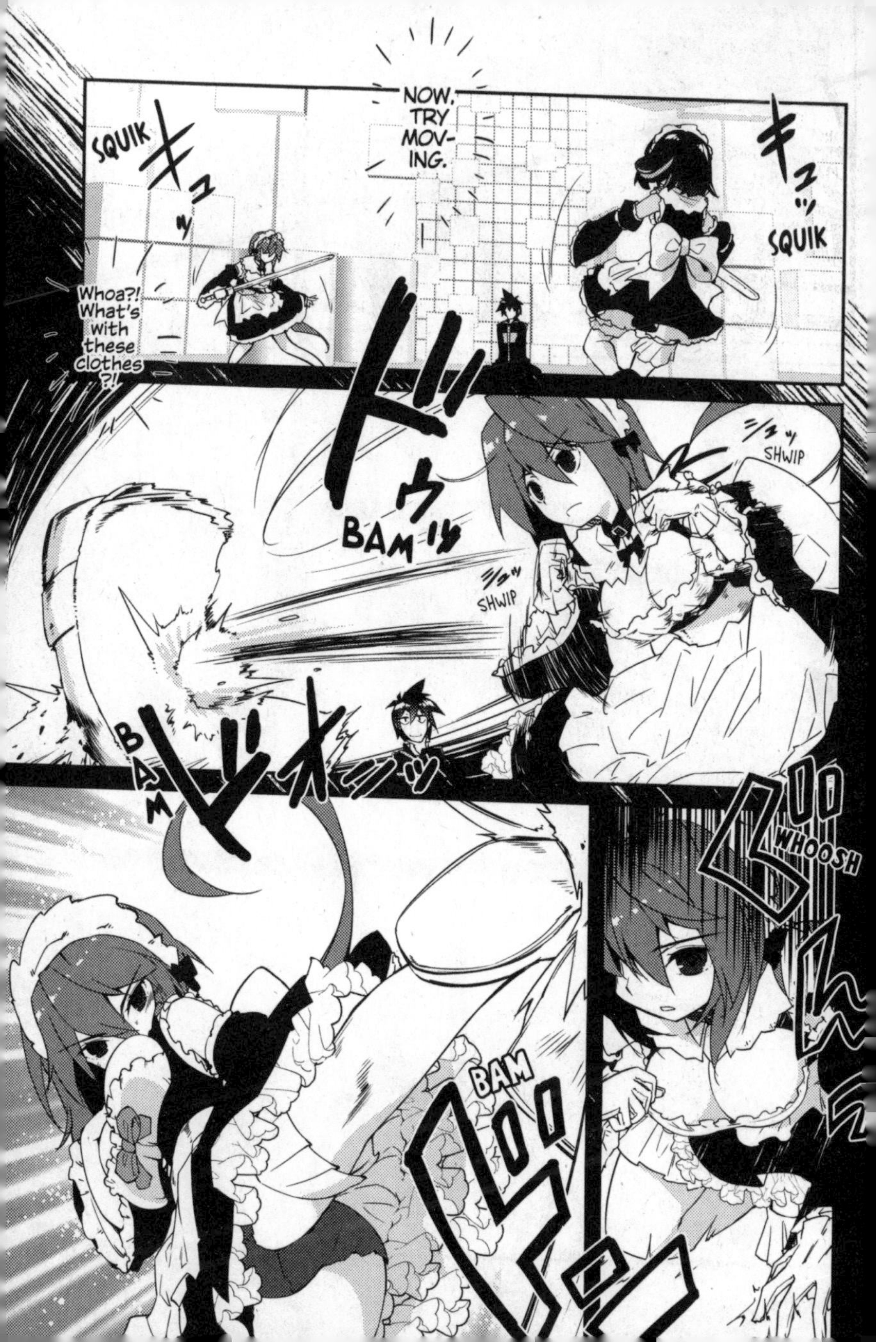

キュッ
SQUIK
NOW. TRY MOVING.
キュッ
SQUIK
Whoa?! What's with these clothes?!
SHWIP
ドゥッ
BAM
SHWIP
BAM
WHOOSH
BAM

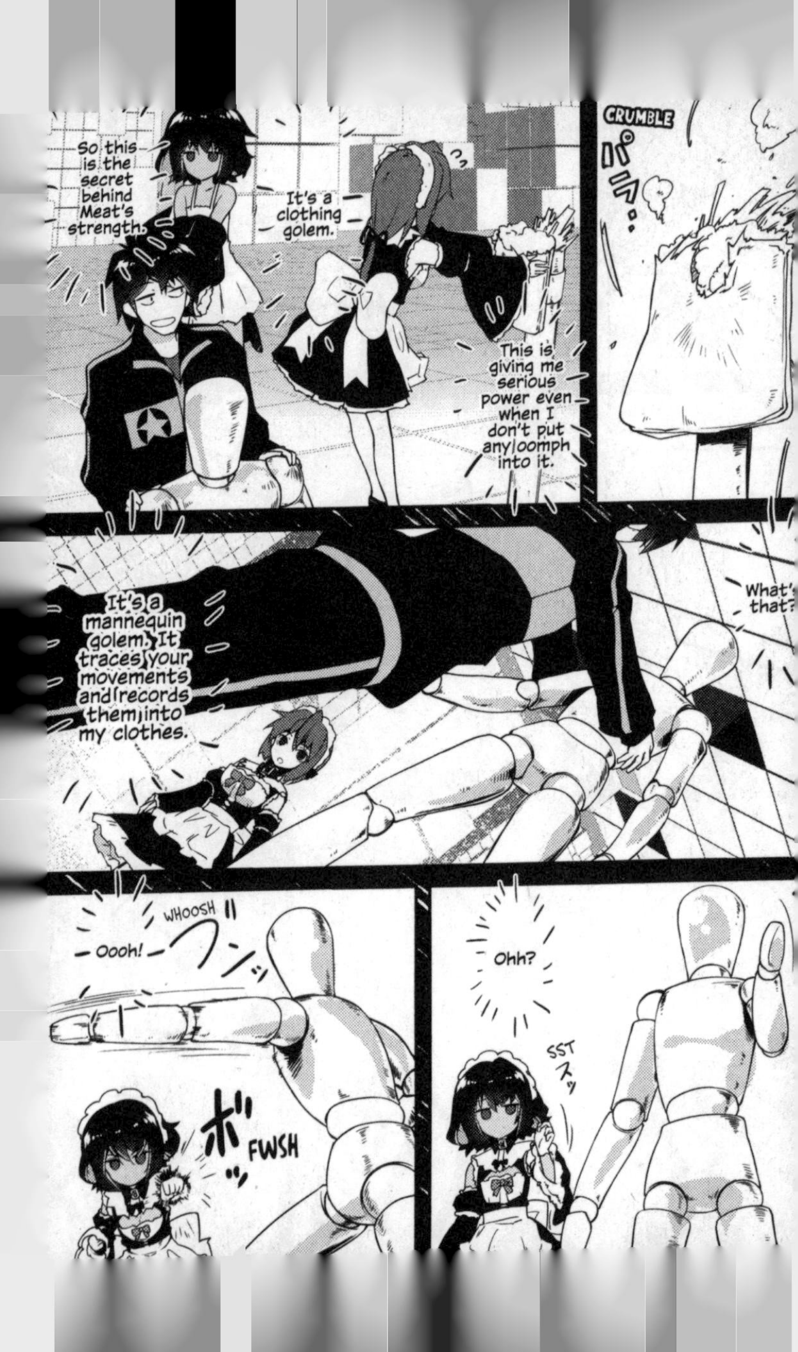
CRUMBLE
So this is the secret behind Meat's strength.
It's a clothing golem.
This is giving me serious power even when I don't put any oomph into it.
What's that?
It's a mannequin golem. It traces your movements and records them into my clothes.
Ohh?
SST
WHOOSH
Oooh!
FWSH

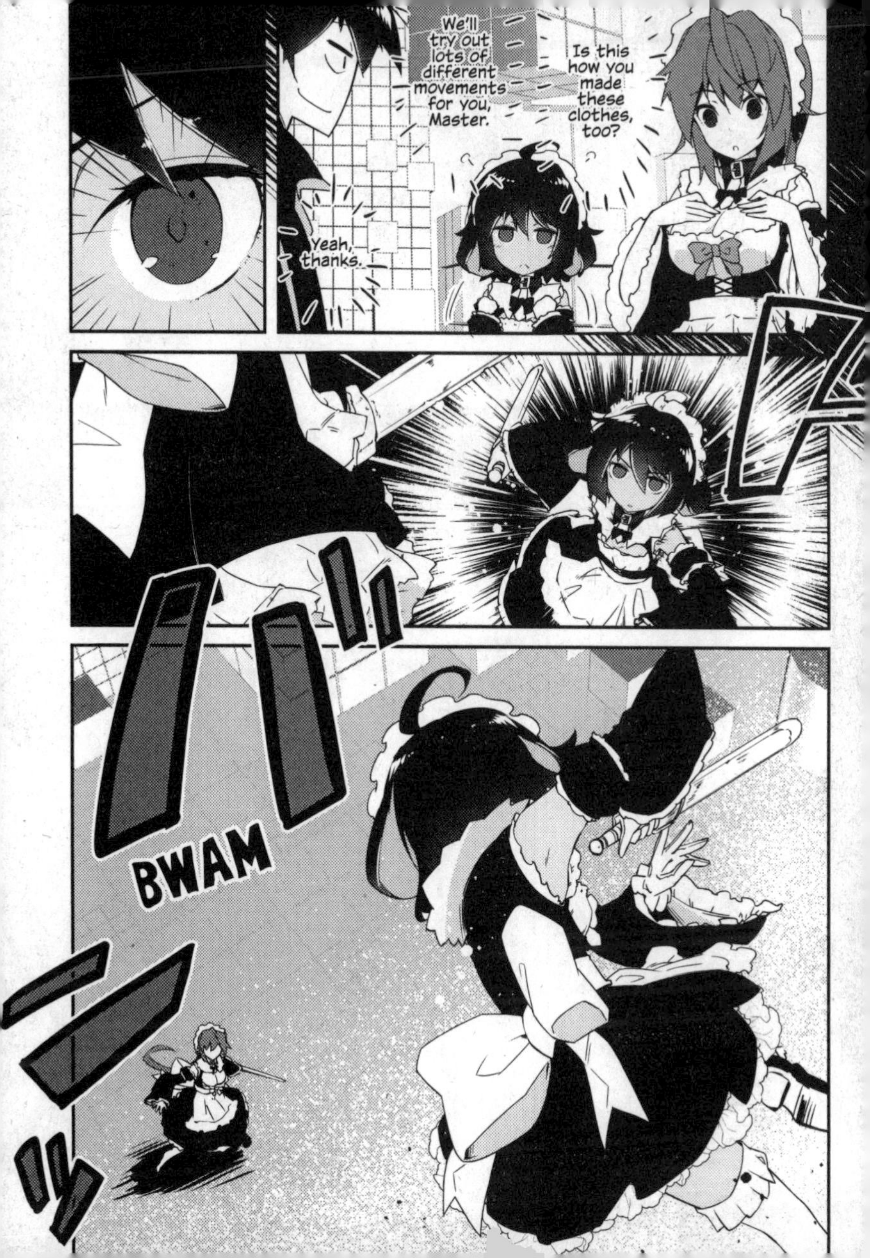
Is this how you made these clothes, too?
We'll try out lots of different movements for you, Master.
Yeah, thanks.
BWAM

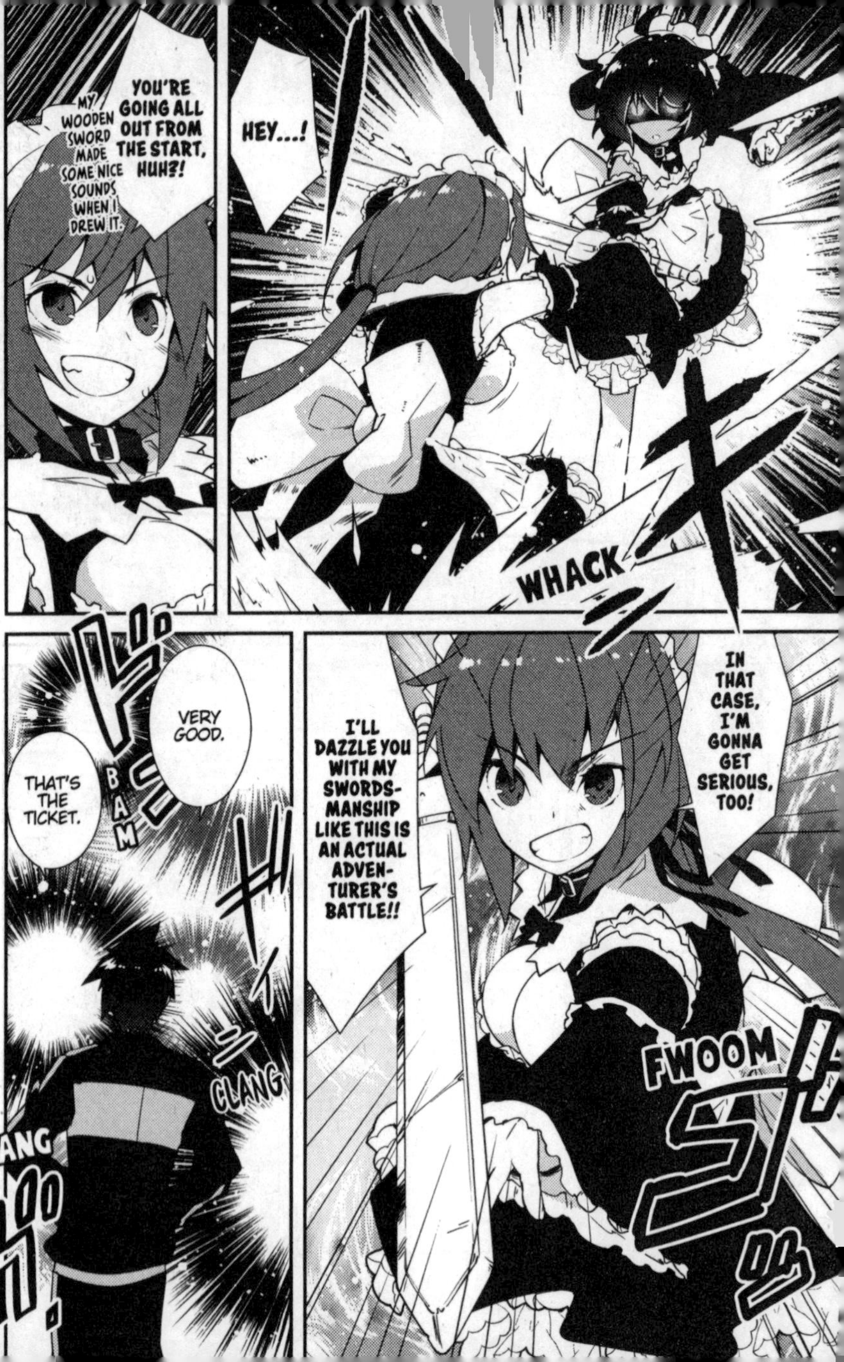
HEY...!
WHACK
YOU'RE GOING ALL OUT FROM THE START, HUH?!
MY WOODEN SWORD MADE SOME NICE SOUNDS WHEN I DREW IT.
IN THAT CASE, I'M GONNA GET SERIOUS, TOO!
I'LL DAZZLE YOU WITH MY SWORDS-MANSHIP LIKE THIS IS AN ACTUAL ADVEN-TURER'S BATTLE!!
FWOOM
VERY GOOD.
THAT'S THE TICKET.
BAM
CLANG
BANG

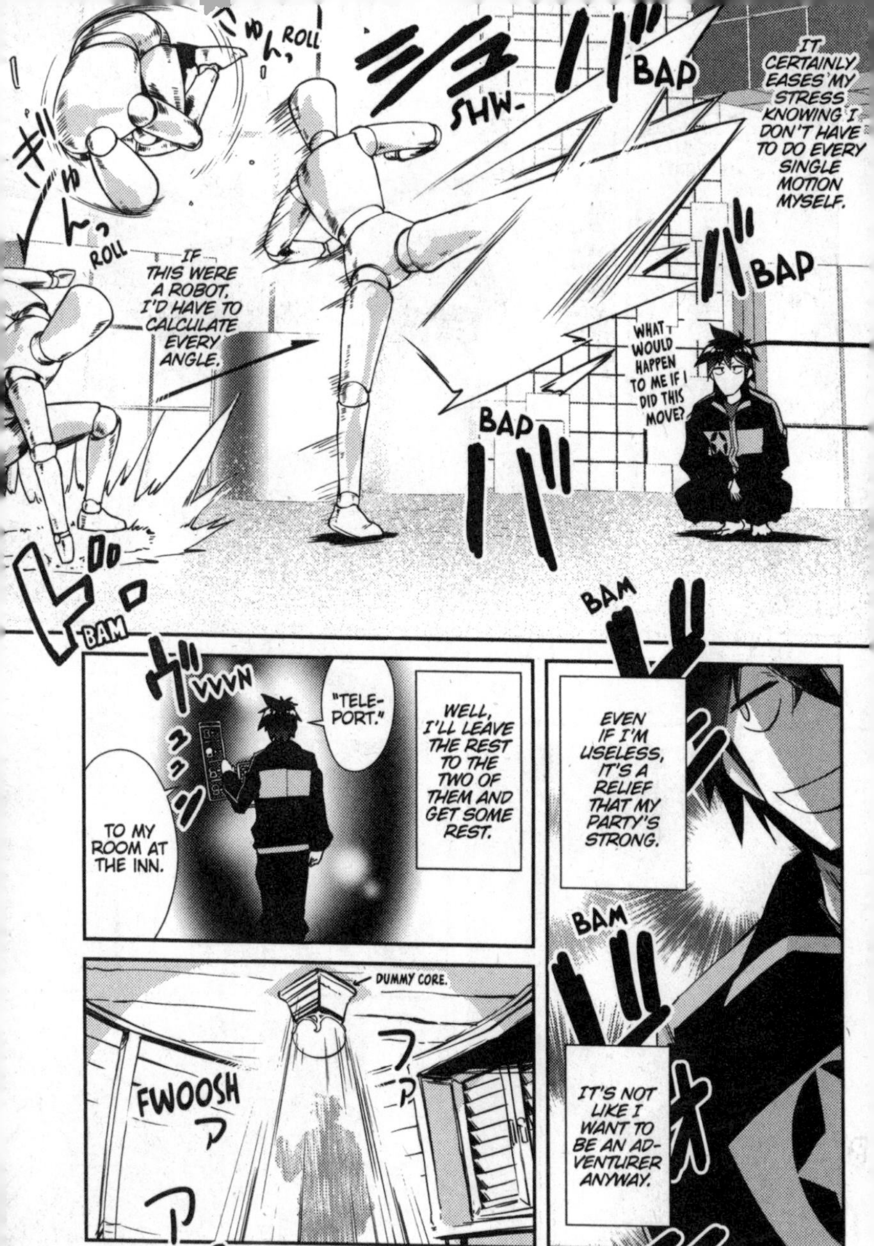
IT CERTAINLY EASES MY STRESS KNOWING I DON'T HAVE TO DO EVERY SINGLE MOTION MYSELF.
BAP
SHW-
ROLL
BAP
WHAT WOULD HAPPEN TO ME IF I DID THIS MOVE?
IF THIS WERE A ROBOT, I'D HAVE TO CALCULATE EVERY ANGLE.
ROLL
BAP
BAM
BAM
EVEN IF I'M USELESS, IT'S A RELIEF THAT MY PARTY'S STRONG.
BAM
IT'S NOT LIKE I WANT TO BE AN ADVENTURER ANYWAY.
WELL, I'LL LEAVE THE REST TO THE TWO OF THEM AND GET SOME REST.
"TELE-PORT."
VVVN
TO MY ROOM AT THE INN.
DUMMY CORE.
FWOOSH

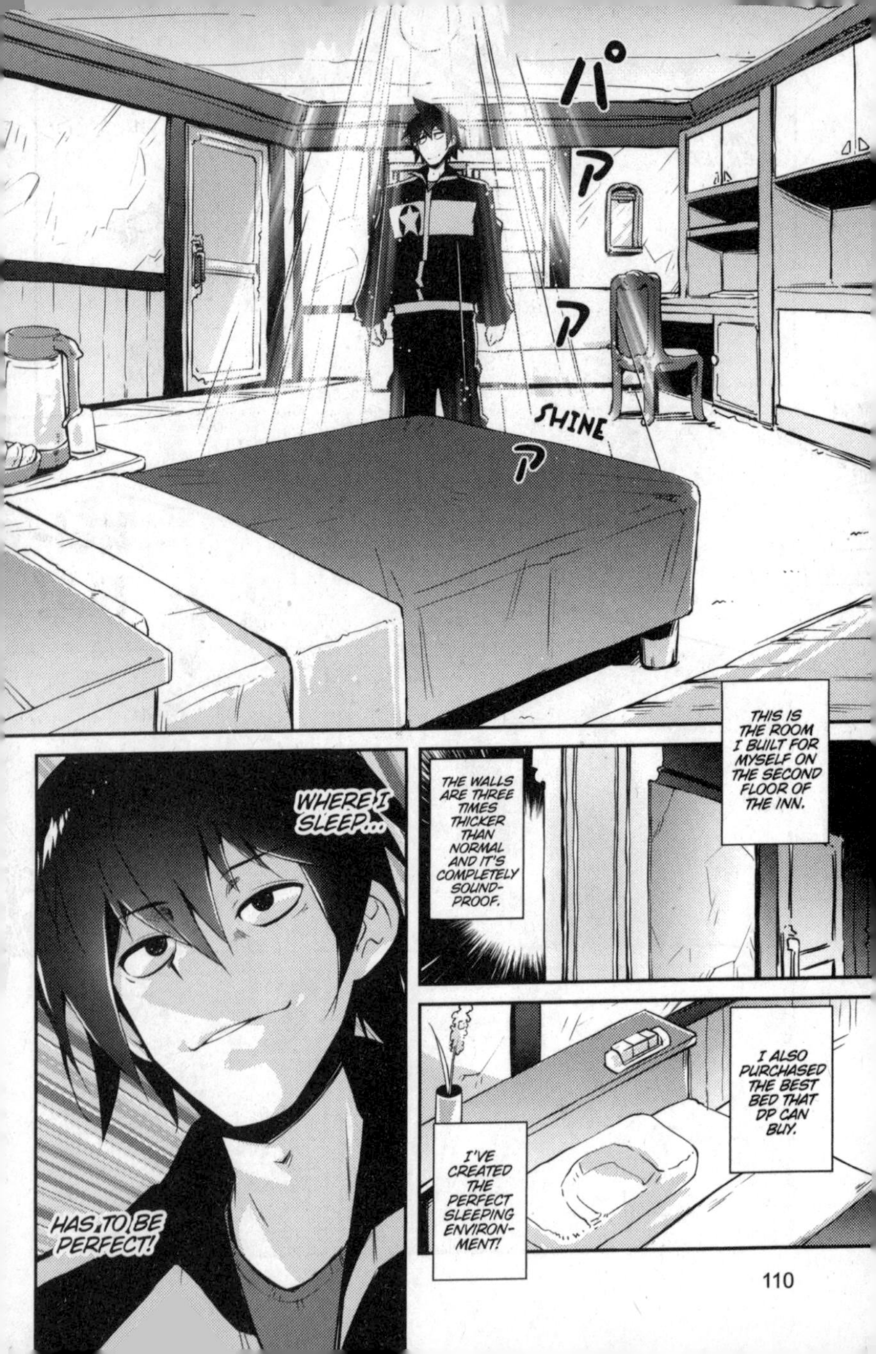
パ
ア
ア
ア
SHINE
THIS IS THE ROOM I BUILT FOR MYSELF ON THE SECOND FLOOR OF THE INN.
THE WALLS ARE THREE TIMES THICKER THAN NORMAL AND IT'S COMPLETELY SOUND-PROOF.
I ALSO PURCHASED THE BEST BED THAT DP CAN BUY.
I'VE CREATED THE PERFECT SLEEPING ENVIRON-MENT!
WHERE I SLEEP...
HAS TO BE PERFECT!

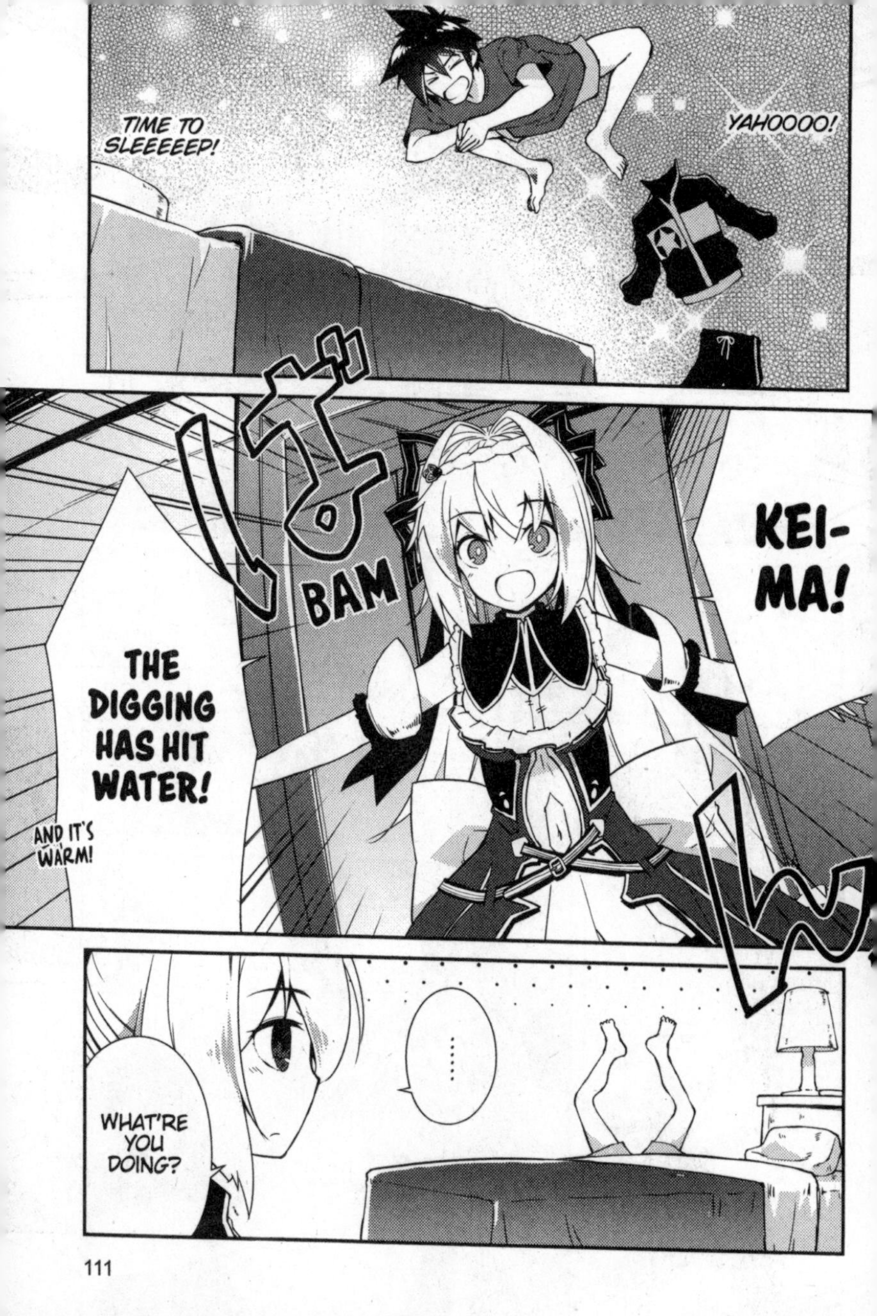

YAHOOOO!
TIME TO SLEEEEEP!
KEI-MA!
BAM
THE DIGGING HAS HIT WATER!
AND IT'S WARM!
......
WHAT'RE YOU DOING?

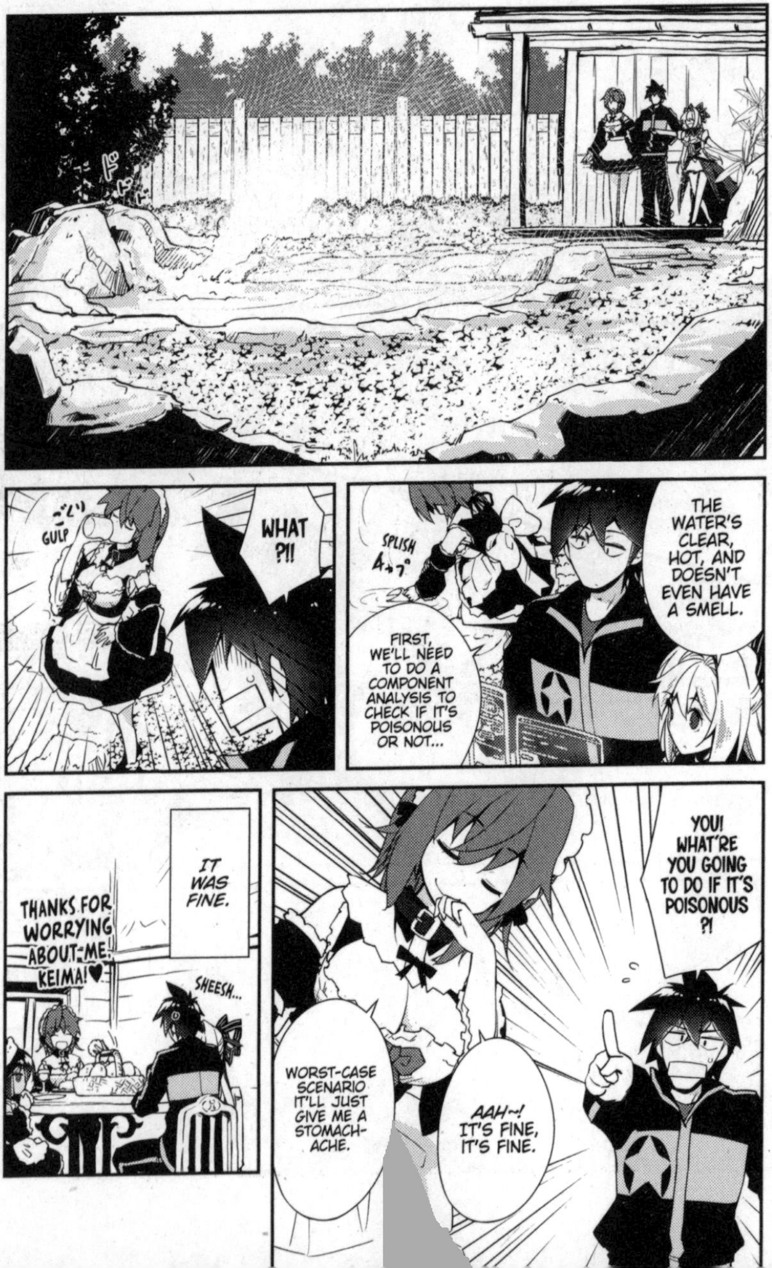
THE WATER'S CLEAR, HOT, AND DOESN'T EVEN HAVE A SMELL.
SPLISH
チャプ
FIRST, WE'LL NEED TO DO A COMPONENT ANALYSIS TO CHECK IF IT'S POISONOUS OR NOT...
WHAT ?!!
GULP
ごくり
YOU! WHAT'RE YOU GOING TO DO IF IT'S POISONOUS ?!
AAH~! IT'S FINE, IT'S FINE.
WORST-CASE SCENARIO IT'LL JUST GIVE ME A STOMACH-ACHE.
IT WAS FINE.
SHEESH...
THANKS FOR WORRYING ABOUT ME, KEIMA!♥

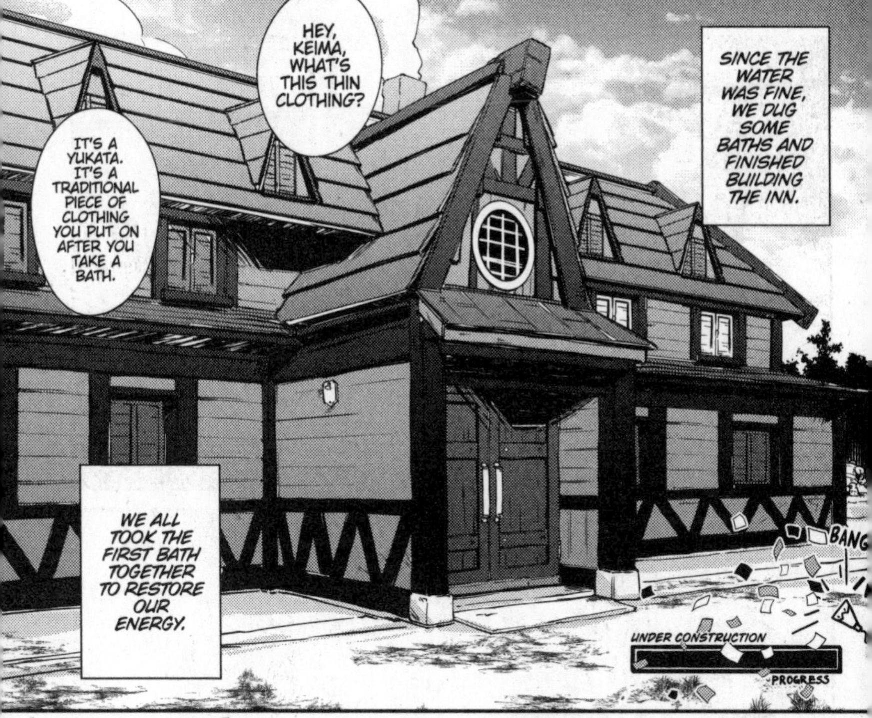
SINCE THE WATER WAS FINE, WE DUG SOME BATHS AND FINISHED BUILDING THE INN.
HEY, KEIMA, WHAT'S THIS THIN CLOTHING?
IT'S A YUKATA. IT'S A TRADITIONAL PIECE OF CLOTHING YOU PUT ON AFTER YOU TAKE A BATH.
WE ALL TOOK THE FIRST BATH TOGETHER TO RESTORE OUR ENERGY.
BANG
UNDER CONSTRUCTION
PROGRESS

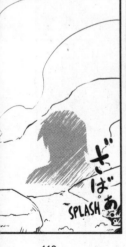

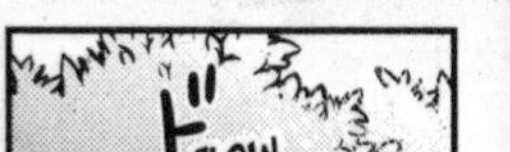
ド FLOW
ド FLOW
ド FLOW
ド FLOW

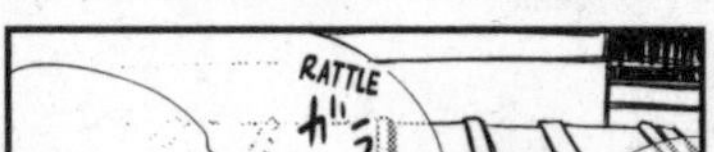
RATTLE ガラ
RATTLE ガラ
RATTLE ガラ

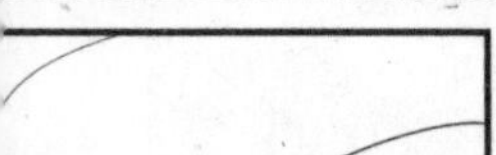
ざばあ
SPLASH

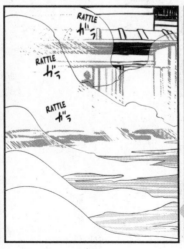

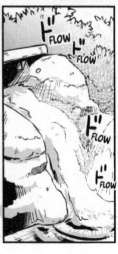

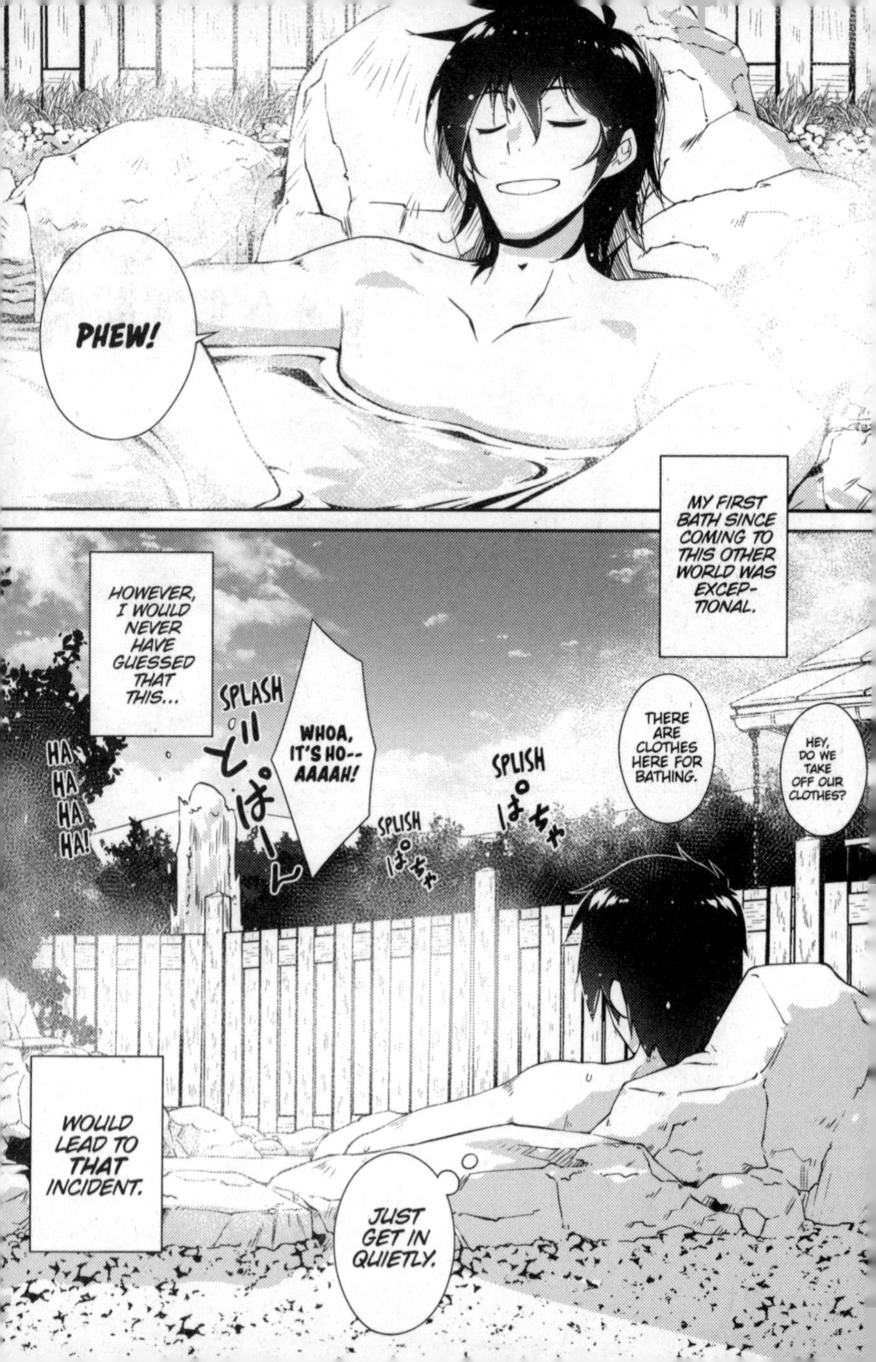
PHEW!
MY FIRST BATH SINCE COMING TO THIS OTHER WORLD WAS EXCEP-TIONAL.
HEY, DO WE TAKE OFF OUR CLOTHES?
THERE ARE CLOTHES HERE FOR BATHING.
SPLISH
ぱちゃ
SPLISH
ぱちゃ
WHOA, IT'S HO--AAAAH!
SPLASH
どぱーん
HA HA HA HA!
HOWEVER, I WOULD NEVER HAVE GUESSED THAT THIS...
JUST GET IN QUIETLY.
WOULD LEAD TO THAT INCIDENT.

LAZY
DUNGEON
MASTER

LAZY
DUNGEON
MASTER

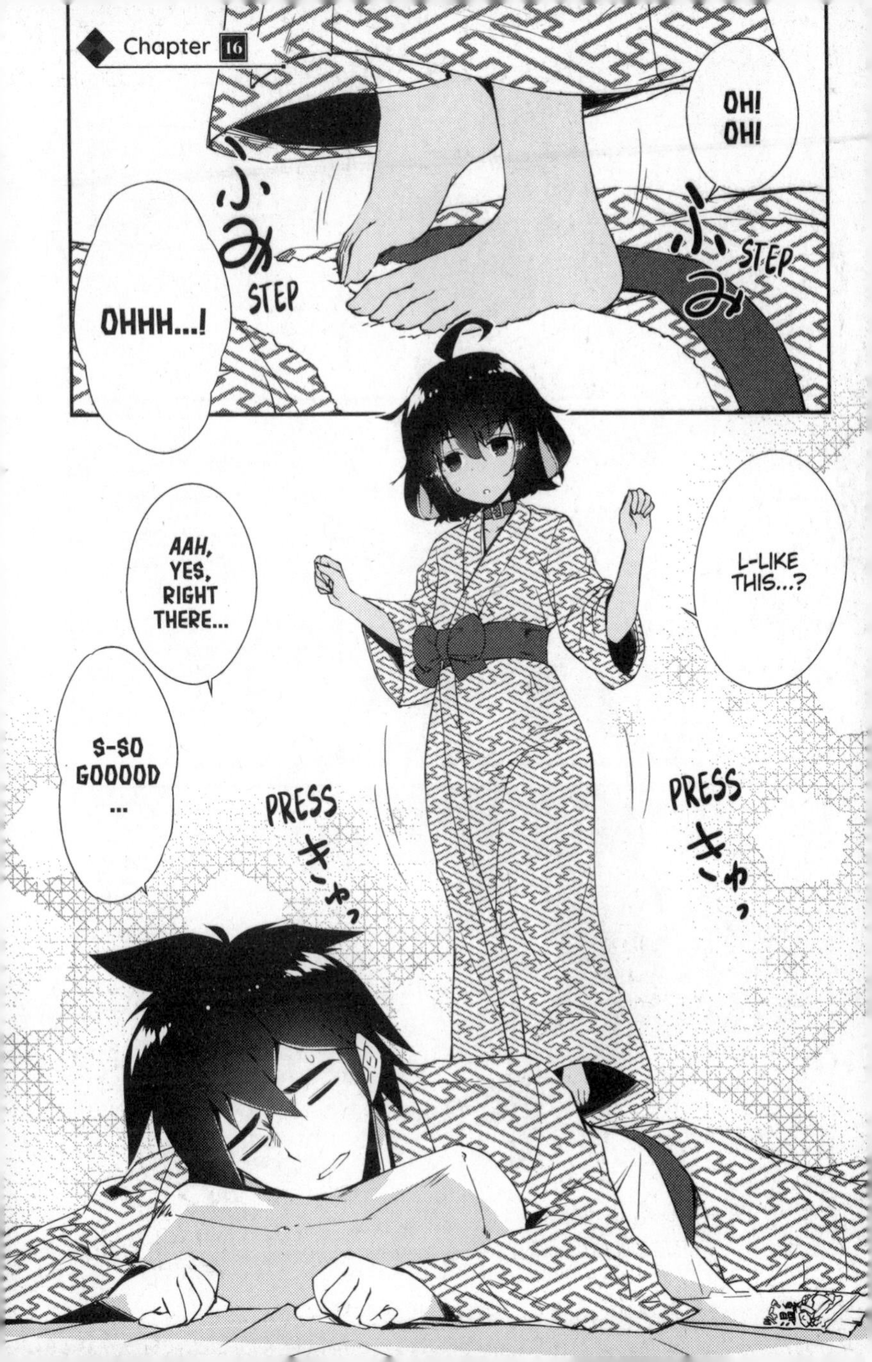
Chapter 16
OH! OH!
ふみ STEP
ふみ STEP
OHHH...!
L-LIKE THIS...?
PRESS きゅっ
AAH, YES, RIGHT THERE...
S-SO GOOOOD ...
PRESS きゅっ

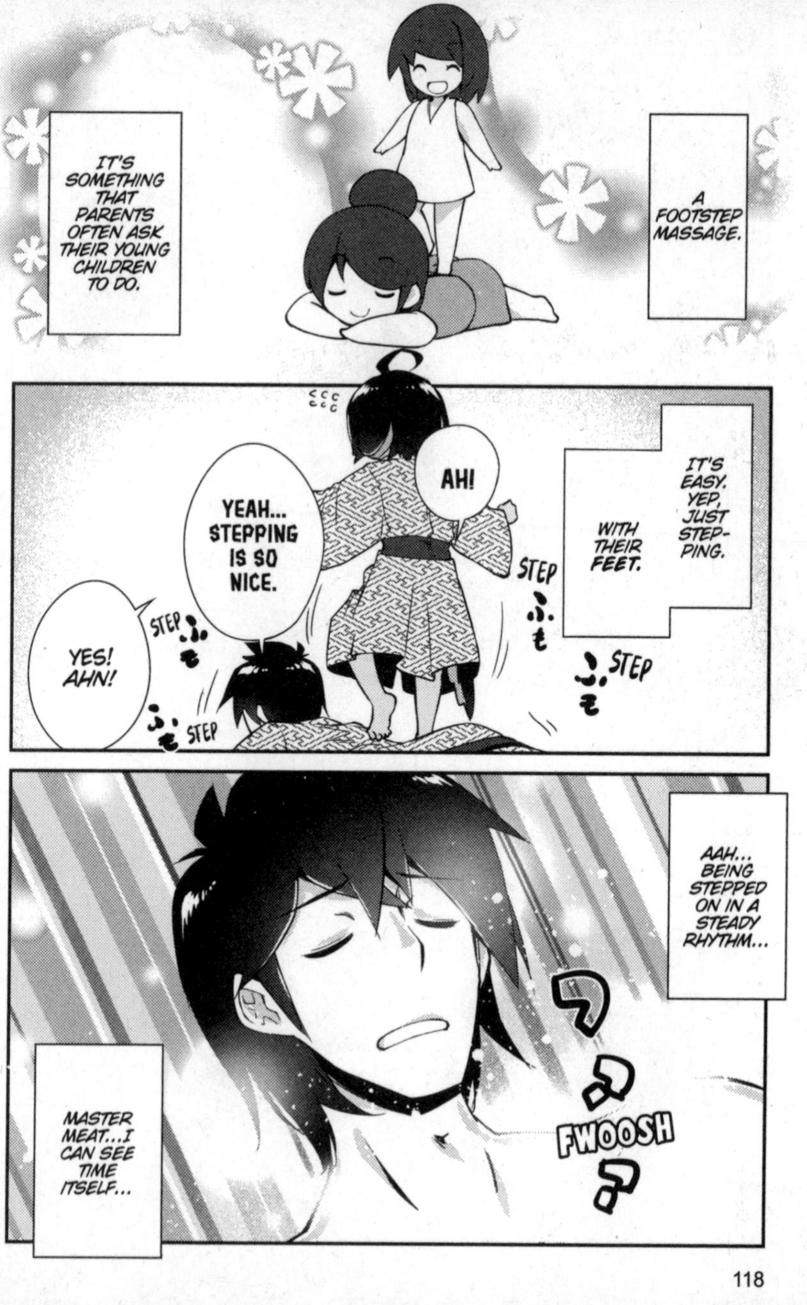
A FOOTSTEP MASSAGE.
IT'S SOMETHING THAT PARENTS OFTEN ASK THEIR YOUNG CHILDREN TO DO.
IT'S EASY. YEP, JUST STEPPING.
WITH THEIR FEET.
STEP
STEP
AH!
YEAH... STEPPING IS SO NICE.
STEP
YES! AHN!
STEP
AAH... BEING STEPPED ON IN A STEADY RHYTHM...
FWOOSH
MASTER MEAT...I CAN SEE TIME ITSELF...

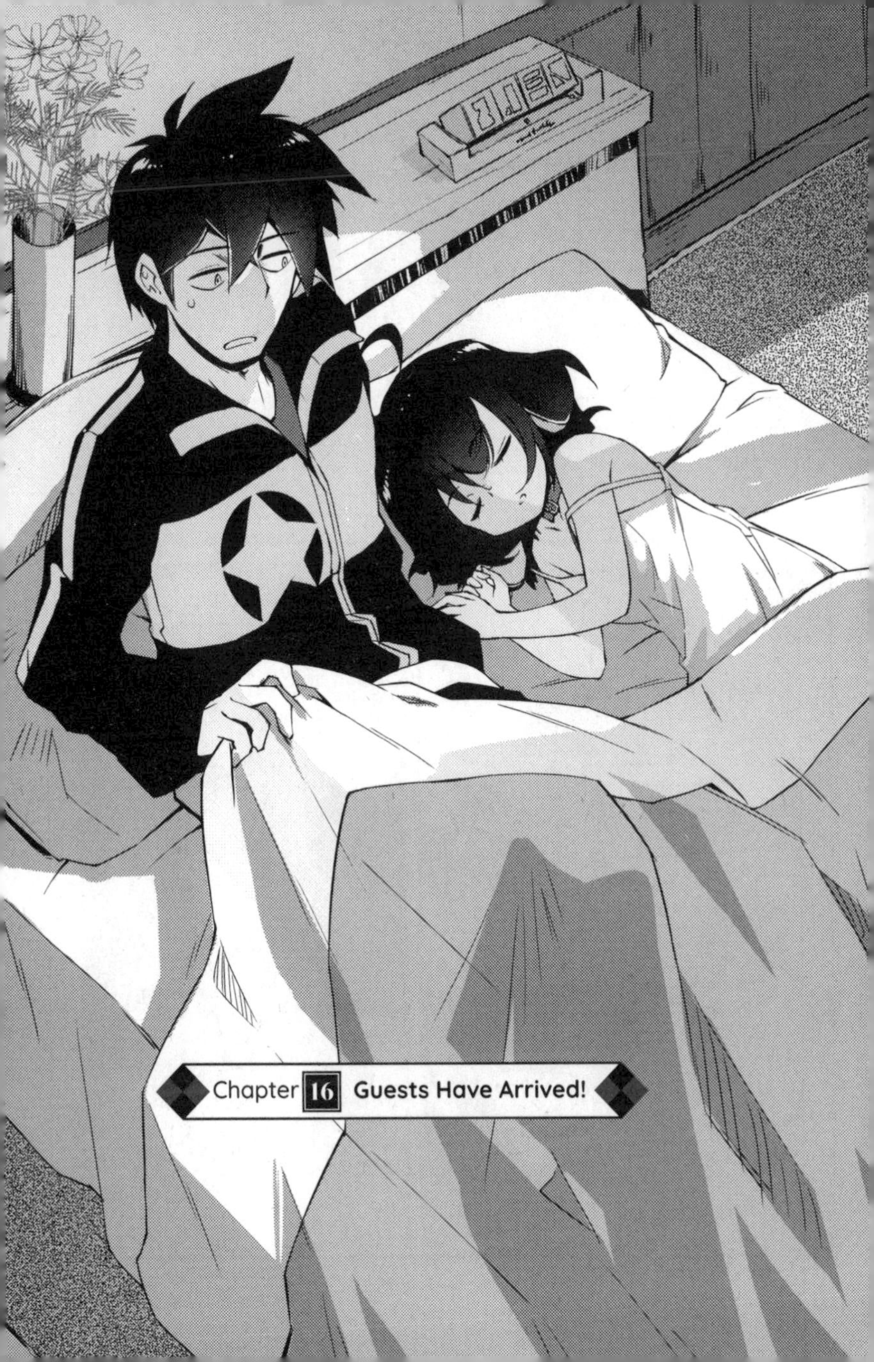
Chapter 16 Guests Have Arrived!

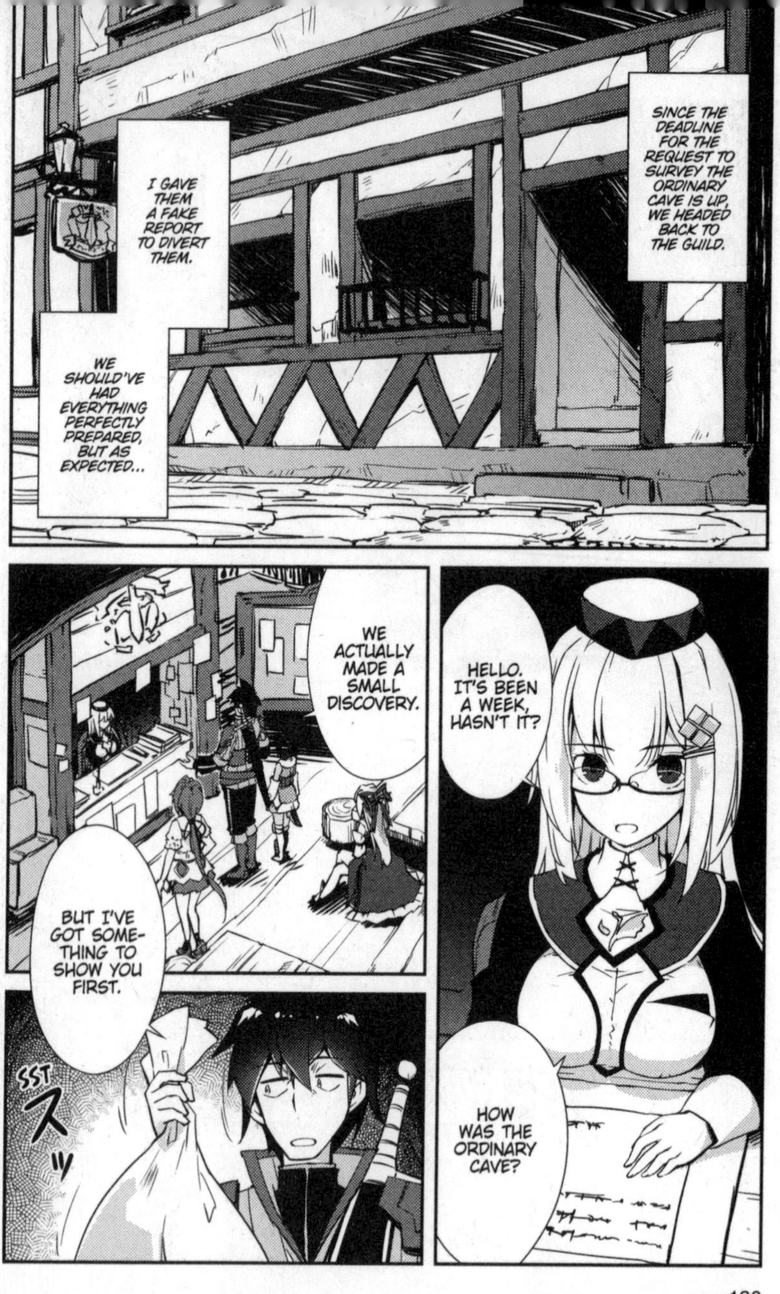
SINCE THE DEADLINE FOR THE REQUEST TO SURVEY THE ORDINARY CAVE IS UP, WE HEADED BACK TO THE GUILD.
I GAVE THEM A FAKE REPORT TO DIVERT THEM.
WE SHOULD'VE HAD EVERYTHING PERFECTLY PREPARED, BUT AS EXPECTED...
HELLO. IT'S BEEN A WEEK, HASN'T IT?
HOW WAS THE ORDINARY CAVE?
WE ACTUALLY MADE A SMALL DISCOVERY.
BUT I'VE GOT SOMETHING TO SHOW YOU FIRST.
......
SST
スッ

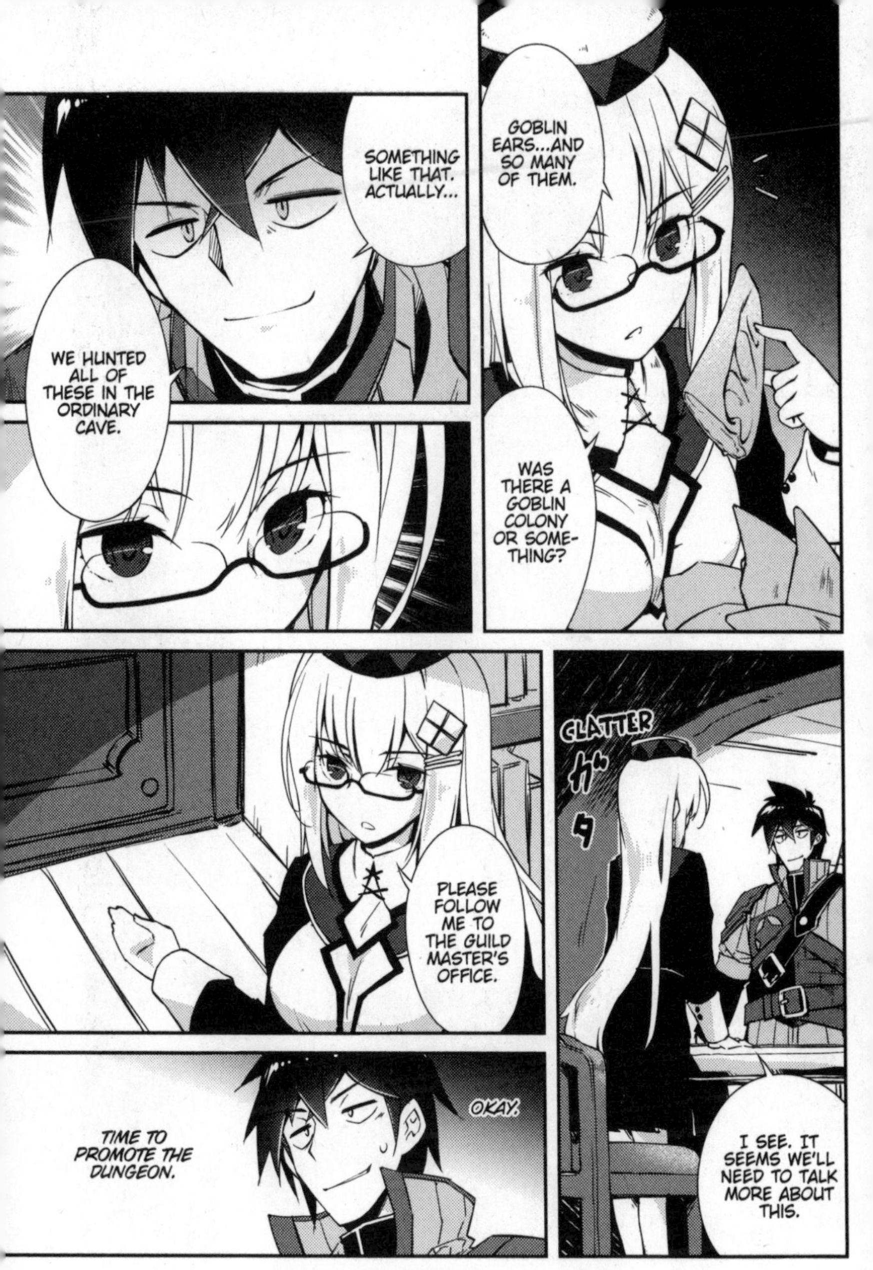
GOBLIN EARS...AND SO MANY OF THEM.
WAS THERE A GOBLIN COLONY OR SOME-THING?
SOMETHING LIKE THAT. ACTUALLY...
WE HUNTED ALL OF THESE IN THE ORDINARY CAVE.
CLATTER
ガタ
I SEE. IT SEEMS WE'LL NEED TO TALK MORE ABOUT THIS.
PLEASE FOLLOW ME TO THE GUILD MASTER'S OFFICE.
OKAY.
TIME TO PROMOTE THE DUNGEON.

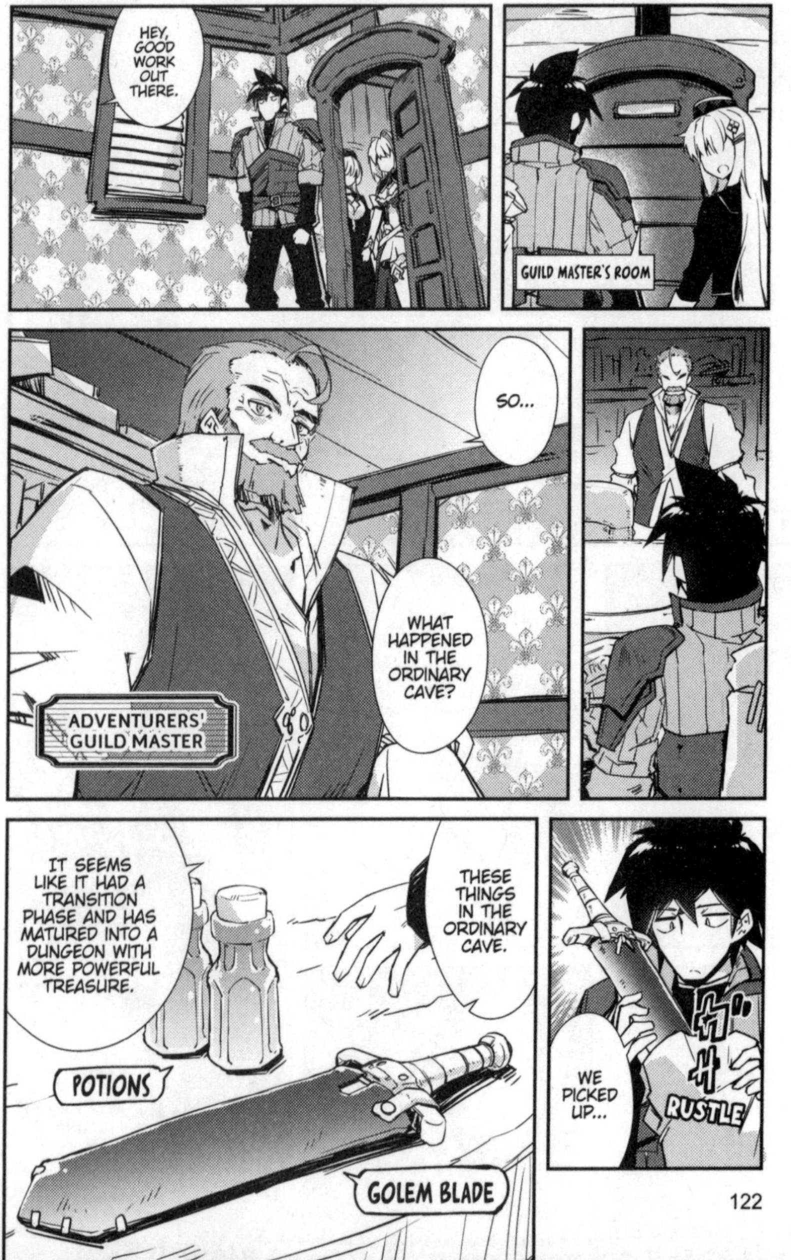
GUILD MASTER'S ROOM
HEY, GOOD WORK OUT THERE.
SO...
WHAT HAPPENED IN THE ORDINARY CAVE?
ADVENTURERS' GUILD MASTER
RUSTLE
WE PICKED UP...
THESE THINGS IN THE ORDINARY CAVE.
IT SEEMS LIKE IT HAD A TRANSITION PHASE AND HAS MATURED INTO A DUNGEON WITH MORE POWERFUL TREASURE.
POTIONS
GOLEM BLADE

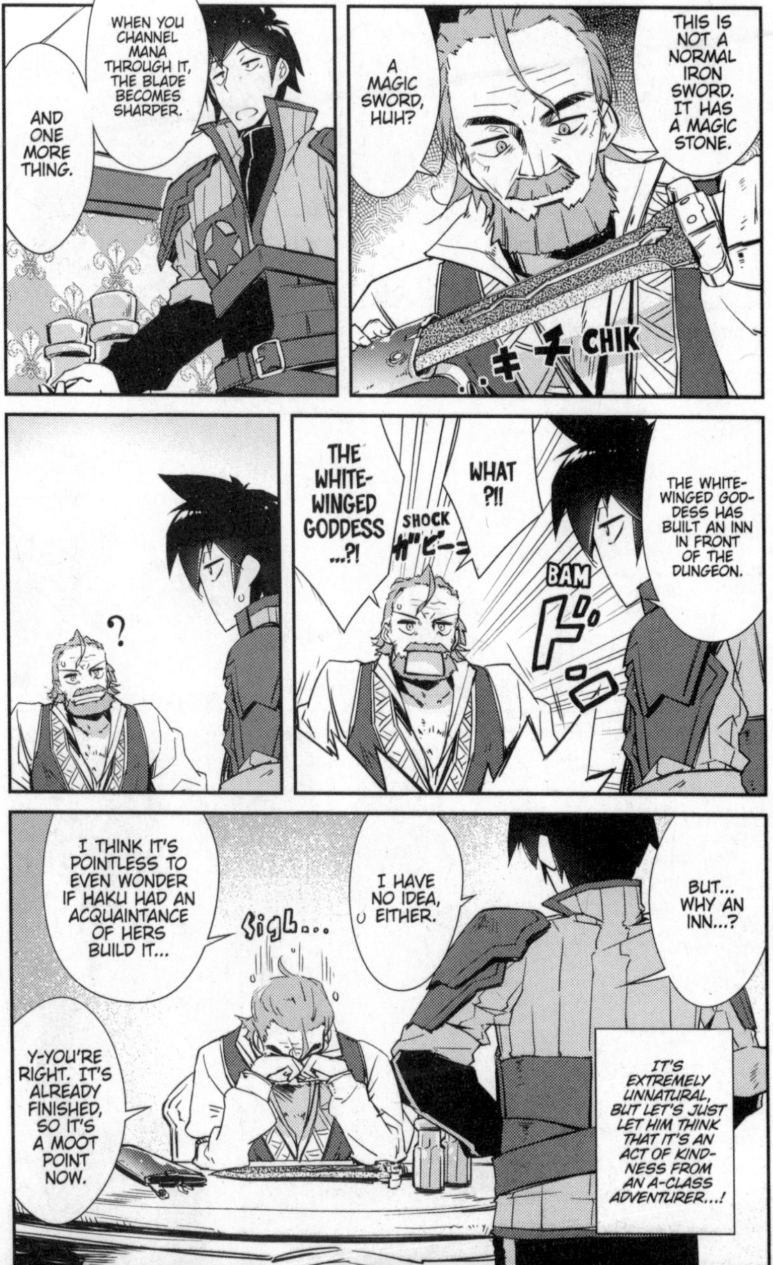
THIS IS NOT A NORMAL IRON SWORD. IT HAS A MAGIC STONE.
A MAGIC SWORD, HUH?
CHIK
WHEN YOU CHANNEL MANA THROUGH IT, THE BLADE BECOMES SHARPER.
AND ONE MORE THING.
THE WHITE-WINGED GODDESS HAS BUILT AN INN IN FRONT OF THE DUNGEON.
BAM
WHAT ?!!
SHOCK
THE WHITE-WINGED GODDESS ...?!
?
BUT... WHY AN INN...?
I HAVE NO IDEA, EITHER.
I THINK IT'S POINTLESS TO EVEN WONDER IF HAKU HAD AN ACQUAINTANCE OF HERS BUILD IT...
sigh...
IT'S EXTREMELY UNNATURAL, BUT LET'S JUST LET HIM THINK THAT IT'S AN ACT OF KINDNESS FROM AN A-CLASS ADVENTURER...!
Y-YOU'RE RIGHT. IT'S ALREADY FINISHED, SO IT'S A MOOT POINT NOW.

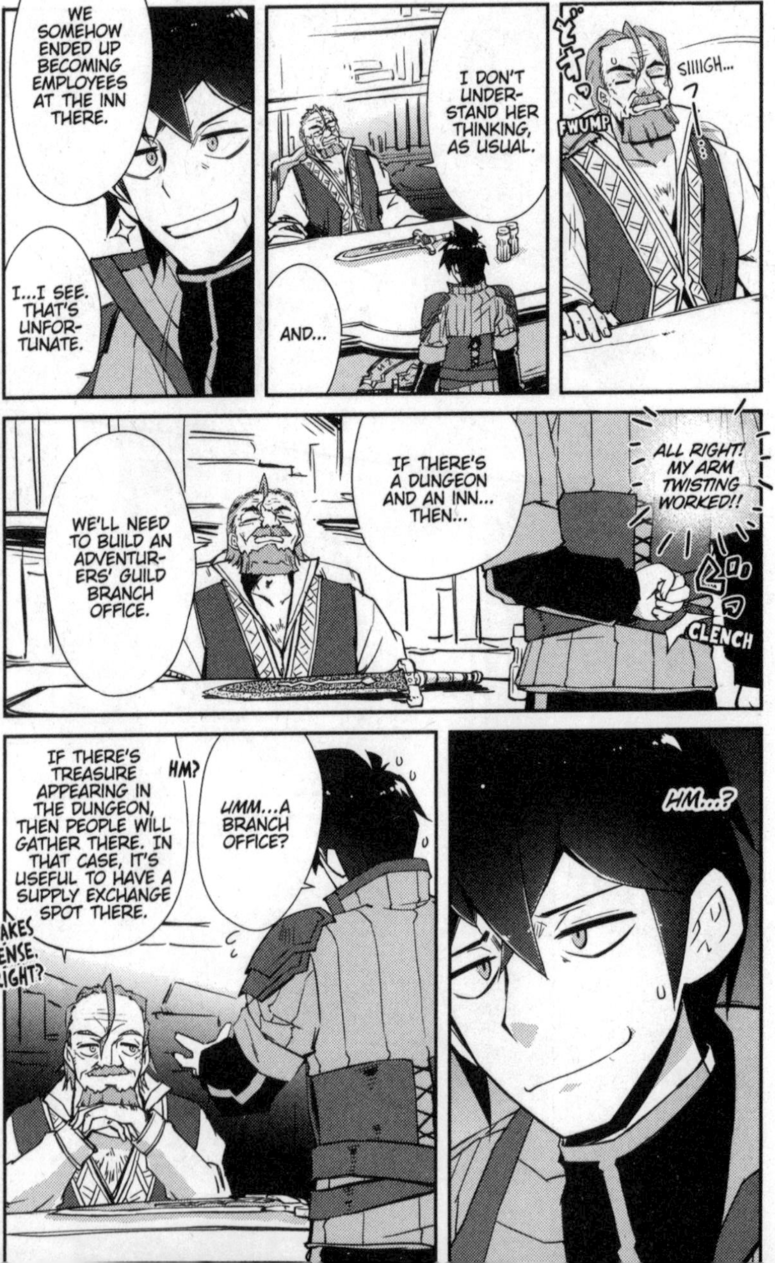
FWUMP
SIIIGH...
...
I DON'T UNDER-STAND HER THINKING, AS USUAL.
AND...
WE SOMEHOW ENDED UP BECOMING EMPLOYEES AT THE INN THERE.
I...I SEE. THAT'S UNFOR-TUNATE.
ALL RIGHT! MY ARM TWISTING WORKED!!
CLENCH
IF THERE'S A DUNGEON AND AN INN... THEN...
WE'LL NEED TO BUILD AN ADVENTUR-ERS' GUILD BRANCH OFFICE.
HM...?
UMM...A BRANCH OFFICE?
HM?
IF THERE'S TREASURE APPEARING IN THE DUNGEON, THEN PEOPLE WILL GATHER THERE. IN THAT CASE, IT'S USEFUL TO HAVE A SUPPLY EXCHANGE SPOT THERE.
MAKES SENSE, RIGHT?

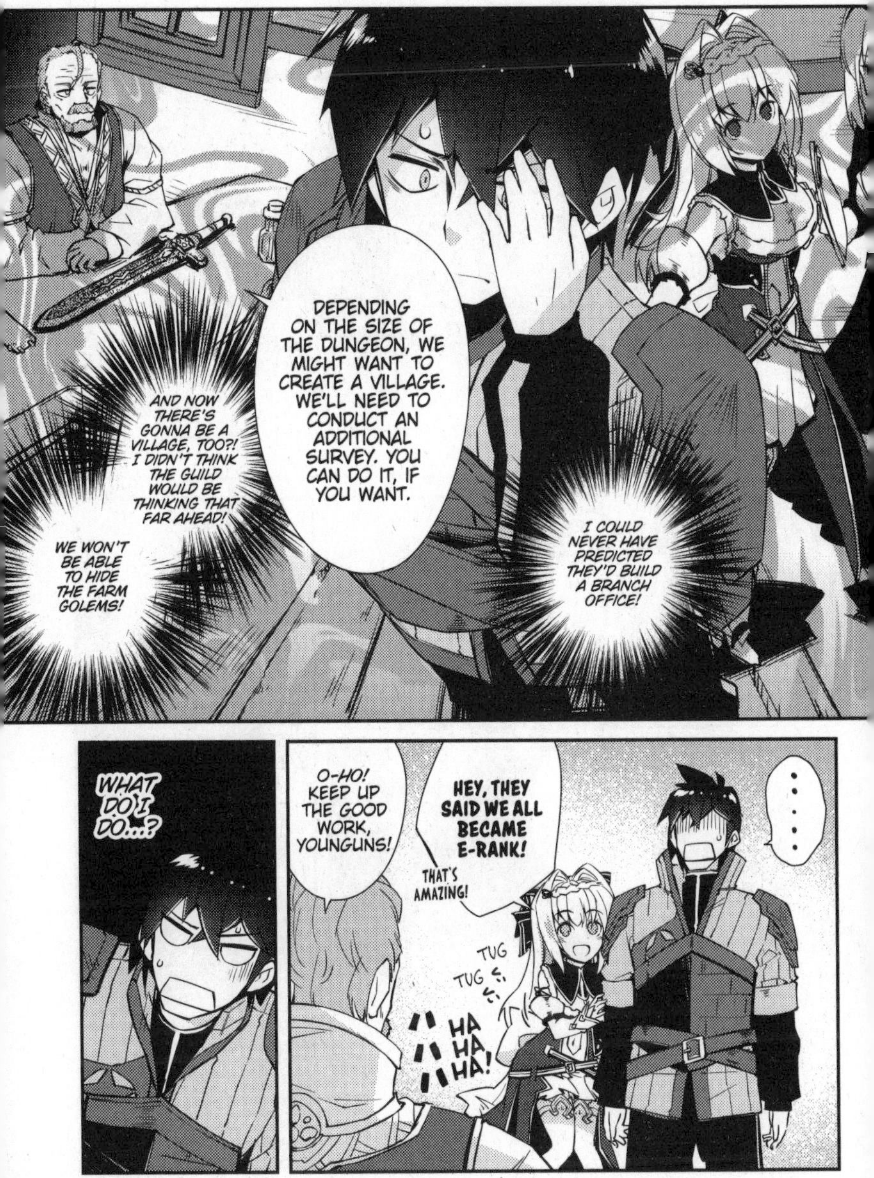
DEPENDING ON THE SIZE OF THE DUNGEON, WE MIGHT WANT TO CREATE A VILLAGE. WE'LL NEED TO CONDUCT AN ADDITIONAL SURVEY. YOU CAN DO IT, IF YOU WANT.
I COULD NEVER HAVE PREDICTED THEY'D BUILD A BRANCH OFFICE!
AND NOW THERE'S GONNA BE A VILLAGE, TOO?! I DIDN'T THINK THE GUILD WOULD BE THINKING THAT FAR AHEAD!
WE WON'T BE ABLE TO HIDE THE FARM GOLEMS!
......
HEY, THEY SAID WE ALL BECAME E-RANK!
O-HO! KEEP UP THE GOOD WORK, YOUNGUNS!
THAT'S AMAZING!
TUG
TUG
HA HA HA!
WHAT DO I DO...?

SINCE THE SITUATION TOOK AN UNEXPECTED TURN, WE HEADED STRAIGHT BACK TO THE DUNGEON.

WE HAVE TO PREPARE EVERYTHING BEFORE ADVENTURERS COME.

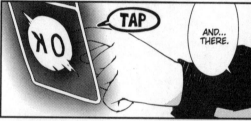

TAP

OK

AND... THERE.

SIGH... WE MADE IT IN TIME SOMEHOW.

GOOD WORK! WANT SOME CURRY BREAD?

SLUMP

NO THANKS.

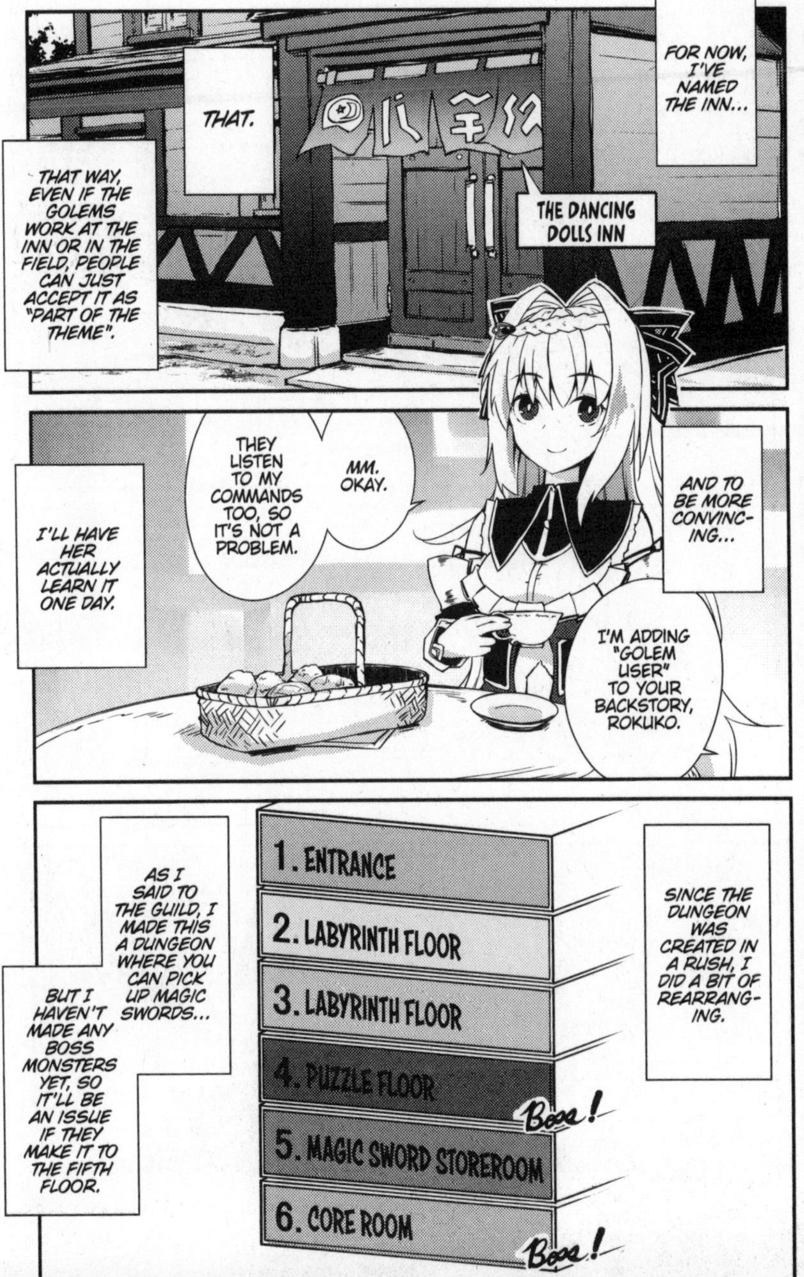
FOR NOW, I'VE NAMED THE INN...
THE DANCING DOLLS INN
THAT.
THAT WAY, EVEN IF THE GOLEMS WORK AT THE INN OR IN THE FIELD, PEOPLE CAN JUST ACCEPT IT AS "PART OF THE THEME".
AND TO BE MORE CONVINC-ING...
I'M ADDING "GOLEM USER" TO YOUR BACKSTORY, ROKUKO.
MM. OKAY.
THEY LISTEN TO MY COMMANDS TOO, SO IT'S NOT A PROBLEM.
I'LL HAVE HER ACTUALLY LEARN IT ONE DAY.
SINCE THE DUNGEON WAS CREATED IN A RUSH, I DID A BIT OF REARRANG-ING.
1. ENTRANCE
2. LABYRINTH FLOOR
3. LABYRINTH FLOOR
4. PUZZLE FLOOR
Boss!
5. MAGIC SWORD STOREROOM
6. CORE ROOM
Boss!
AS I SAID TO THE GUILD, I MADE THIS A DUNGEON WHERE YOU CAN PICK UP MAGIC SWORDS...
BUT I HAVEN'T MADE ANY BOSS MONSTERS YET, SO IT'LL BE AN ISSUE IF THEY MAKE IT TO THE FIFTH FLOOR.

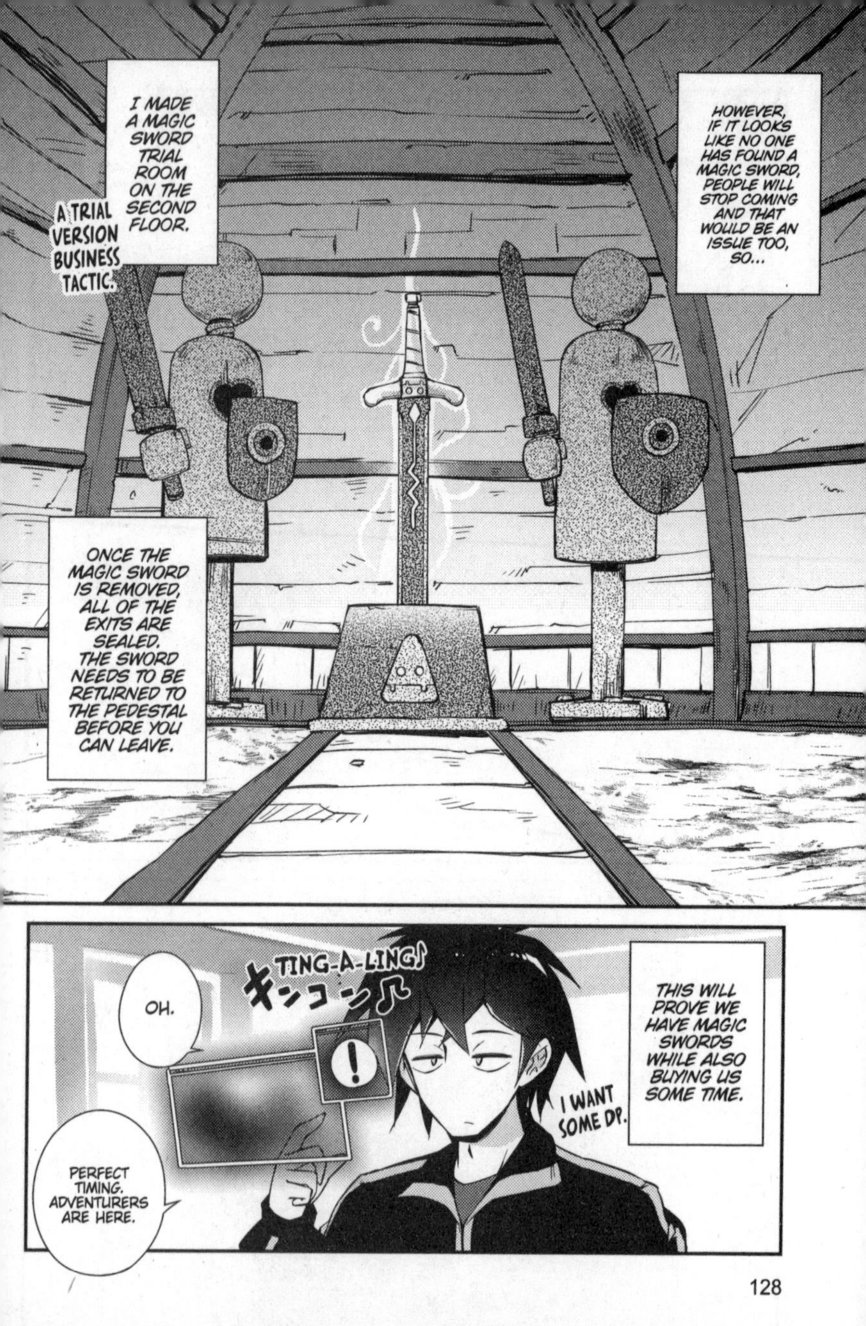
HOWEVER, IF IT LOOKS LIKE NO ONE HAS FOUND A MAGIC SWORD, PEOPLE WILL STOP COMING AND THAT WOULD BE AN ISSUE TOO, SO...
I MADE A MAGIC SWORD TRIAL ROOM ON THE SECOND FLOOR.
A TRIAL VERSION BUSINESS TACTIC.
ONCE THE MAGIC SWORD IS REMOVED, ALL OF THE EXITS ARE SEALED. THE SWORD NEEDS TO BE RETURNED TO THE PEDESTAL BEFORE YOU CAN LEAVE.
THIS WILL PROVE WE HAVE MAGIC SWORDS WHILE ALSO BUYING US SOME TIME.
I WANT SOME DP.
TING-A-LING♪
OH.
PERFECT TIMING. ADVENTURERS ARE HERE.

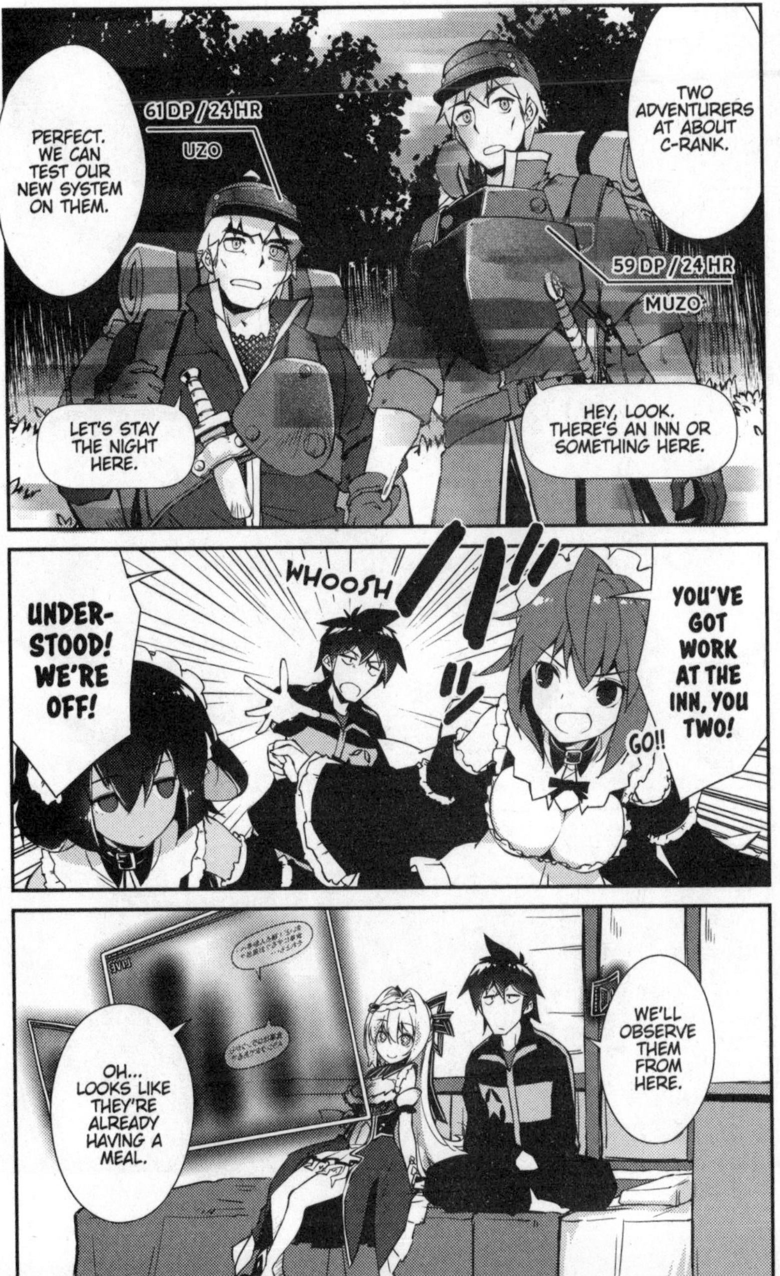
TWO ADVENTURERS AT ABOUT C-RANK.
PERFECT. WE CAN TEST OUR NEW SYSTEM ON THEM.
61 DP / 24 HR
UZO
59 DP / 24 HR
MUZO
HEY, LOOK. THERE'S AN INN OR SOMETHING HERE.
LET'S STAY THE NIGHT HERE.
YOU'VE GOT WORK AT THE INN, YOU TWO!
GO!!
WHOOSH
UNDER-STOOD! WE'RE OFF!
WE'LL OBSERVE THEM FROM HERE.
OH... LOOKS LIKE THEY'RE ALREADY HAVING A MEAL.

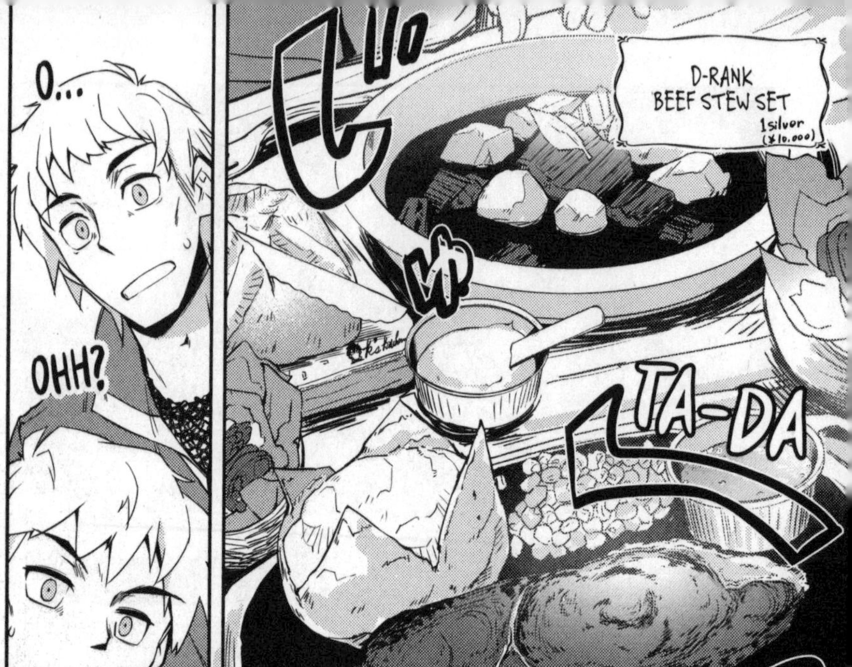
D-RANK
BEEF STEW SET
1silver
(¥10,000)
TA-DA
C-RANK
STEAK SET
5 silver
(¥50,000)
O...
OHH?

*10,000 yen is roughly $100 USD.

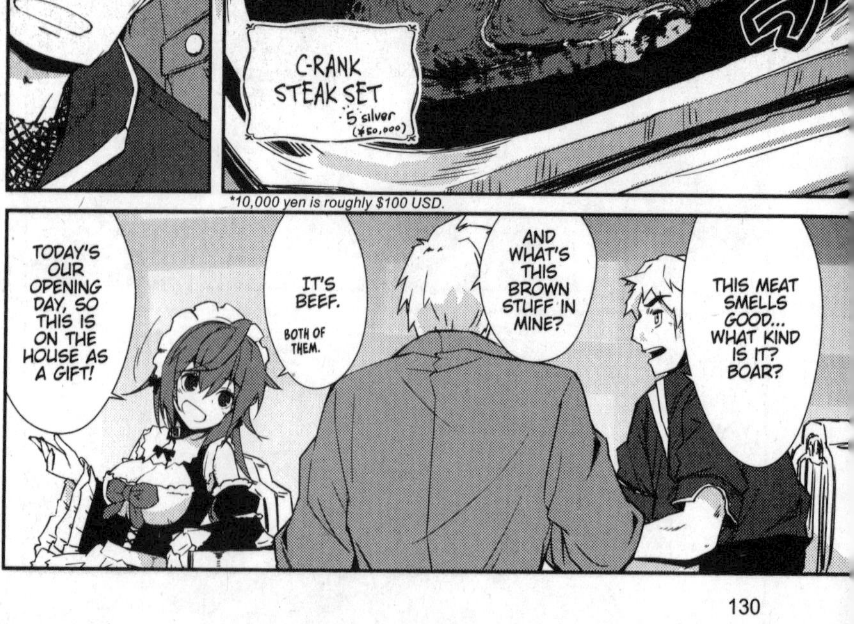
THIS MEAT SMELLS GOOD... WHAT KIND IS IT? BOAR?
AND WHAT'S THIS BROWN STUFF IN MINE?
IT'S BEEF.
BOTH OF THEM.
TODAY'S OUR OPENING DAY, SO THIS IS ON THE HOUSE AS A GIFT!

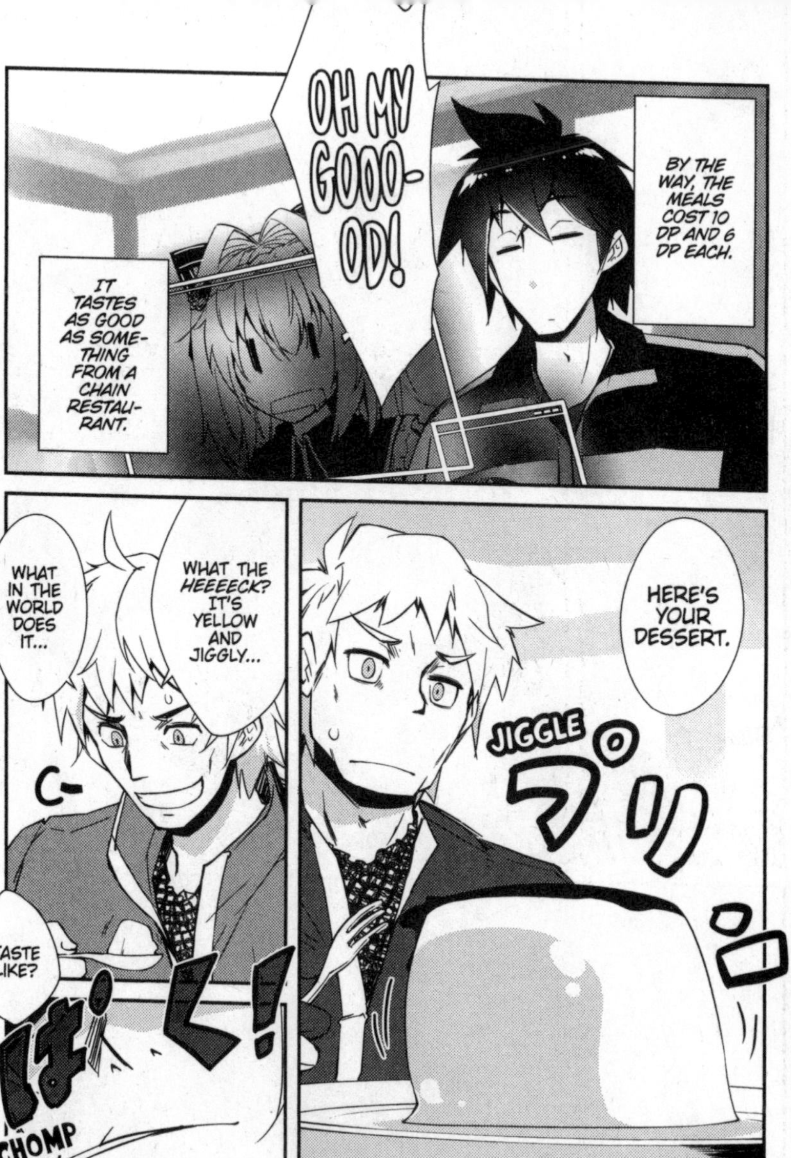
OH MY GOOO-OD!
IT TASTES AS GOOD AS SOME-THING FROM A CHAIN RESTAU-RANT.
BY THE WAY, THE MEALS COST 10 DP AND 6 DP EACH.
HERE'S YOUR DESSERT.
JIGGLE
プリ
WHAT THE HEEEECK? IT'S YELLOW AND JIGGLY...
WHAT IN THE WORLD DOES IT...
C-
TASTE LIKE?
ぱく!
CHOMP

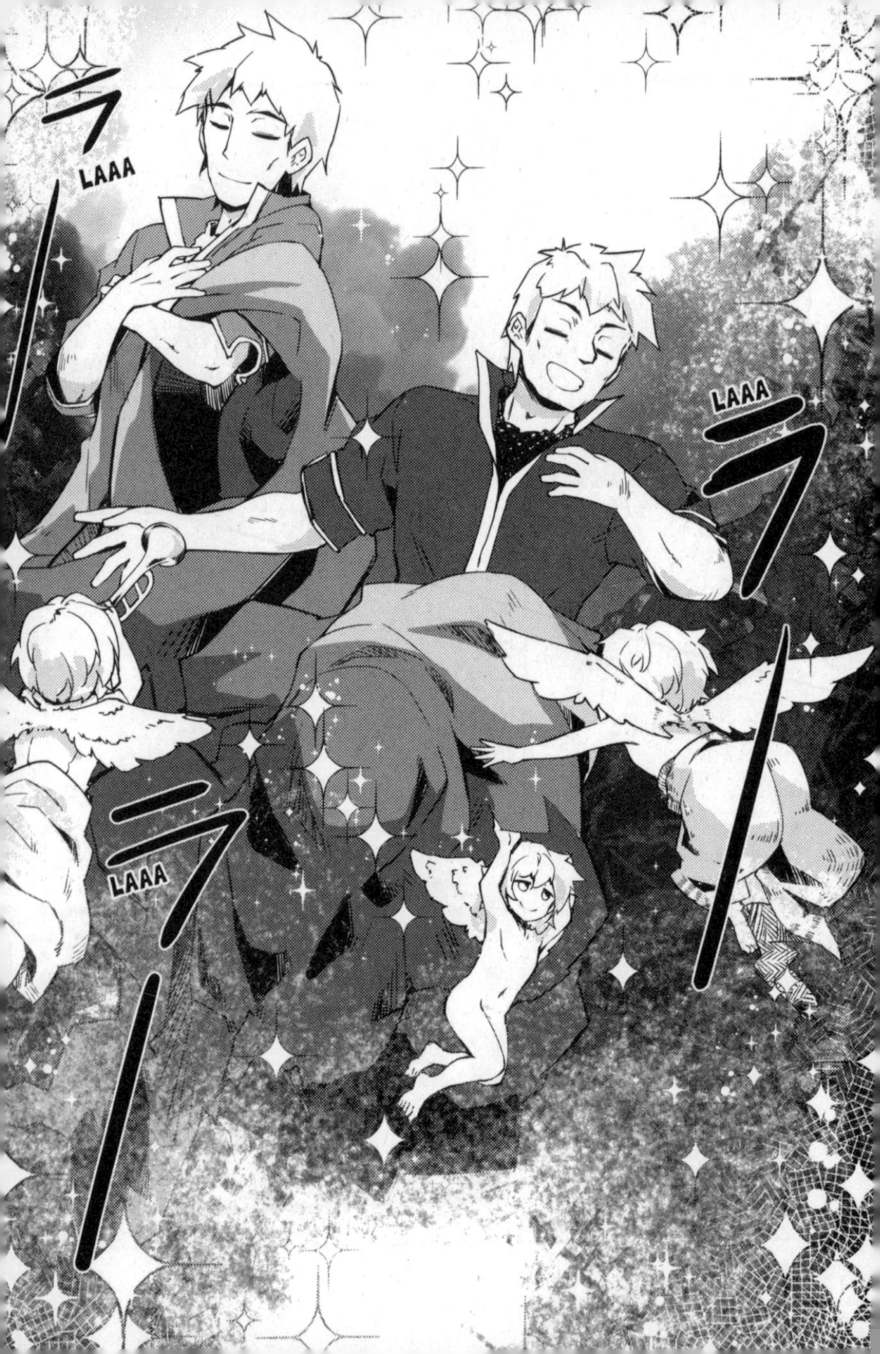

ラー
LAAA
ラー
LAAA
ラー
LAAA

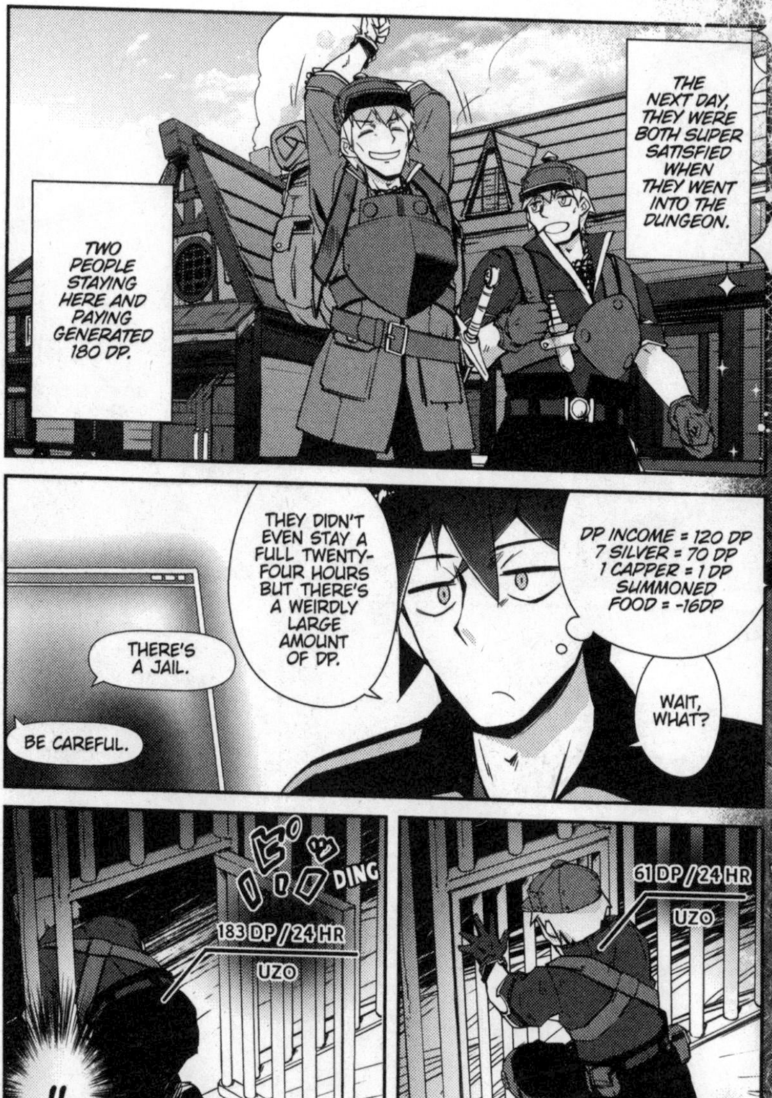
THE NEXT DAY, THEY WERE BOTH SUPER SATISFIED WHEN THEY WENT INTO THE DUNGEON.
TWO PEOPLE STAYING HERE AND PAYING GENERATED 180 DP.
DP INCOME = 120 DP
7 SILVER = 70 DP
1 CAPPER = 1 DP
SUMMONED FOOD = -16DP
WAIT, WHAT?
THEY DIDN'T EVEN STAY A FULL TWENTY-FOUR HOURS BUT THERE'S A WEIRDLY LARGE AMOUNT OF DP.
THERE'S A JAIL.
BE CAREFUL.
61 DP / 24 HR
UZO
DING
183 DP / 24 HR
UZO
!!

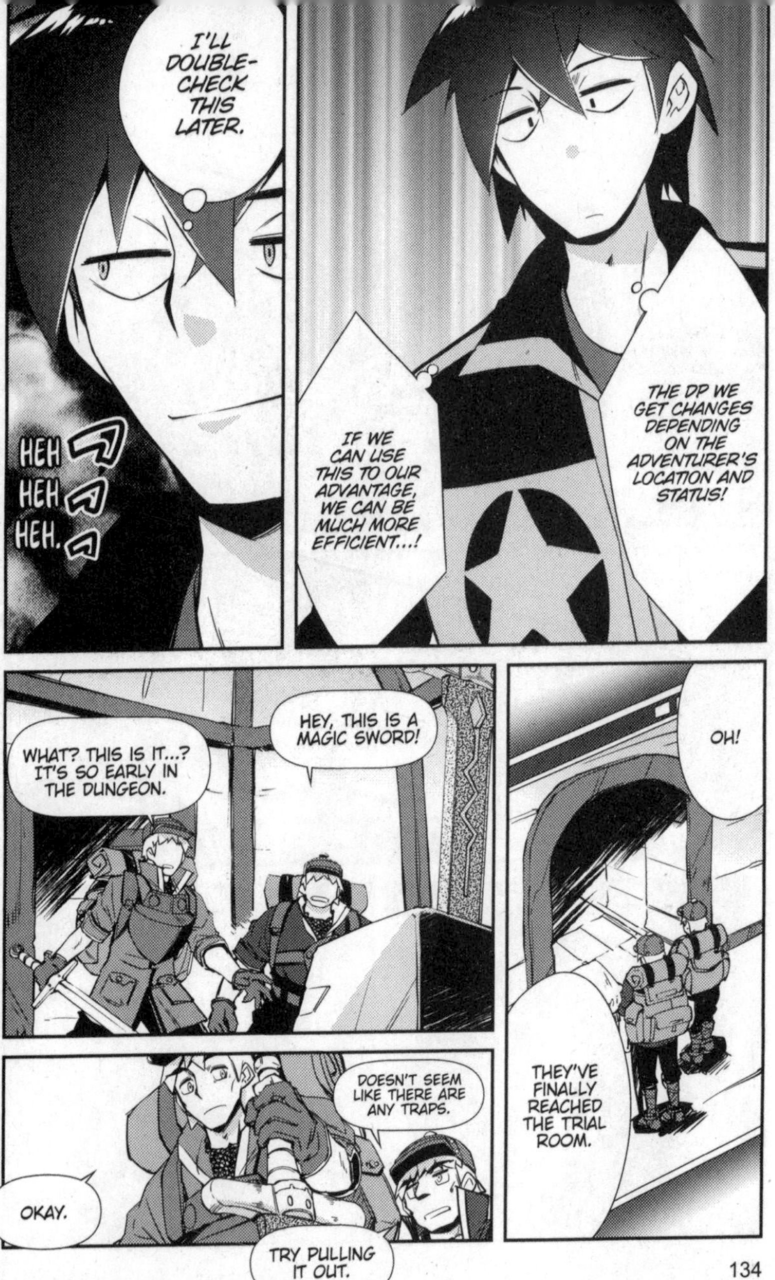
THE DP WE GET CHANGES DEPENDING ON THE ADVENTURER'S LOCATION AND STATUS!
IF WE CAN USE THIS TO OUR ADVANTAGE, WE CAN BE MUCH MORE EFFICIENT...!
I'LL DOUBLE-CHECK THIS LATER.
HEH HEH HEH.
OH!
THEY'VE FINALLY REACHED THE TRIAL ROOM.
HEY, THIS IS A MAGIC SWORD!
WHAT? THIS IS IT...? IT'S SO EARLY IN THE DUNGEON.
DOESN'T SEEM LIKE THERE ARE ANY TRAPS.
TRY PULLING IT OUT.
OKAY.

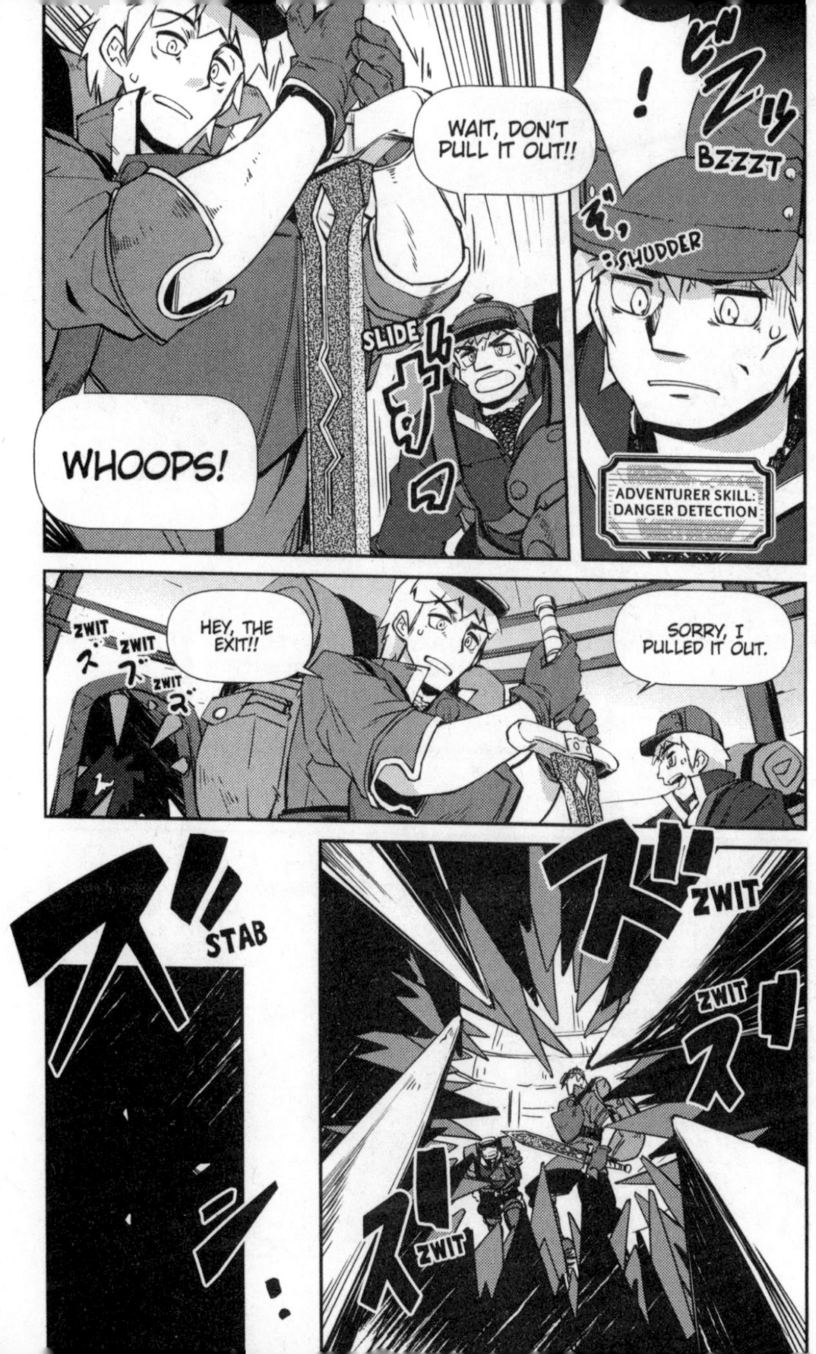
!
BZZZT
SHUDDER
ADVENTURER SKILL: DANGER DETECTION
WAIT, DON'T PULL IT OUT!!
SLIDE
WHOOPS!
SORRY, I PULLED IT OUT.
HEY, THE EXIT!!
ZWIT
ZWIT
ZWIT
ZWIT
ZWIT
ZWIT
STAB

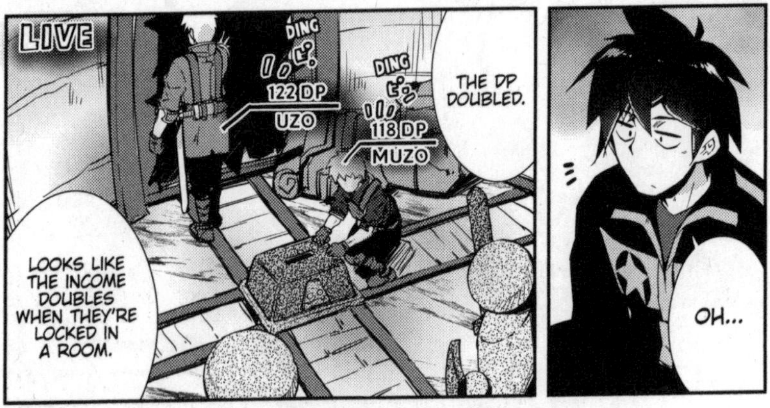
OH...
THE DP DOUBLED.
DING
DING
118 DP
MUZO
122 DP
UZO
LOOKS LIKE THE INCOME DOUBLES WHEN THEY'RE LOCKED IN A ROOM.
LIVE

DP INCOME RULE
INTRUDER SECTION

KEEPING INTRUDERS TRAPPED IN A ROOM DOUBLES THE AMOUNT OF DP AVAILABLE FROM EACH INTRUDER.

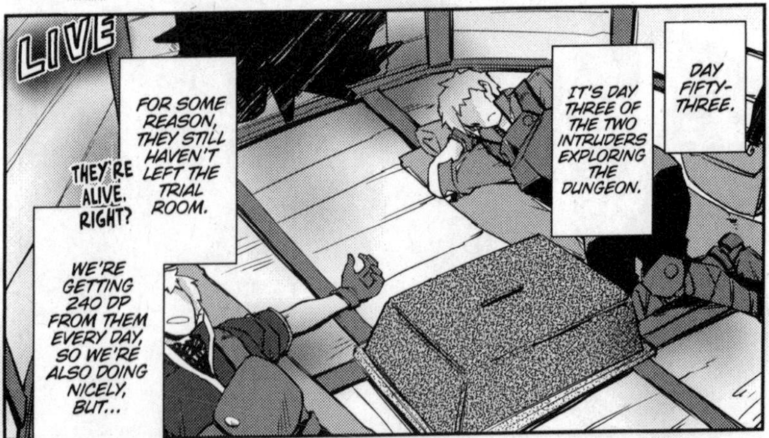
LIVE
DAY FIFTY-THREE.
IT'S DAY THREE OF THE TWO INTRUDERS EXPLORING THE DUNGEON.
FOR SOME REASON, THEY STILL HAVEN'T LEFT THE TRIAL ROOM.
THEY'RE ALIVE, RIGHT?
WE'RE GETTING 240 DP FROM THEM EVERY DAY, SO WE'RE ALSO DOING NICELY, BUT...

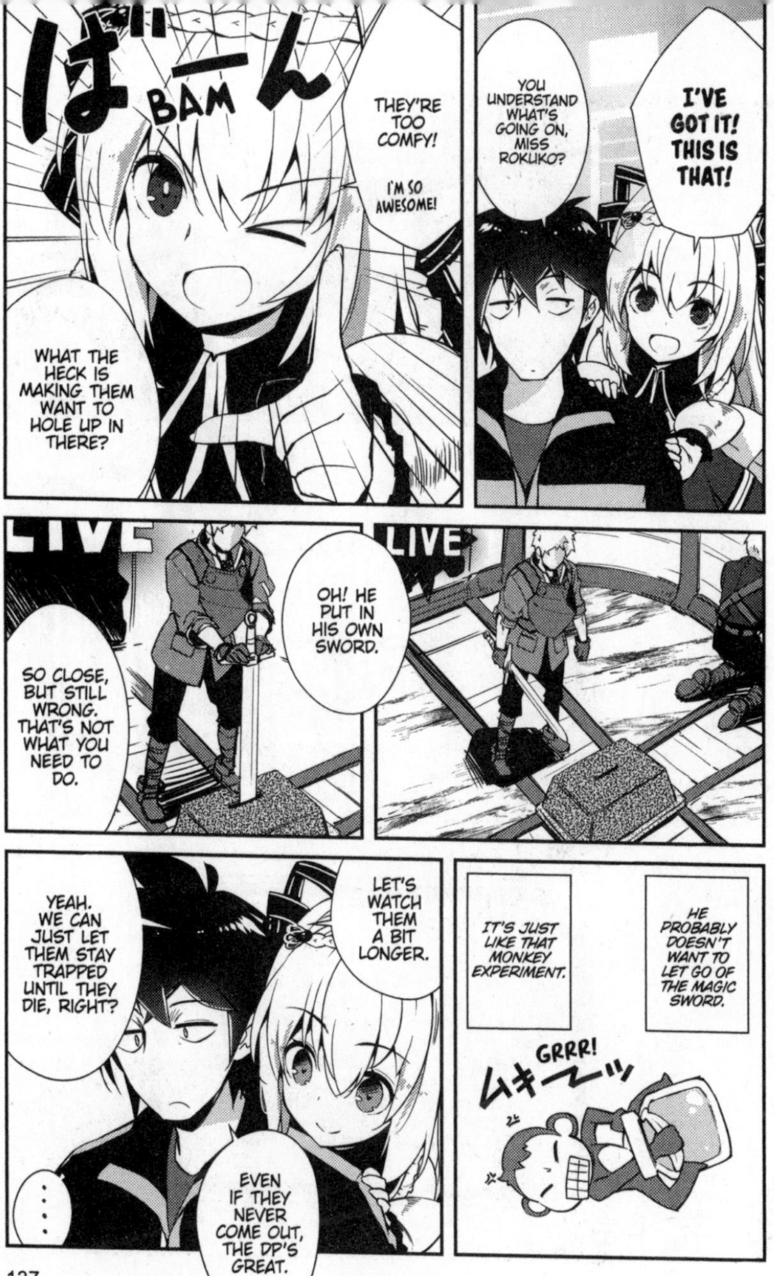
I'VE GOT IT! THIS IS THAT!
YOU UNDERSTAND WHAT'S GOING ON, MISS ROKUKO?
THEY'RE TOO COMFY!
I'M SO AWESOME!
ばーん
BAM
WHAT THE HECK IS MAKING THEM WANT TO HOLE UP IN THERE?
LIVE
OH! HE PUT IN HIS OWN SWORD.
LIVE
SO CLOSE, BUT STILL WRONG. THAT'S NOT WHAT YOU NEED TO DO.
HE PROBABLY DOESN'T WANT TO LET GO OF THE MAGIC SWORD.
IT'S JUST LIKE THAT MONKEY EXPERIMENT.
ムキーッ
GRRR!
LET'S WATCH THEM A BIT LONGER.
YEAH. WE CAN JUST LET THEM STAY TRAPPED UNTIL THEY DIE, RIGHT?
EVEN IF THEY NEVER COME OUT, THE DP'S GREAT.
....

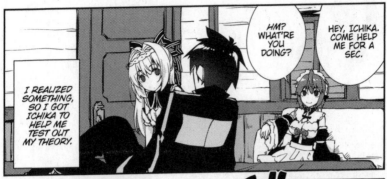

HEY, ICHIKA. COME HELP ME FOR A SEC.
HM? WHAT'RE YOU DOING?
I REALIZED SOMETHING, SO I GOT ICHIKA TO HELP ME TEST OUT MY THEORY.
ドスーンッ
KA-THUD
BEEP
ピ
WHHHY?! WHAT DID I DO?!
RATTLE
がっしゃ
OH! HER DP TRIPLED.
がっしゃ
RATTLE

WHICH IS HOW I CLEARED UP A FEW THINGS.

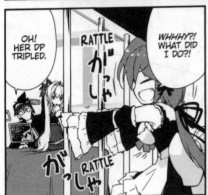

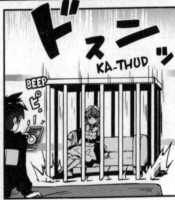

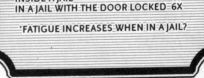

DP INCOME RULE #2

LOCKED IN A ROOM WITH A KEY	2X
INSIDE A JAIL	3X
IN A JAIL WITH THE DOOR LOCKED	6X

*FATIGUE INCREASES WHEN IN A JAIL?

LET'S LOCK THE DOORS OF THE INN AT NIGHT.

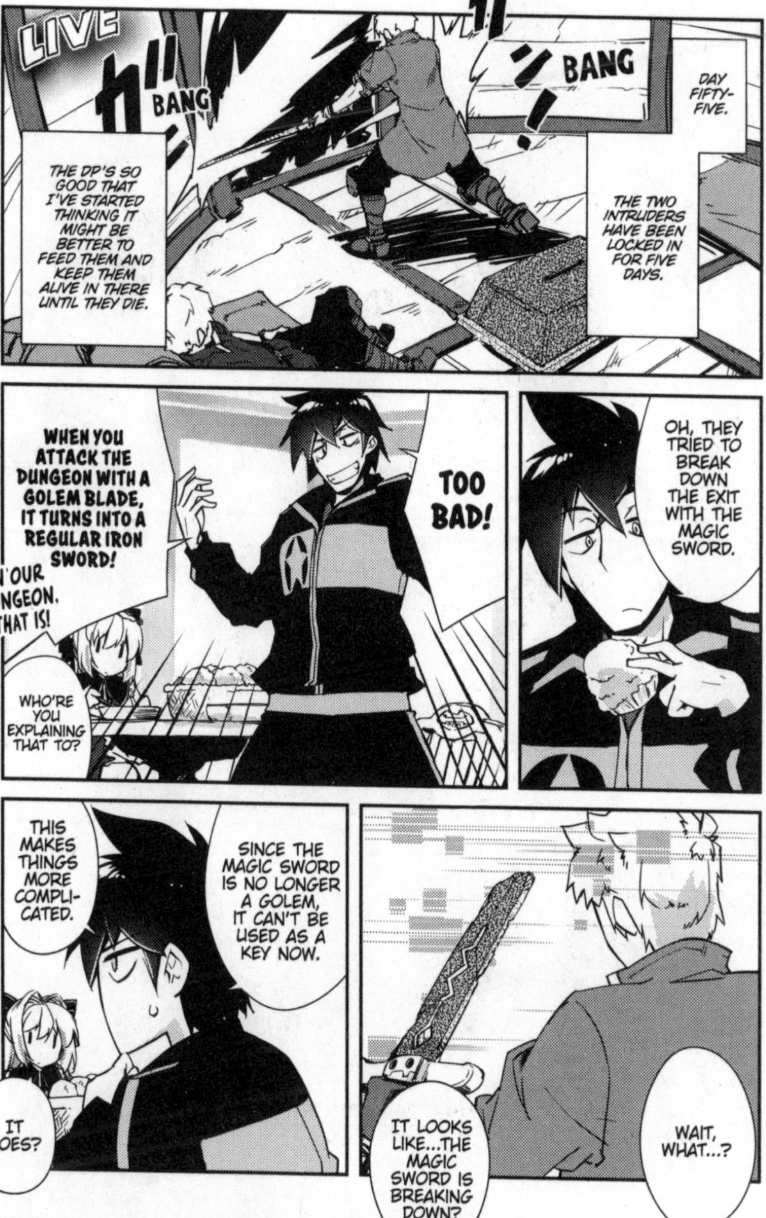
BANG
DAY FIFTY-FIVE.
THE TWO INTRUDERS HAVE BEEN LOCKED IN FOR FIVE DAYS.
LIVE
BANG
THE DP'S SO GOOD THAT I'VE STARTED THINKING IT MIGHT BE BETTER TO FEED THEM AND KEEP THEM ALIVE IN THERE UNTIL THEY DIE.
OH, THEY TRIED TO BREAK DOWN THE EXIT WITH THE MAGIC SWORD.
TOO BAD!
WHEN YOU ATTACK THE DUNGEON WITH A GOLEM BLADE, IT TURNS INTO A REGULAR IRON SWORD!
IN OUR DUNGEON, THAT IS!
WHO'RE YOU EXPLAINING THAT TO?
WAIT, WHAT...?
IT LOOKS LIKE...THE MAGIC SWORD IS BREAKING DOWN?
SINCE THE MAGIC SWORD IS NO LONGER A GOLEM, IT CAN'T BE USED AS A KEY NOW.
THIS MAKES THINGS MORE COMPLICATED.
IT DOES?

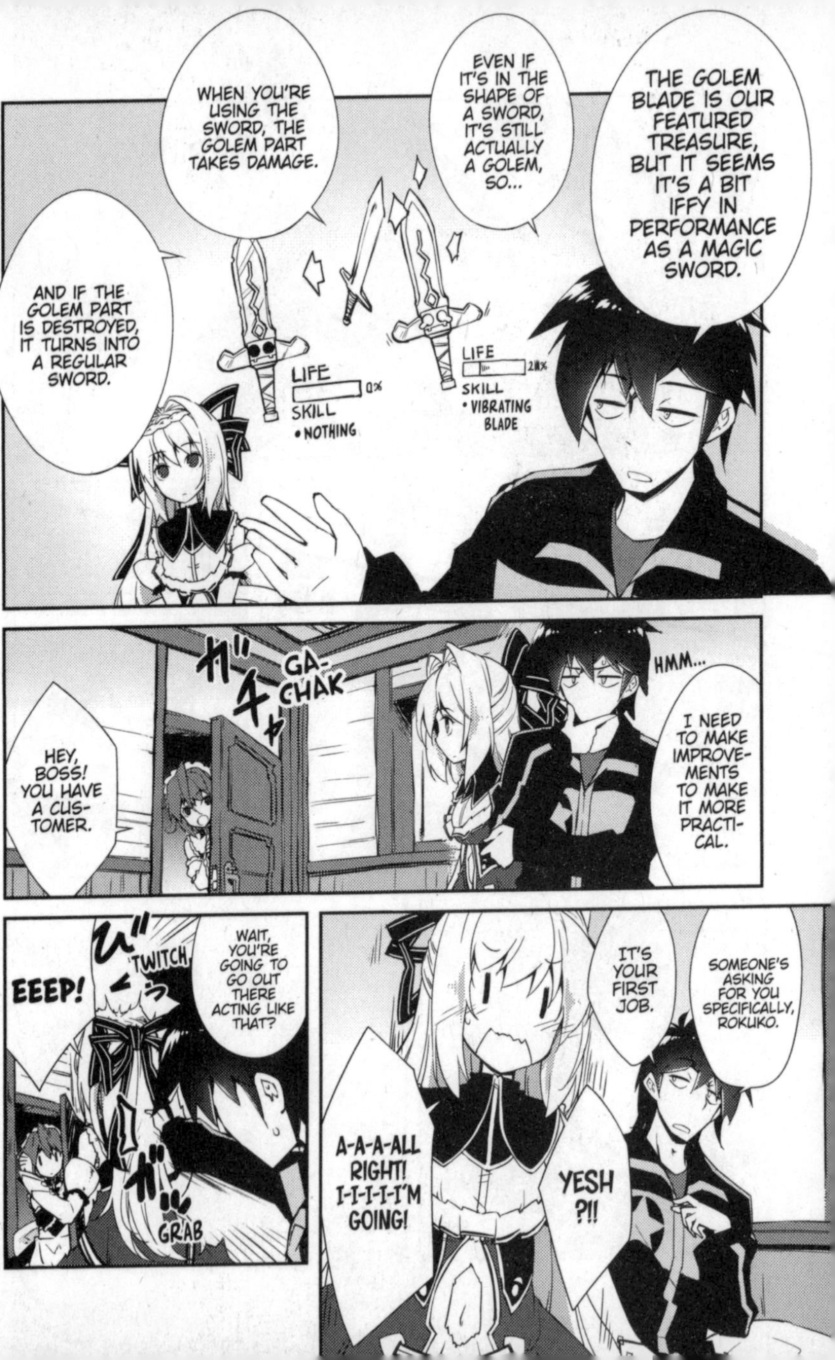
THE GOLEM BLADE IS OUR FEATURED TREASURE, BUT IT SEEMS IT'S A BIT IFFY IN PERFORMANCE AS A MAGIC SWORD.
EVEN IF IT'S IN THE SHAPE OF A SWORD, IT'S STILL ACTUALLY A GOLEM, SO...
WHEN YOU'RE USING THE SWORD, THE GOLEM PART TAKES DAMAGE.
LIFE
SKILL
• VIBRATING BLADE
LIFE 0%
SKILL
• NOTHING
AND IF THE GOLEM PART IS DESTROYED, IT TURNS INTO A REGULAR SWORD.
HMM...
I NEED TO MAKE IMPROVEMENTS TO MAKE IT MORE PRACTICAL.
GA-CHAK
HEY, BOSS! YOU HAVE A CUSTOMER.
SOMEONE'S ASKING FOR YOU SPECIFICALLY, ROKUKO.
IT'S YOUR FIRST JOB.
YESH ?!!
A-A-A-ALL RIGHT! I-I-I-I-I'M GOING!
WAIT, YOU'RE GOING TO GO OUT THERE ACTING LIKE THAT?
TWITCH
EEEP!
GRAB

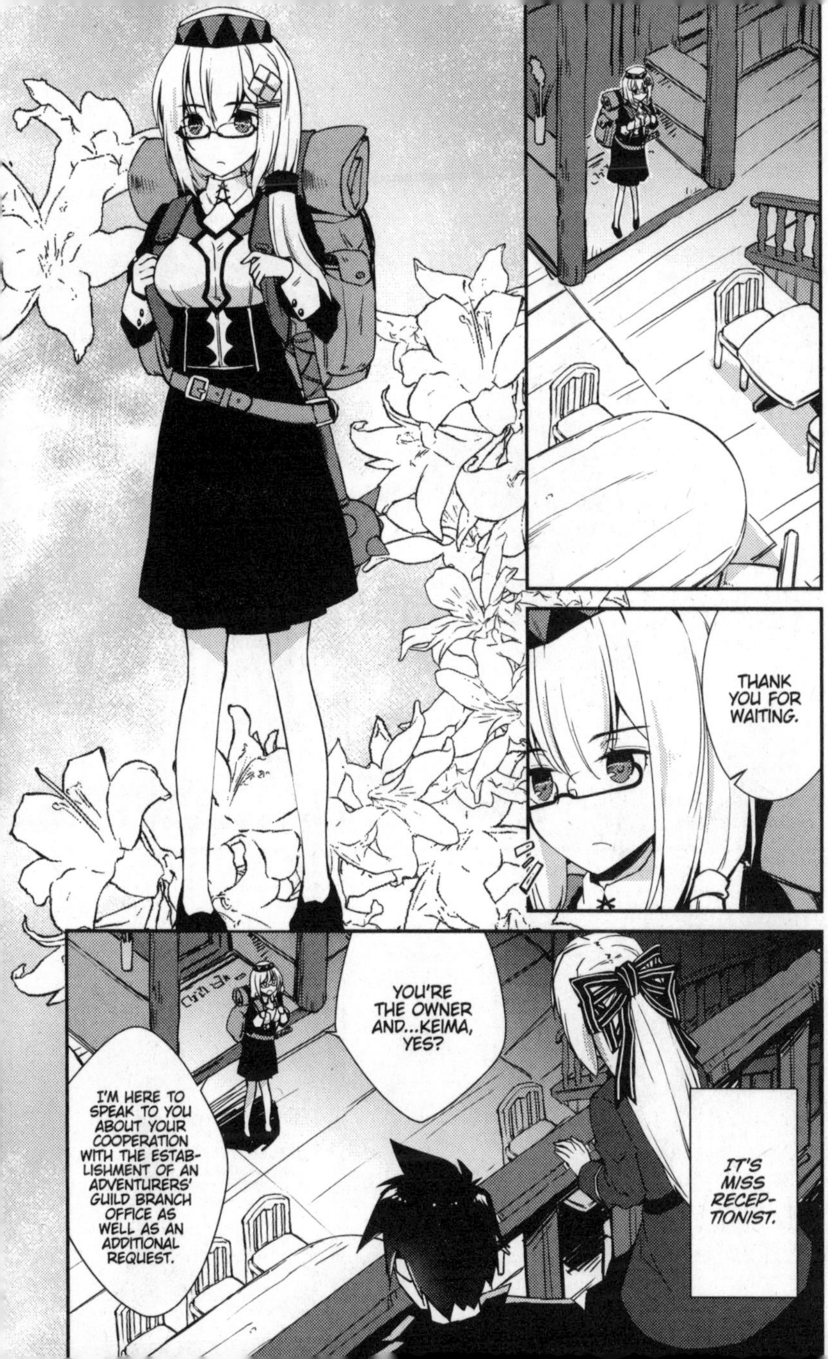
THANK YOU FOR WAITING.
IT'S MISS RECEPTIONIST.
YOU'RE THE OWNER AND...KEIMA, YES?
I'M HERE TO SPEAK TO YOU ABOUT YOUR COOPERATION WITH THE ESTABLISHMENT OF AN ADVENTURERS' GUILD BRANCH OFFICE AS WELL AS AN ADDITIONAL REQUEST.

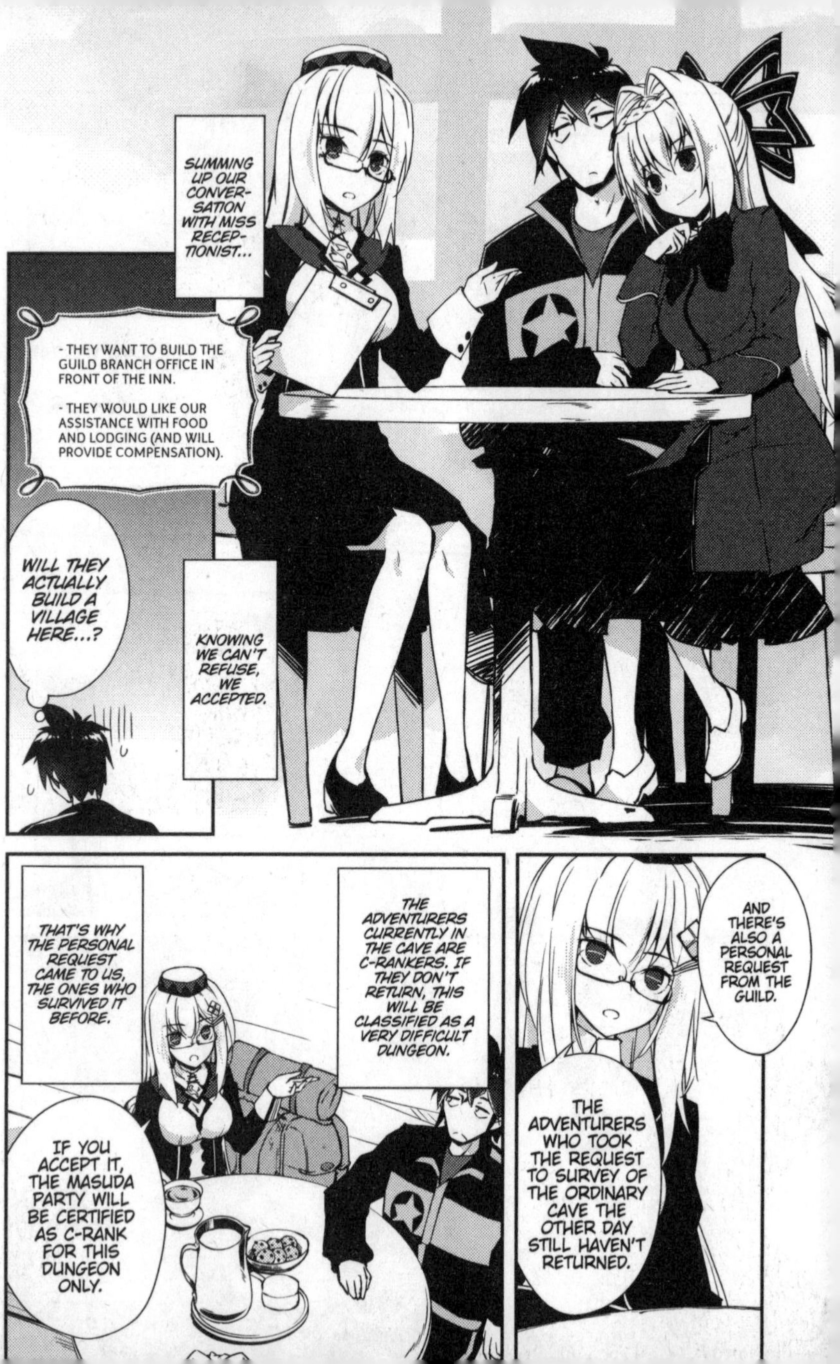
SUMMING UP OUR CONVERSATION WITH MISS RECEPTIONIST...
- THEY WANT TO BUILD THE GUILD BRANCH OFFICE IN FRONT OF THE INN.
- THEY WOULD LIKE OUR ASSISTANCE WITH FOOD AND LODGING (AND WILL PROVIDE COMPENSATION).
KNOWING WE CAN'T REFUSE, WE ACCEPTED.
WILL THEY ACTUALLY BUILD A VILLAGE HERE...?
AND THERE'S ALSO A PERSONAL REQUEST FROM THE GUILD.
THE ADVENTURERS WHO TOOK THE REQUEST TO SURVEY OF THE ORDINARY CAVE THE OTHER DAY STILL HAVEN'T RETURNED.
THE ADVENTURERS CURRENTLY IN THE CAVE ARE C-RANKERS. IF THEY DON'T RETURN, THIS WILL BE CLASSIFIED AS A VERY DIFFICULT DUNGEON.
THAT'S WHY THE PERSONAL REQUEST CAME TO US, THE ONES WHO SURVIVED IT BEFORE.
IF YOU ACCEPT IT, THE MASUDA PARTY WILL BE CERTIFIED AS C-RANK FOR THIS DUNGEON ONLY.

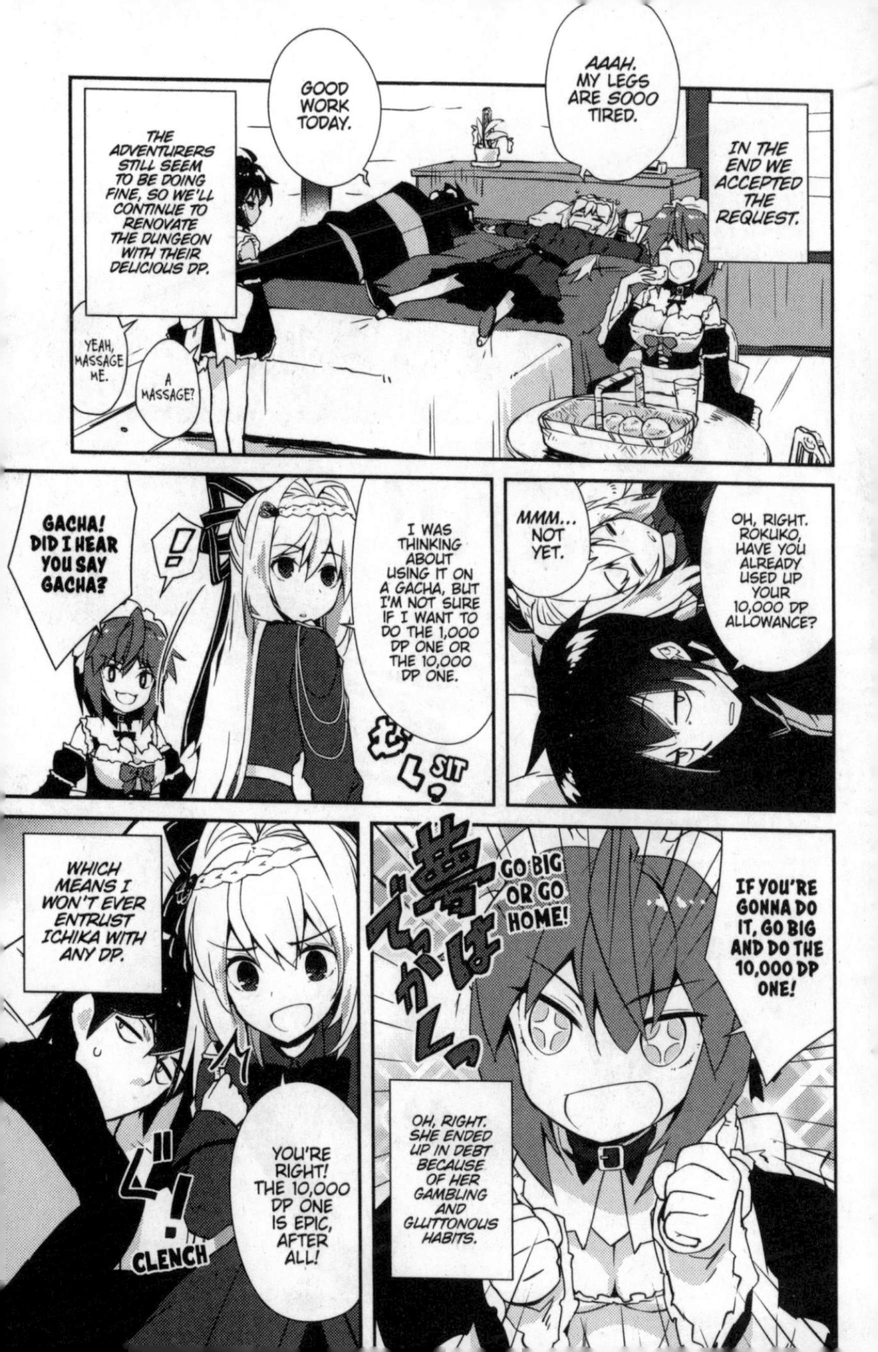
IN THE END WE ACCEPTED THE REQUEST.
AAAH. MY LEGS ARE SOOO TIRED.
GOOD WORK TODAY.
THE ADVENTURERS STILL SEEM TO BE DOING FINE, SO WE'LL CONTINUE TO RENOVATE THE DUNGEON WITH THEIR DELICIOUS DP.
A MASSAGE?
YEAH, MASSAGE ME.
OH, RIGHT. ROKUKO, HAVE YOU ALREADY USED UP YOUR 10,000 DP ALLOWANCE?
MMM... NOT YET.
I WAS THINKING ABOUT USING IT ON A GACHA, BUT I'M NOT SURE IF I WANT TO DO THE 1,000 DP ONE OR THE 10,000 DP ONE.
!
SIT
GACHA! DID I HEAR YOU SAY GACHA?
IF YOU'RE GONNA DO IT, GO BIG AND DO THE 10,000 DP ONE!
GO BIG OR GO HOME!
OH, RIGHT. SHE ENDED UP IN DEBT BECAUSE OF HER GAMBLING AND GLUTTONOUS HABITS.
WHICH MEANS I WON'T EVER ENTRUST ICHIKA WITH ANY DP.
YOU'RE RIGHT! THE 10,000 DP ONE IS EPIC, AFTER ALL!
CLENCH

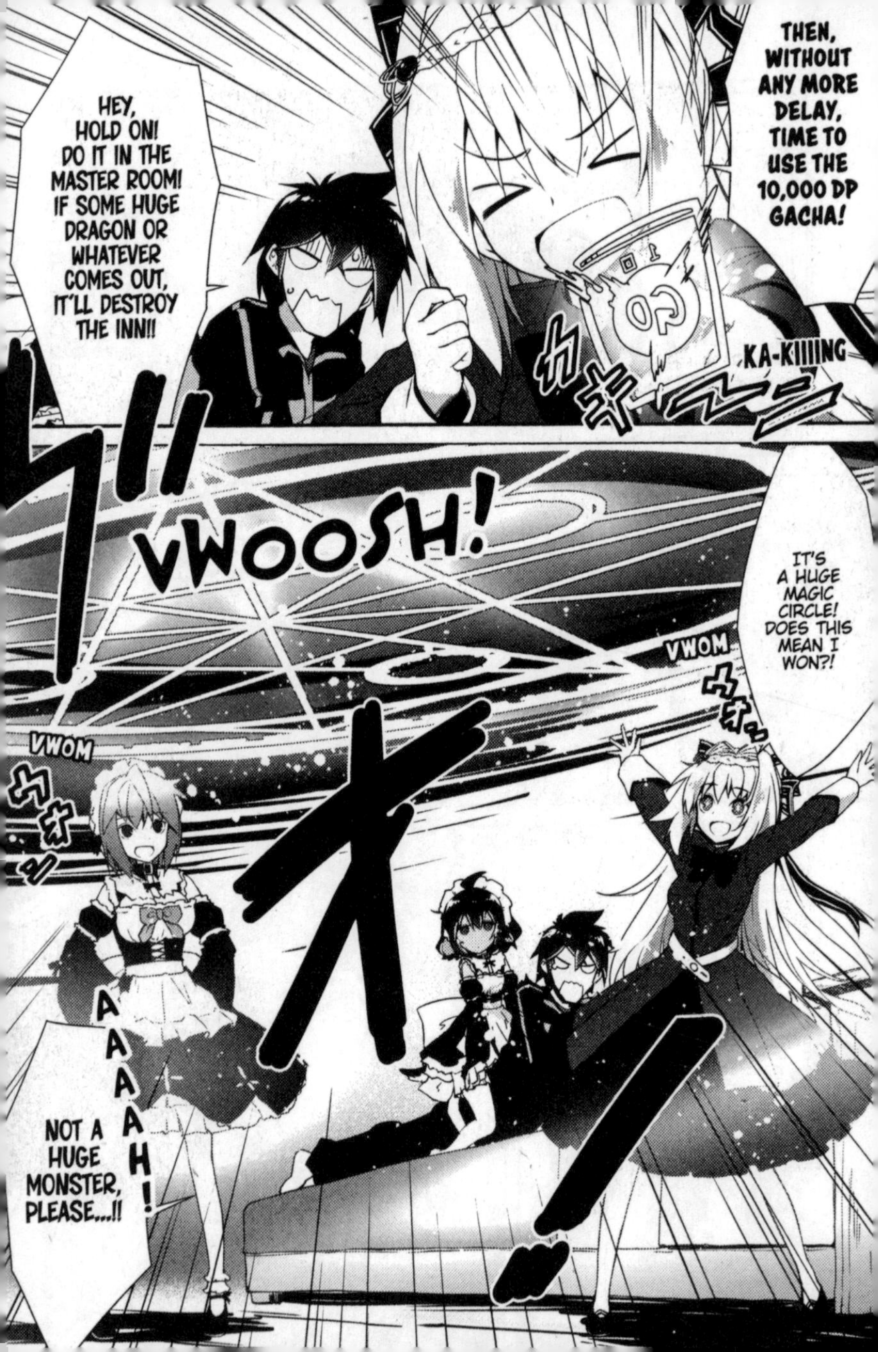
THEN, WITHOUT ANY MORE DELAY, TIME TO USE THE 10,000 DP GACHA!
KA-KIIIING
HEY, HOLD ON! DO IT IN THE MASTER ROOM! IF SOME HUGE DRAGON OR WHATEVER COMES OUT, IT'LL DESTROY THE INN!!
IT'S A HUGE MAGIC CIRCLE! DOES THIS MEAN I WON?!
VWOM
VWOOSH!
VWOM
AAAAAH!
NOT A HUGE MONSTER, PLEASE...!!

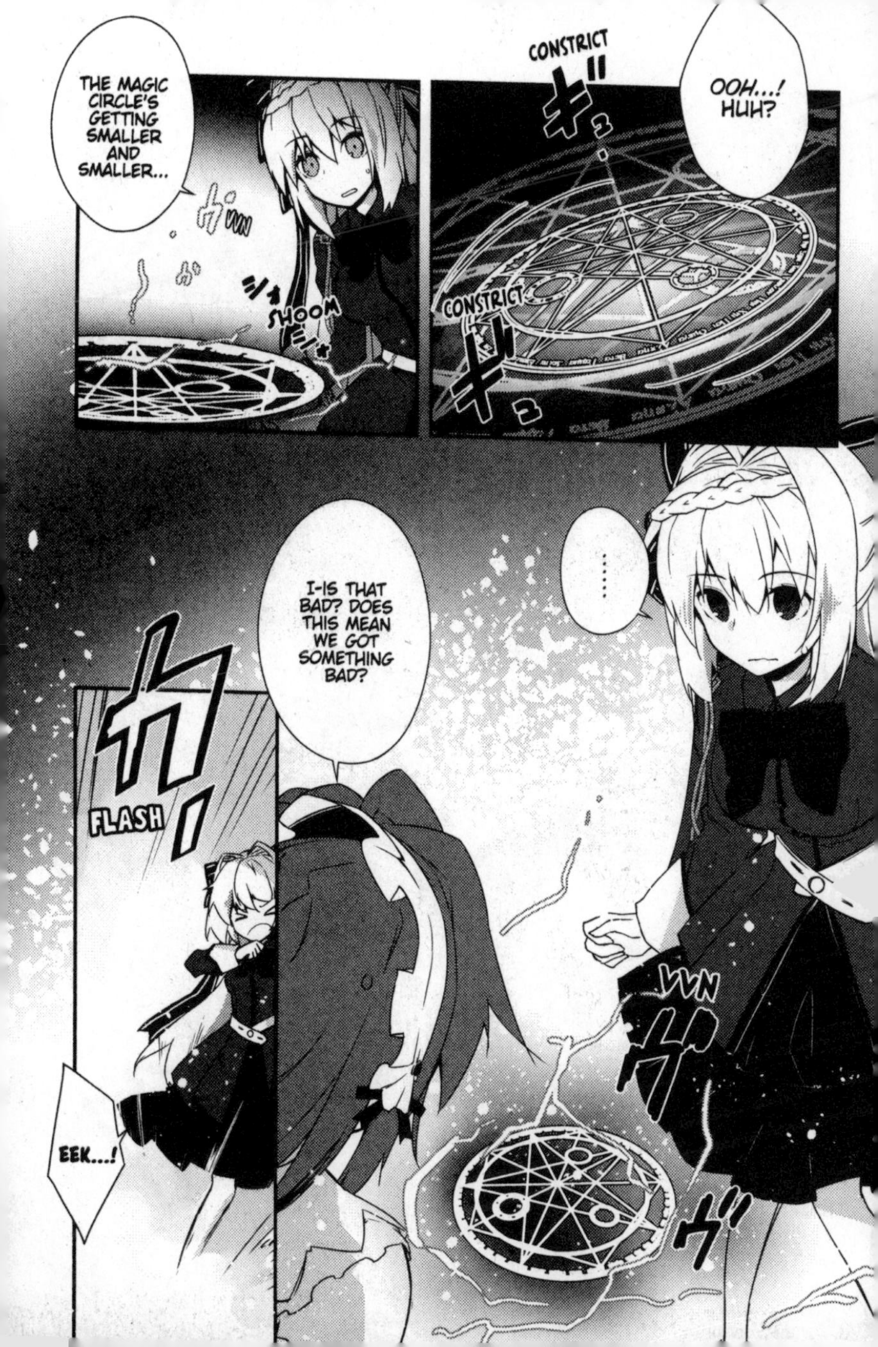

OOH...! HUH?
CONSTRICT
CONSTRICT
THE MAGIC CIRCLE'S GETTING SMALLER AND SMALLER...
VVN
SHOOM
......
I-IS THAT BAD? DOES THIS MEAN WE GOT SOMETHING BAD?
VVN
FLASH
EEK...!

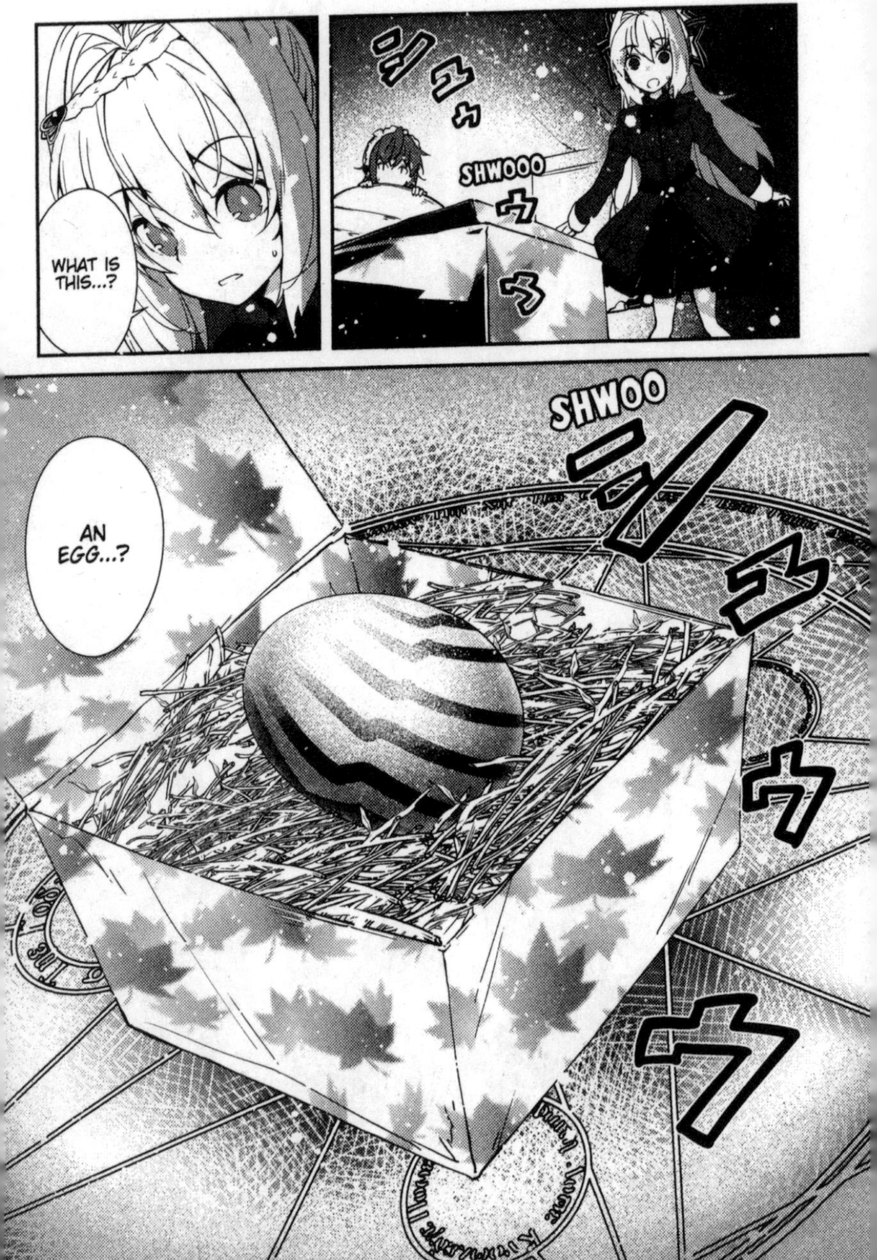
SHWOOO
WHAT IS THIS...?
SHWOO
AN EGG...?

LAZY DUNGEON MASTER

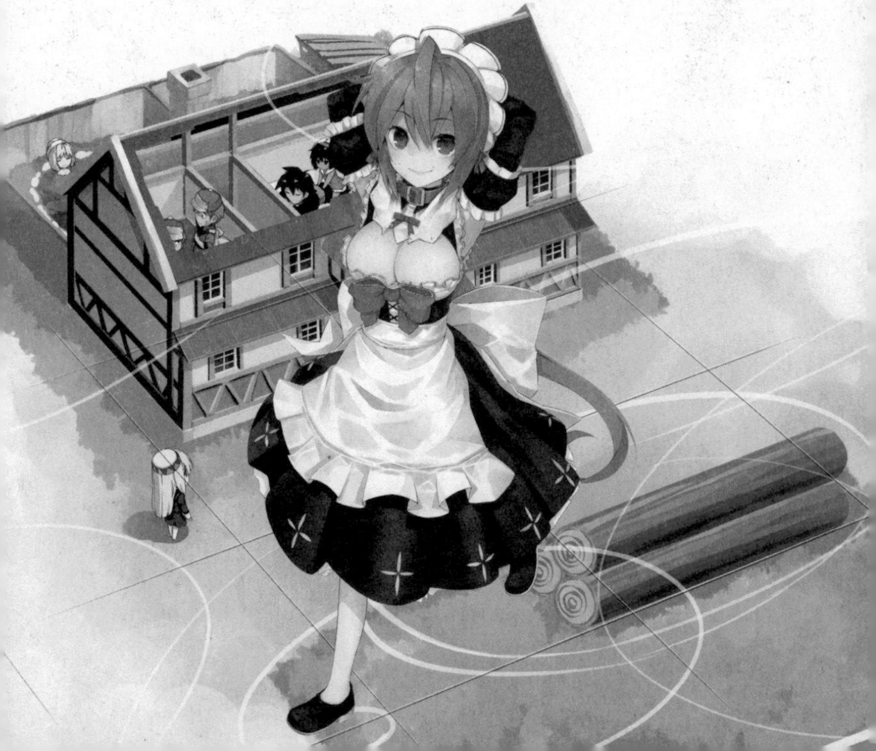

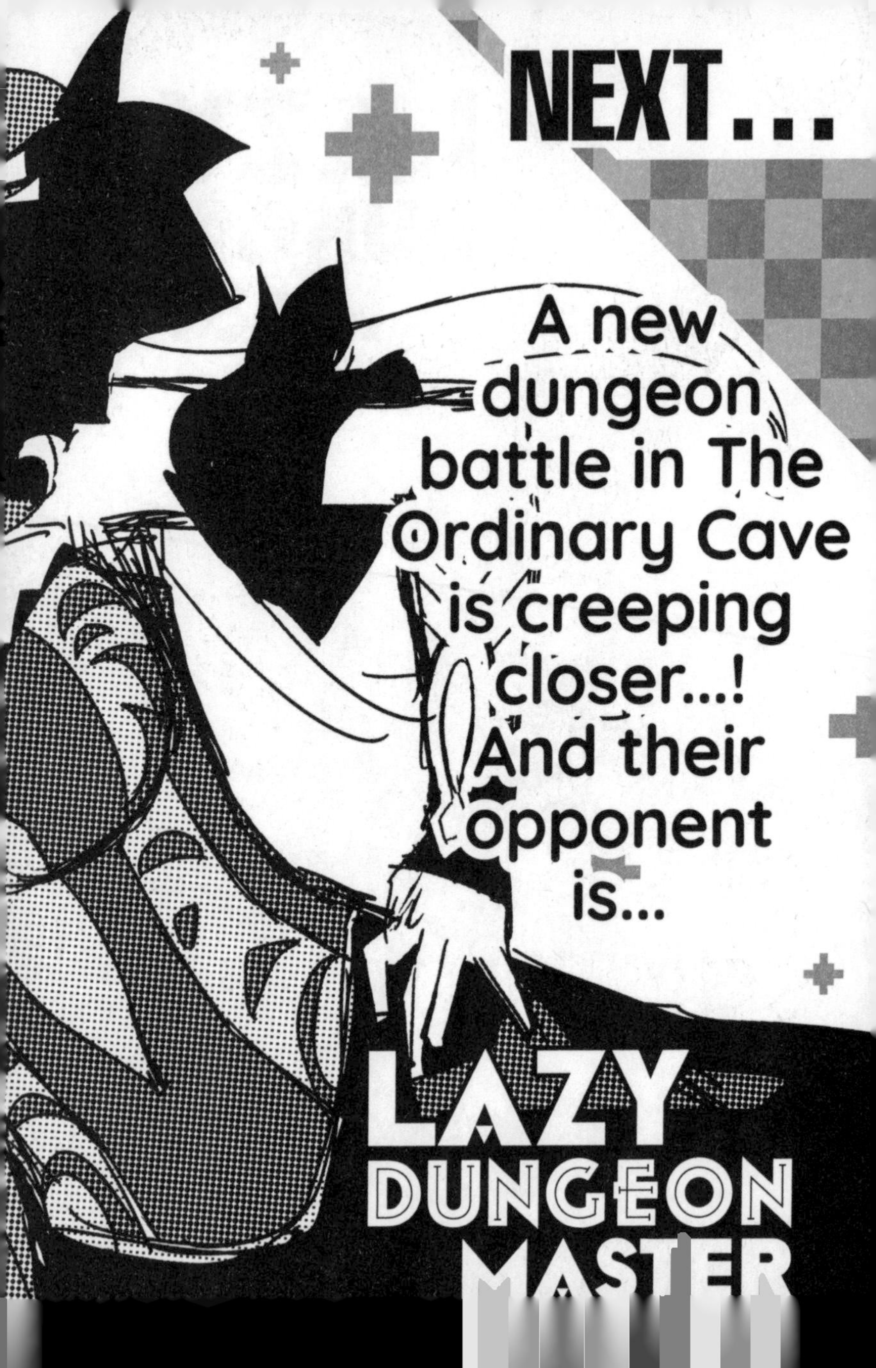
NEXT...
A new dungeon battle in The Ordinary Cave is creeping closer...! And their opponent is...
LAZY DUNGEON MASTER

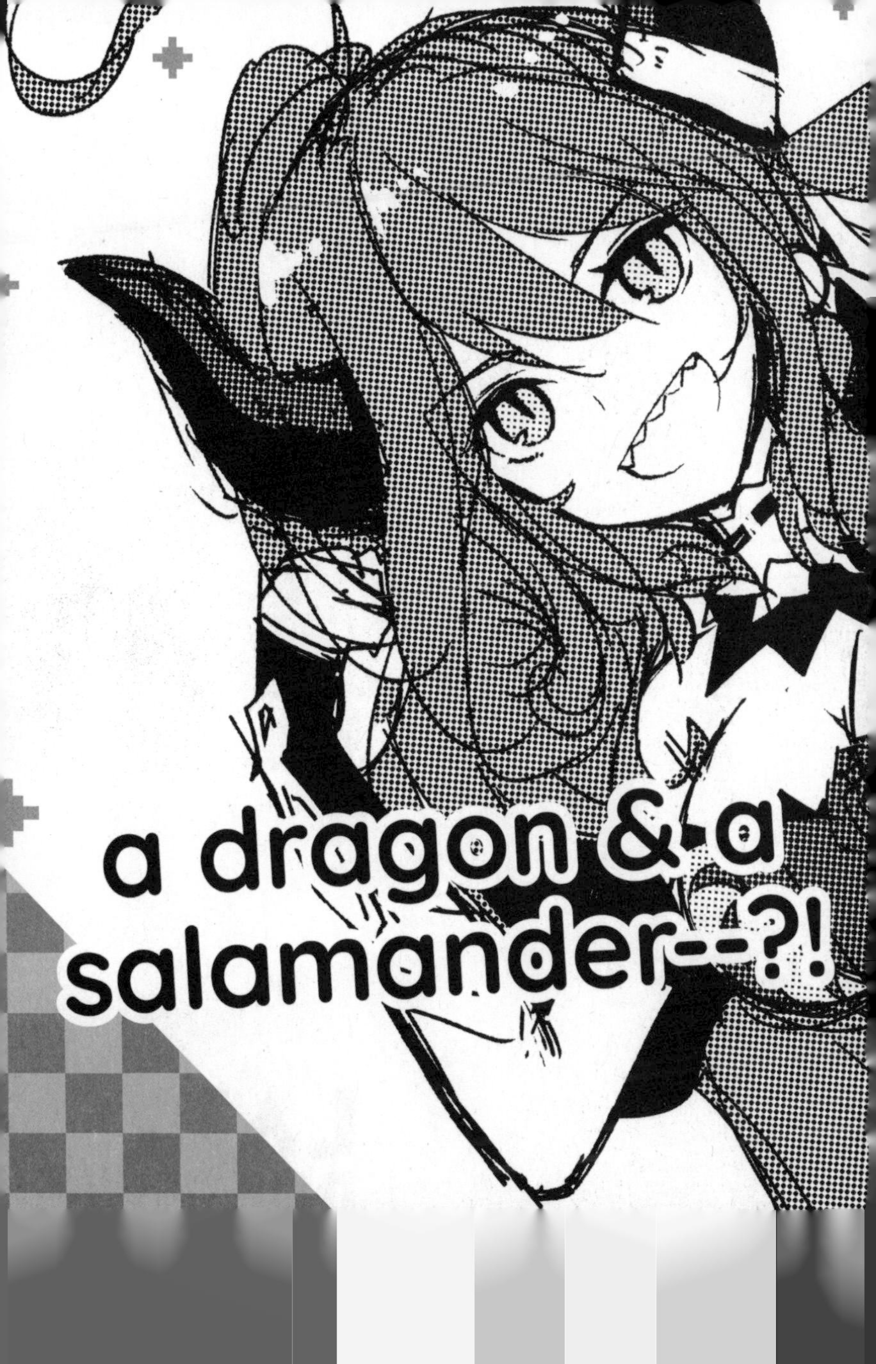
a dragon & a salamander--?!

LAZY
DUNGEON
MASTER

The Secret Backstory for the Inn that We Can't Talk About

◆ ◆ ◆ ━━◄━ ━►━━ ◆ ◆ ◆

Haku Laverio, an A-rank adventurer who also went by the name "White-Winged Goddess," had taken an extraordinary interest in a dungeon known as The Ordinary Cave. It was newly formed and, while educationally valuable, was on the small side and only attracted goblins. Since it was far too weak for her, Haku requested that the guild place the dungeon under probation and observe it on the grounds that it needed to be protected.

The Guild Master made a special exception for this to happen, but since Haku was the one making the request, the whole thing was a mere formality. And thus, The Ordinary Cave became a guild-controlled dungeon.

※*It's an open secret that the A-rank adventurer Haku Laverio, the Grand Master, the founder of the Laverio Empire, the primary deity of the of the White God Religion, and the White Goddess, are all the same person. Because of this, while she's working as an adventurer, she's not referred to as the White Goddess, but the White-Winged Goddess.*

For a few years, there weren't any particular changes in the dungeon and management was carried out only once a month. It was a very peaceful situation.

At least, until the bandits came.

The bandits dug so deep into The Ordinary Cave that they ended up changing the dungeon's very shape. After removing them, however, the dungeon became larger and less valuable educationally.

Even so, this was the dungeon that Haku found, and she still insisted it be watched carefully. No one objected to her wish.

"We'll need to observe it more carefully from now on," she decided. And with that in mind, she set out to establish an observation base.

"Field Analysis... Hmm."

Upon analyzing the area, Haku learned it had a hot spring. The fact that there was a perfectly good source of water eliminated many of the common problems that came with establishing a base. Taking this into account, Haku immediately hired a contractor. However, these sorts of construction jobs take time and unless Haku built her base quickly, the risk of even more bandits arriving to occupy the dungeon was high.

Thus, Haku decided to call upon an acquaintance of hers, a magician called Narikin, who specialized in architecture magic. Being both a Grand Master and an A-rank adventurer, Haku teleported to Narikin's home deep in the mountains with ease, despite the fact that this particular magic normally required many special rituals.

"Dear me, Haku. You want a vacation home?" Narikin asked.

"Something like that. Let's see...I'd like something reminiscent of the heroes' homeland. Could you build me a hot spring inn?"

"As you wish. When do you need it finished by?"

"Preferably as soon as you can. Would three days be enough time?"

"Understood. If I work hard, I should have it done in two. It will cost you, of course."

After closing the deal, Haku teleported again, this time with Narakin in tow, and arrived at the entrance of The Ordinary Cave. Then, just as Narakin said, the inn was completed in two days. Satisfied with the workmanship, Haku paid them a fair wage.

"Well, here you are. I hope I can count on your patronage in the future."

"Yes, I'll call upon your services again."

Haku used *Teleport* to send Narakin back to their home. Alone once more, she went inside to take a look at the building.

The inn certainly was good enough to double as a base for Haku, even if it was a bit too showy for her tastes. There was also plenty of room, which would allow not only Haku but all of her followers to stay there as well. It was a fully functioning inn, just as she had intended.

"Now I need some people to run this place."

The words had barely left her mouth when she saw a girl walking by outside.

"What a wonderful inn!" the stranger remarked. "To think I'd find a place like this after getting lost so deep in the mountains!"

The girl walked right up to the inn and entered without hesitation. That's when she came across Haku, who was still pondering about her lack of staff.

"Oh my."

"Well now."

Their eyes met. Haku felt something at that moment, something that told her this was fate.

"You're so cute. What's your name?"

"I'm Rokuko. What's your name, Miss?"

"Ah, let's see. Please call me Haku."

"Okay, Big Sis Haku."

And this is how Haku met Rokuko. You could say it was love at first sight.

"Where are you from, Rokuko?"

"Oh. Well, I'm from…I-I…h-huh? Why, I can't remember where I'm from! I can only remember my name!"

Rokuko clearly didn't have any connections to Zia and instead seemed to have come from some other place altogether. Haku was sure a fairy or something had likely spirited her away from her home as a trick.

"I see. I've heard of things like that happening before."

"Now I can't return home…" Rokuko lamented.

"How convenient for me though. Why don't I give you this inn?"

It was perfect. Haku could now kill two birds with one stone *and* protect Rokuko by leaving the inn in her hands. In other words...

One could say that, as an act of favoritism, she bestowed the inn upon Rokuko as a gift.

"Use it however you like. If you end up making money as well, all the better."

"Thank you so much, Big Sis Haku! But I don't know what to do with such an amazing inn."

"Hmm. Shall I arrange some servants for you?"

She *did* need workers, after all.

"You'll need competent staff. Here, take this," Haku said as she handed Rokuko a scroll.

"What's this, Big Sis Haku?"

"This is the *Create Golem Scroll*. You can use it to create clay golems who will do all the hard labor for you."

"It makes golems, huh? That'll sure come in handy."

Due to the way Rokuko gracefully manipulated those golems, Haku named the inn *The Dancing Dolls*.

"I'm still a bit nervous about being here alone, even though there are golems around. And if I get attacked by bandits when you're not here, Big Sis Haku, I'll have nowhere to stay."

"That's true. Whatever shall we do about that?"

After all, bandits appeared only yesterday and settled in The Ordinary Cave. Clay golems wouldn't be enough on their own.

It was at that moment that they saw an adventurer who just happened to be passing by.

"Whoa. There's an inn all the way out here? I thought this was just The Ordinary Cave."

"I was so surprised my legs almost gave way, Master."

Correction. It was an adventurer *and* his slave.

"This is perfect. Let's make that adventurer your bodyguard. That way he can lend us his slave. You there, adventurer." Haku called out. "Come over here for a moment."

"Holy crap, the White-Winged Goddess? Guess I'd better do as she says."

"I'll go along with whatever you decide, Master," said his slave.

Once he was summoned by Haku, the adventurer prostrated himself before her. She *was* an A-rank adventurer after all.

"We require manpower to run this inn, so please lend us your slave. You needn't give her to me."

"As you wish, White-Winged Goddess."

Then, the obedient adventurer was given permission to use a room at the inn whenever he liked in exchange for lending out his slave.

"However, if we're going to work here, I'd like to bring on one more person. This girl here is too young, and people will look down on her if she's the one receiving guests."

"Very well. I'll give you a single gold coin so you can purchase a slave in Zia. We'll stay behind and prepare a meal."

"Wow, I'm so happy. Thank you, Big Sis Haku!"

"Tee-hee. It's all for you, my cute little sister."

And thus, the inn Haku prepared now had a proprietor and was open for business.

"And that's the backstory. What do you think? The adventurer is me and the slave is Meat."

"Yeah, we kinda figured that part out."

Keima was in the process of coordinating everyone's backstories for the inn: how the inn was built, how they, the adventurer Keima and his slave, Meat, had nothing to do with the contractor, and why Rokuko was so unfamiliar with the world. A fairy's mischievous influence also provided the perfect excuse for her strange growth patterns, and why she either didn't grow at all or grew all at once in a spurt. At least, that's what Keima thought.

"And after this you buy me, right?" asked Ichika.

"Yep. I'm counting on you to make it seem like that's what happened."

"Got it. That's what I'll tell people," she replied with a nod.

As a slave, she didn't have any objections.

"You're okay with this too, right, Meat?"

"Yes. I'll do my best."

The tiny, dog-eared girl huffed energetically through her nose. Her expression was blank, but her wagging tail betrayed her excitement.

Watching her companions, Rokuko, who had been listening the whole time, sighed.

"Keima, shouldn't you just be a writer or something?"

"Never thought we'd end up in a mess like this, though..." Keima thought.

Yet even after all that, they never ended up needing the backstory, and the inn was accepted, courtesy of her majesty, the A-rank adventurer Haku.

LAZY DUNGEON MASTER

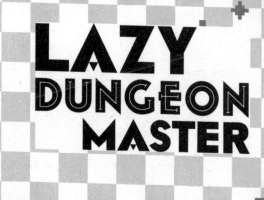

Chapter 15 B Side/Newly Drawn Bonus Illustration

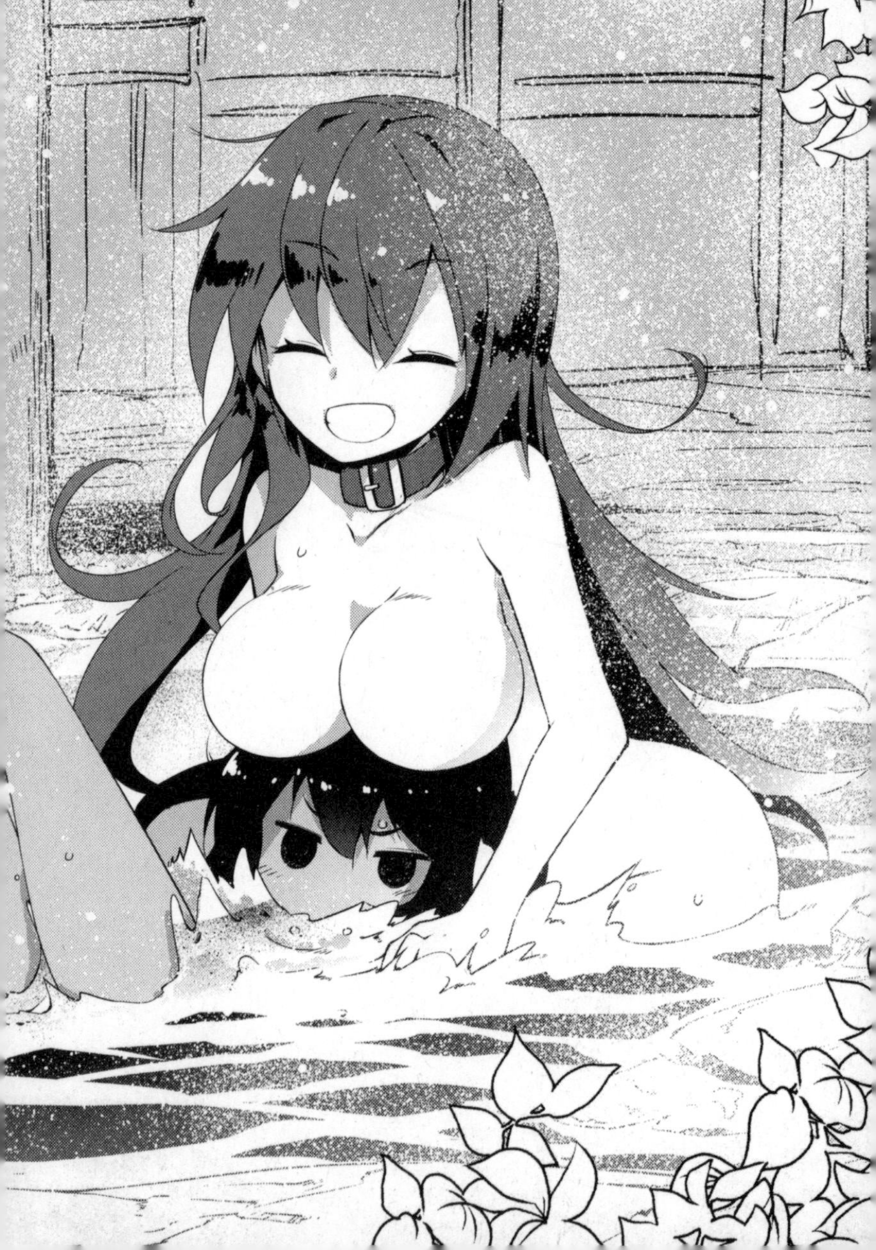

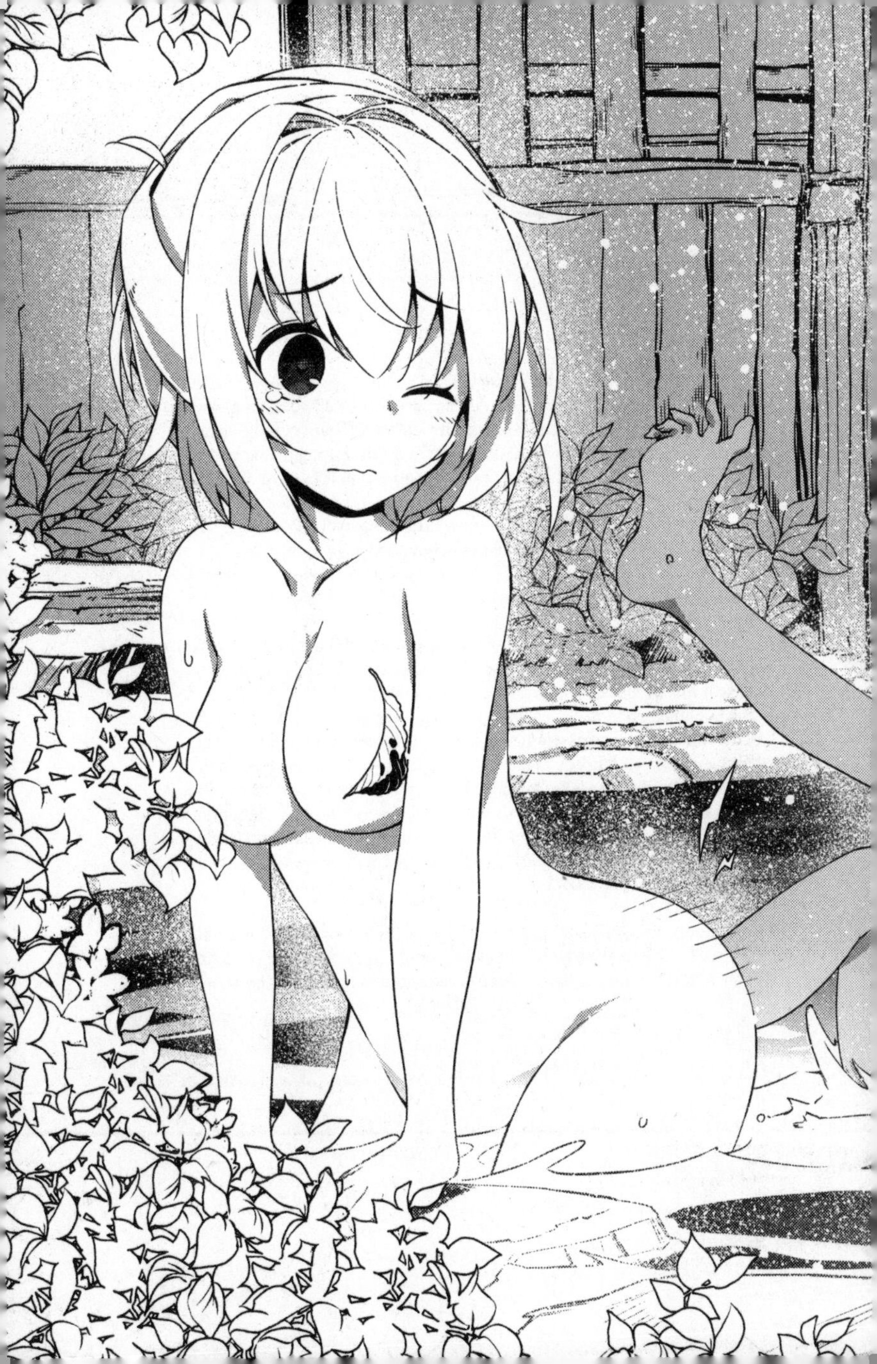

Afterword

We're now at volume 3 of the comic. Volume 2 of the novel is split into one chapter each, you know? At this pace, I have 33 volumes and about 15 years of stock. This'll be an incredibly long serialization, huh? Also, thanks to you readers, the novel will continue. I'm waiting on the anime offer. Making it into a CR is also possible. My dream is to buy a fan comic of my work at somewhere like Comiket. You don't actually have to wait for an anime of this to make one, you know? If you do make one, I'll go buy it, so tell me on Twitter and the like. I'm not good at Googling myself. I'm also waiting for reports of fan art! So! Please, I'd appreciate it so much! I'd appreciate it so much! (It's super important, so I said it twice.)

Now then, in the third volume of the comic, Ichika joins their group. Although she has a personality and career that seem insane from a common-sense mindset, since she knows the world better than Rokuko and Keima, who are holed up in the cave, and Meat, who was bought by bandits to be a body pillow, she becomes someone they can rely on. Definitely. Probably. Maybe. However, Ichika's boobs would be irresistible for any normal man. Keima is all about the legs, though. However, since how nice the slave's legs were is used as basic criteria at the slave shop, there's no doubt hers are the sort of legs Keima likes. This means that Rokuko has to also emphasize her legs and seduce Keima. So please add more foot service scenes like that, Nanaroku-sensei. Please!

Looks like I'm running out of space for the afterword in this volume, too. Let's meet again next time in either volume 13 of the novel or volume 4 of the comic. Or maybe they'll be released at the same time? Who knows.

Supana Onikage

AFTERWORD

*THE TEMPERATURE NEEDS TO BE ABOVE 60 DEGREES CELSIUS TO KILL THE MITES!!

THANK YOU FOR PURCHASING VOLUME 3. I'M THINKING OF PUTTING IN SOME FUTON MATERIAL IN EVERY VOLUME, SO THIS TIME IT'S ABOUT MAINTENANCE. BASICALLY, YOU DRY THE FUTON BECAUSE IT GETS DAMP, BUT IT'S NOT SUITABLE FOR KILLING MITES, SO YOU NEED TO WASH THE FUTON COMPLETELY (WITHOUT TAKING IT APART) TO DO THAT.

THEREFORE, I RECOMMEND A "WASHABLE FUTON" WHICH YOU CAN STUFF INTO A COIN LAUNDRY MACHINE, AND BY INSERTING A COIN, YOU CAN COMFORTABLY SPEND YOUR TIME ON A CLEAN FUTON THAT'S HAD THE MITES WASHED OUT OF IT!

A WASHABLE FUTON IS NICE! IT TAKES A PRETTY PENNY TO CLEAN IT, BUT IT'S ONLY ABOUT 3,000 YEN AT C.L.? BY THE WAY, IT DOESN'T SEEM TO BE VERY GOOD TO BEAT THE FUTON. WELL, SEE YOU NEXT TIME.

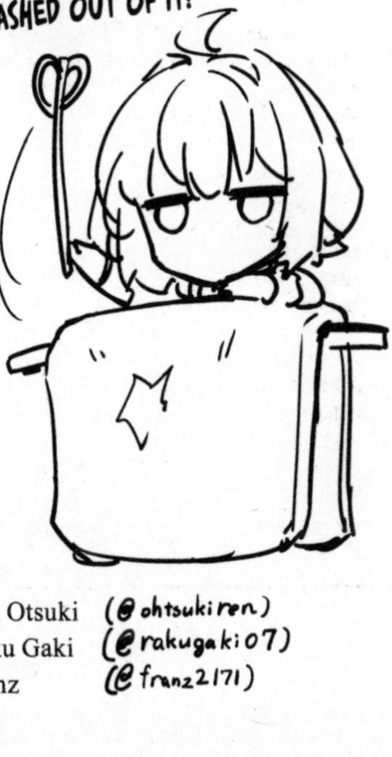

2020.1

Assistants: Ren Otsuki (@ohtsukiren)
Raku Gaki (@rakugaki07)
Franz (@franz2171)

Monologue Woven For You

STORY & ART BY Syu Yasaka   VOLUME 1

MY BRAIN IS DIFFERENT

Stories of ADHD and Other Developmental Disorders

MONZUSU

My Deer Friend Nokotan

1

Story and art by Oshioshio

ART Yamomichan   STORY JAKI   MANGA 1

THE MOST NOTORIOUS TALKER RUNS THE WORLD'S GREATEST CLAN

1

Reincarnated as a Sword

Another Wish

ART BY Hinako Inoue
STORY BY Yuu Tanaka
LLo

Restart After Growing Hungry

story and art by cocomi

Sheeply Horned Witch Romi

Story & art by Yoichi Abe   1

TOKYO Revengers

STORY & ART BY KEN WAKUI   1-2

01

YAKUZA REINCARNATION

ART BY HIROKI MIYASHITA
STORY BY TAKESHI NATSUHARA

Explore all these and more at
SevenSeasEntertainment.com

SEVEN SEAS ENTERTAINMENT PRESENTS

ZY DUNGEON MASTER

PANA ONIKAGE   art by **NANAROKU**   character designs by **YOUTA**   **VOLUME THREE**

TRANSLATION
Jessica Latherow

ADAPTATION
Molly Muldoon

LETTERING
Jamil Stewart

COVER DESIGN
H. Qi

PROOFREADER
Tori Bowler

COPY EDITOR
B. Lillian Martin

EDITOR
McKenzie Carnahan

PRODUCTION DESIGNER
Christina McKenzie

PRODUCTION MANAGER
Lissa Pattillo

PREPRESS TECHNICIAN
Melanie Ujimori
Jules Valera

EDITOR-IN-CHIEF
Julie Davis

ASSOCIATE PUBLISHER
Adam Arnold

PUBLISHER
Jason DeAngelis

Lazy Dungeon Master (Manga) Vol. 3
©2020 Nanaroku
©Supana Onikage/OVERLAP
First published in Japan in 2020 by OVERLAP Inc., Ltd., Tokyo.
English translation rights arranged with OVERLAP Inc., Ltd., Tokyo.

Seven Seas press and purchase enquiries can be sent to Marketing Manager Lianne Sentar at press@gomanga.com. Information regarding the distribution and purchase of digital editions is available from Digital Manager CK Russell at digital@gomanga.com.

ISBN: 978-1-63858-864-1
Printed in Canada
First Printing: March 2023
10 9 8 7 6 5 4 3 2 1

READING DIRECTIONS

This book reads from *right to left*, Japanese style. If this is your first time reading manga, you start reading from the top right panel on each page and take it from there. If you get lost, just follow the numbered diagram here. It may seem backwards at first, but you'll get the hang of it! Have fun!!

Follow us online: www.SevenSeasEntertainment.com